"As a biblical counselor, I love Wayne an[...] used it over and over again with folks who struggle w[...] the folks I counsel are not the only ones who have benefitted from this book; as a person who can easily be overpowered by fear, I have been the first to benefit. I have been blessed as I have reminded myself repeatedly of the principles this book teaches. The Macks' work stands out among a number of good resources on the subject. I would encourage you to use it first to bless your own life and then to use it to bless the lives of everyone you know who might experience the emotion of fear (wouldn't that be all of us?)."

—**Amy Baker,** Counselor, Faith Biblical Counseling Ministries

"Dr. Mack and his son Josh have been dear friends and mentors to me for over twenty years now. They practice what they preach! They have both personally helped me fight my fears biblically, and they will do the same for you through this super book. Dive in!"

—**Tim Cantrell,** Pastor-Teacher, Antioch Bible Church, Johannesburg, South Africa

"Tragically, fear grips many, many Christians in their daily walk. I say 'tragically' because, while this reality of ongoing fear should not be such a debilitating part of any believer's life, it nevertheless continues to plague countless beleaguered souls. But what to do about it? The answer, of course, is to avail yourself of large doses of God's inerrant Word, out of which crippling fear—whatever kind of fear it may be—can be victoriously overcome. And this is simply but marvelously what Wayne Mack's book *Courage* attempts to do, taking Holy Scripture and applying it to the fearful person's woes. If you are one of those professing Christians whose most significant struggle is fear, you've now found in this book a treasure trove of biblical teaching that can wonderfully liberate you from your fear factor."

—**Lance Quinn,** Pastor, Grace Advance at Grace Community Church, Sun Valley, California

"*Courage* tops the list of books that I regularly recommend for discipleship and counseling. There are few books written that are as helpful a resource to nearly every counselee who walks through my door. Though the subject matter seems broad, it is presented in a biblically sound and comprehensive way that speaks into the lives of hurting people, teaching them to live in the fear of the Lord."

—**John D. Street,** President, Association of Certified Biblical Counselors; Professor and Chair of Biblical Counseling, The Master's College and Seminary

"Every one of us knows what it is like to be gripped by fear and doubt. Wayne and Josh Mack have served Christ's church well with their new book on how to develop biblical courage. You can always be sure of two things whenever the Macks write a book: it will be filled with helpful truth from Scripture and be extremely relevant to the challenges we are facing today. This book will be a helpful resource to study personally and to give to others in need."

—**Steve Viars,** Pastor, Faith Baptist Church, Lafayette, Indiana

COURAGE

ALSO BY WAYNE A. MACK

A Fight to the Death (with Joshua Mack)

Down, But Not Out

God's Solutions to Life's Problems (with Joshua Mack)

*Homework Manual for Biblical Living, Vol. 1:
Personal and Interpersonal Problems*

*Homework Manual for Biblical Living, Vol. 2:
Family and Marital Problems*

Humility (with Joshua Mack)

In-Laws

"It's Not Fair!" (with Deborah Howard)

Life in the Father's House (with Dave Swavely)

Maximum Impact

Preparing for Marriage God's Way

Reaching the Ear of God

Strengthening Your Marriage

Sweethearts for a Lifetime (with Carol Mack)

Your Family, God's Way

Betty Graham
October 3, 2016

COURAGE

FIGHTING FEAR WITH FEAR

WAYNE A. MACK
JOSHUA MACK

P U B L I S H I N G
P.O. BOX 817 • PHILLIPSBURG • NEW JERSEY 08865-0817

Originally published in 2002 by Hensley Publishing as *The Fear Factor: What Satan Doesn't Want You to Know*

P&R Publishing edition 2014

ISBN: 978-1-59638-926-7 (pbk)
ISBN: 978-1-59638-927-4 (ePub)
ISBN: 978-1-59638-928-1 (Mobi)

Printed in the United States of America

CONTENTS

Foreword   7

1. You Can Be Courageous!   9

2. Guard Your Heart   29

3. Face to Face with Fear   49

4. Trapped!   71

5. Getting to the Heart of the Problem   91

6. Throw Off the Covers   111

7. The Way Up Is Down   127

8. God's Game Plan   149

9. Be Afraid—Be Very Afraid   167

10. The Fear That Is Good for You   187

11. The Fear That Overcomes Fear   211

12. Yes, but How?   231

13. Learning from the Master   261

14. A Call for Courage   279

FOREWORD

AS I WRITE THESE WORDS, our nation is under threat of more terrorist attacks, our stock market is in shambles, and companies struggling to operate at a profitable level are laying off many competent employees. Unusual weather patterns are creating severe drought in some areas of the country, with floods in others. All these circumstances are creating fear in the hearts of people in America.

I believe, however, that the most universal source of fear is what the Bible calls "the fear of man" (Prov. 29:25). Even in the best of times, we are afraid of what people will think or say about us. We are afraid they will ridicule or reject us. But as Proverbs 29:25 points out, "The fear of man brings a snare." The fear of man—that is, of other people—can prevent us from living our lives as God intends. How then can we combat this universal tendency that seems to control our lives?

Dr. Wayne Mack and his son Joshua give us the answer in this book. In summary they teach us that the fear of God, rightly lived out in our lives, drives out the fear of man. We all know, however, that is not as simple as it sounds. The fear of man is very complex, having many facets. And the fear of God is little understood by believers today. So Dr. Mack and Joshua do not leave us with a single sentence prescription. They plumb the depths of the fear of man and, at the same time, open wide to our minds the true biblical meaning of the fear of God. Then they show us how the fear of God is the only true antidote to the fear of man.

Wayne and Joshua remind me of the Puritans in their writings. When those godly English pastors of the seventeenth century wrote on a subject, there was little that was left unsaid. To use a modern idiom, they covered all the bases. This is what Wayne and Joshua have done in *Courage: Fighting Fear with Fear*. They have given us a comprehensive treatment on human fear—both of other people and of circumstances—and have shown us how a true biblical fear of God addresses both problems. To drive home the truth, they have included very searching, personal application questions at the end of each chapter.

Some years ago the late Dr. John Murray wrote, "The fear of God is the soul of godliness."[1] Every Christian who desires to be a godly person will profit from prayerfully reading and reflecting on the truths of *Courage*.

Jerry Bridges
Bible teacher, author of *The Joy of Fearing God* and *The Pursuit of Holiness*

1. John Murray, *Principles of Conduct* (Grand Rapids: Eerdmans, 1957), 233.

1

YOU CAN BE COURAGEOUS!

SOMEONE ONCE SAID, "A man who is afraid will do anything." History has proven that statement true. Fear is a powerful emotion. Fear will prevent you from doing things you normally would do and cause you to do things you normally wouldn't do. Fear has caused proud men to beg, strong men to cry, loving men to hate, and peaceful men to be filled with fury. Like a slave master, fear is controlling.

You know this from experience. We've all heard others say, "I don't want to talk to that person about Christ; I'm too afraid of his reaction." "I don't want to open up about what is really going on in my life; I'm afraid of what others might think." "I don't want to obey God; I'm scared of what that will require." "I don't want people to get too close to me; then they'll find out what's really going on in my heart." "I don't want to share my testimony; I'm scared." "I know I should talk to that person, but I'm afraid of what she'll think of me."

Many Christians are controlled by fear. As a result, they are crippled spiritually. They come to church, read the Scriptures, hear God's Word preached, and know what God wants them to do. But they don't obey because they are frightened. So they compromise. They live their Christian lives incognito, going to church on Sundays and living like the world the rest of the week. They neglect their gifts and are ashamed of Christ—all as a result of sinful fear.

9

Fear is a problem for everyone, and it's a major problem in the Christian life. The Bible makes it clear that fear can paralyze even great men. The apostle Paul was well aware of that. In fact, that was one of Paul's primary concerns for Timothy as he wrote his second letter to him. Paul was concerned that fear would stop Timothy from living all out for Christ.

Paul wrote this second letter to Timothy from prison. He was anticipating martyrdom. The emperor Nero was acting irrationally; he had just torched the city of Rome and was blaming it on the Christians. Persecution was intensifying. This was not an easy time to be a believer. A number of Paul's friends had even given up the faith and abandoned him because of their fears (2 Tim. 1:15).

Paul understood that fear could cripple Timothy's effectiveness for Christ. That's why he exhorted Timothy, "I remind you to kindle afresh the gift of God" (2 Tim. 1:6). Step up, be bold, and use the gift God has given you. In verse 8 Paul went on to encourage Timothy, "Do not be ashamed of the testimony of our Lord or of me His prisoner, but join with me in suffering for the gospel according to the power of God."

Paul didn't want Timothy to become so afraid of the future that he would stop living for Christ in the present. This was not a time for weakness, it was a time for strength; not a time to hide gifts, rather a time to use them; not a time to shrink back, but to stand strong; not a time for fear, rather a time for courage. "You therefore, my son, be strong in the grace that is in Christ Jesus," Paul wrote (2:1). Why? "God has not given us a spirit of fear" (1:7 NKJV).

When we read this passage from the comfort of our recliners, it's very easy to miss the impact of Paul's words. Think carefully about what Paul was telling Timothy. He didn't write, "Timothy, you have nothing to be afraid of. The Christian life is easy!" No, Paul was very blunt. He told Timothy there were going to be consequences for being a Christian. He wrote in verse 8, "Join with me in suffering." You are going to suffer, but you must not fear!

Paul didn't mean we aren't to have any old kind of fear. It's not wrong to jump when someone says, "Boo!" or to be startled when you're placed in a frightening situation. The word Paul used for *fear* describes moral cowardice. He was referring to a sinful fear that would keep Timothy from obeying God and fulfilling his responsibilities. In other words, Paul was telling Timothy, "You must not be controlled by sinful fear. It's not from God."

If Paul said this to Timothy, we can be sure he would say the same to us today. Yes, there's a cost for following after Christ. Yes, difficulties will come into your life. But stop riding the fence. Stop playing both sides. Start wholeheartedly obeying Christ despite what may come. Don't allow your fear of the future to stop you from fully obeying God now. You don't have to be paralyzed by fear.

That's a shocking statement. How could Paul expect us to be courageous when life is so frightening? Isn't it normal to be afraid of suffering? Doesn't it make sense to try to avoid it? If you look to the future and know that if you take a particular route you will certainly suffer, wouldn't it make sense to take a different route? Why shouldn't we be afraid? Why shouldn't we shrink back?

THE REASON FOR COURAGE

That's the question Paul answered in verse 7. He wrote, "For God has not given us a spirit of timidity, but of power and love and discipline."

Paul wrote "For," or in other words, "This is the reason why . . ." You should be courageous because God has not given you a spirit of fear.

To whom was Paul referring? Who is the *us* in this verse? Just naturally confident people? People with all sorts of abilities? No. Paul meant all believers, regardless of personality, regardless of natural talents and abilities. Not one believer has a right to be characterized by a spirit of fear. That spirit, that attitude is not from God.

Timothy was a naturally timid person, but notice that Paul didn't allow him to use that as an excuse. He didn't say, "Poor Timothy. You're a fearful person. That's okay. Just hang in there." Instead Paul began by rebuking Timothy: "Timothy, stop being afraid. It's not from God. The reason you're dominated by fear and anxiety is because you're in sin."

If you are a non-Christian, you are trapped by your personality. Oh, you may learn some gimmicks and tricks that help you cope with life despite your personality, but you are, basically, enslaved to it. If you are a Christian, however, you have been freed from this kind of slavery.

Dr. Lloyd-Jones explains:

> Here is the miracle of redemption. We are given our temperaments by God. . . . All our temperaments are different and that also is of God. Yes, but it must never be true of us as Christians that we are controlled by our temperaments. We must be controlled by the Holy Ghost. You must put them in that order. Here are powers and capacities and here is your particular temperament that uses them, but the vital point is that as a Christian you should be controlled by the Holy Spirit. What is so tragically wrong in a Christian is that he should allow himself to be controlled by his temperament. The natural man is always controlled by his temperament, he cannot help himself; but the difference that regeneration makes is that there is now a higher control even over temperament. The moment the Holy Spirit enters in, He controls everything including our temperament, and so He enables you to function in your own particular way through your temperament. That is the miracle of redemption. Temperament remains, but temperament no longer controls. The Holy Spirit now controls.[1]

So if you are saying, "I'm fearful because that's my personality," or "I just don't have the strength to be courageous in this situation," it's time to throw those excuses out the window. They just don't work. You may have a naturally timid personality, but you still can be courageous.

Perhaps you are wondering how we can say that when we don't know your situation—that we couldn't help but be scared if we were in your shoes.

If those are your thoughts, you are considering yourself to still be the same person you were before God saved you. But you are not the person you used to be. When you see your situation the same way you would if you were still an unbeliever, you are failing to realize what a great gift God has given you.

---

1. Martyn Lloyd-Jones, *Spiritual Depression* (Grand Rapids: Eerdmans, 1965), 101.

That was precisely Paul's point. He was telling Timothy, "You've got to pull yourself together and understand that you are not just like everyone else anymore. God has given you the Holy Spirit." And He is not the "spirit of slavery leading to fear again, but you have received a spirit of adoption as sons by which we cry out, 'Abba! Father!'" (Rom. 8:15).

Once again Dr. Lloyd-Jones explains:

Our fears are due to our failure to stir up, a failure to think, a failure to take ourselves in hand. You find yourself looking to the future and then you begin to imagine things and you say: "I wonder what is going to happen?" And then your imagination runs away with you. You are gripped by the thing; you do not stop to remind yourself of who and what you are, this thing overwhelms you and you go down. Now the first thing you need to do is take a firm grip of yourself, and speak to yourself. As the Apostle puts it, we have to remind ourselves of certain things.... The big thing Paul is saying to Timothy is, "Timothy, you seem to be thinking about yourself and your life and all you have to do as if you are still an ordinary person. But Timothy, you are not an ordinary person. You are a Christian, you have the Spirit of God within you."[2]

Something tremendous has happened in our lives. We're not who we used to be. God has given us the Holy Spirit, and He is not a spirit of cowardice. This means there is hope. Your situation may be difficult, but you are not alone!

THE SPIRIT WITHIN YOU

Recently good friends of ours took a trip to Canada. They were on a tight budget, so they carefully planned for the trip, not wanting to spend a cent more than necessary. The wife packed meals for the entire family for each and every day. They stayed in a nice hotel, but ate all their meals in their room. At the end of the week, as they checked out of the hotel, they learned that the hotel had been offering a special that

2. Ibid., 99–100.

week—lunch at the hotel restaurant had been included in the price of the room! They had missed out on having free lunches because they were unaware of the resources available to them.

Many Christians live their lives the same way. They've never considered the resources that are available to them in Christ, so they fail to take advantage of the privileges that belong to them. The result? They live like nonbelievers.

You see, the world says, "The key to courage is self-confidence." But face the facts. You aren't that great; you aren't that powerful; you don't have control over all situations; and if you are trusting in yourself, you're going to be sorely disappointed. You're going to let yourself down. You can believe in yourself all you want, but that's not going to stop your plane from crashing. You can be completely self-confident, but that won't protect you from failure. Don't close your eyes to reality. If you're trying to become courageous by trusting in yourself, you're eating sandwiches in your hotel room when you should be dining in the restaurant!

Biblical courage is not based on foolish self-confidence. Paul doesn't point Timothy toward Timothy. He points Timothy toward God. Think about the great resource God has given you. He's given you the Spirit! You should be courageous, not because of who you are and what you've done, but because of who God is and what He has done!

The Spirit of Power

Paul wanted us to think specifically about the Spirit God has given us. Yes, you are weak, but the Spirit God has given you isn't. He is the Spirit of power.

You are frightened. You look to the future, and you get all worked up. You think, "There is no way I can handle this, I'm not that strong; I'm going to fail!" You start to lose hope.

Do you want to know what your problem really is?

You don't understand how powerful the Spirit who is at work within you really is. You are unaware of the resources that are available to you in Christ.

Picture a great king who is very powerful. He has all sorts of body-guards who are with him wherever he goes. One snap of his fingers and two dozen Navy SEALs and Army Rangers will be at his side.

Then one day the king goes out for a walk, and a scrawny four-year-old boy cries out, "King, come over here. I'm going to beat you up!" The king hears this threat and immediately is seized with fear. "What am I going to do? I don't want to get beaten up! He's threatening me. I'm in trouble."

The great king trembles and is paralyzed with fear because of the threats of a four-year-old boy. Finally someone goes to him and says, "King, remember you're the king. Remember all the resources at your disposal. You've got a dozen bodyguards around you and armies at your disposal. With all those incredible resources, why are you afraid of the threats of a puny little boy?"

Yes, it's a silly story. Yet that's often how we respond to the troubling circumstances of life. Our most difficult circumstances are nothing when compared to the power of the Spirit. Our problems arise because we don't realize just how powerful the Spirit really is. We think we need more power, when instead we need to realize the power that is already available to us. In Ephesians 1:18–19, Paul wrote to the believers, "I pray that the eyes of your heart may be enlightened, so that you will know . . . what is the surpassing greatness of His power toward us who believe." Paul didn't pray for us to have more power; he prayed that we might know the power that is ours in Christ. The power that is ours in Christ is "surpassingly great"!

If you need proof that He's powerful enough to help you in your time of weakness, consider this: what is the greatest problem anyone will ever face? Death. Yet the Spirit has already overcome that.

Paul wrote in Romans 8:11, "If the Spirit of Him who raised Jesus from the dead dwells in you, He who raised Christ Jesus from the dead will also give life to your mortal bodies through His Spirit who dwells in you." In other words, the same Spirit who raised Jesus from the dead is in you, and if He could raise Jesus from the dead, He certainly is able to give you the strength to deal with the problems that are going to arise in your life.

You think about your future and think, "I couldn't handle that, I'm not strong enough." But you aren't in that situation yet, so your lack of strength is no reason to be afraid. God's not going to give you the strength for a situation until you are in that situation. Instead of fearing the future, trust God for the strength for today. Remember you are not alone. You have incredible resources. The Spirit of power dwells in you.

The Christian is a person of great strength. The Christian has the power to endure great hardship, to stand strong when life is difficult, and to hang on in the midst of great pain.

Why can Christians stand strong? Is it because in and of themselves they are naturally strong people? No! Believers can stand strong because the Spirit within them is so powerful.

Often we tend to put courageous people on a pedestal, thinking that we could never do what they have done because we are not as strong as they are. Scripture won't allow us to do that. The Bible goes to great lengths to show us that many of the men and women who accomplished great things for God were very, very normal. In fact, sometimes it seems as though God went out of His way to choose the weakest individuals just to make the point that it wasn't about them and their abilities to make the difference; it is about God and His power.

Think of Moses. Here was a great man. He stood up to Pharaoh and an entire nation. He led God's people out of Egypt. Surely he must have been a man endowed with a naturally bold and courageous personality! But was he? How did he respond when God called him to this great task? "Not me, Lord," he said. "Anybody but me. Please no, Lord." Reading the story, we are almost embarrassed by Moses' lack of courage. (We say "almost," because most of us would have probably responded the exact same way!)

Think of Joshua. What a leader. He took over after Moses' death. He led God's people into the Promised Land. He was one of the greatest military commanders of all time. He must have been a naturally courageous person, right? It doesn't appear so. God had to tell him over and over and over again, "Be strong and courageous." Why would

God have to say that so many times? Because Joshua was tempted to be weak and afraid.

Think of Paul. Here was a man's man. Though he was stoned and beaten for preaching the gospel, no man could stop him from spreading the message. Paul stood boldly before great leaders and large crowds, never shrinking back. Yet even Paul seems to have struggled with fear. To the Corinthians Paul wrote that he came to them with much weakness and in fear and trembling (1 Cor. 2:3).

The point is this: these men were just like us, yet they were able to be incredibly courageous. How? Because of the Spirit's work within them. Because they relied on God! Don't say, "I can't be courageous, I'm too weak." God hasn't changed. The same God who enabled Moses, Joshua, and Paul to stand courageously for Christ and for God's glory is at work within you! Stop looking to yourself for courage. Stop making excuses. Start relying on God!

The Spirit of Love

What's the opposite of a spirit of fear? Most people would automatically say the answer is a spirit of power. It makes sense. But according to the Bible the opposite of a spirit of fear is a spirit of love.

You must understand this. If you are dominated by sinful fear, worry, and anxiety, your problem is that you are too self-centered. You are a selfish person. You are thinking about yourself too much.

That's why John wrote, "There is no fear in love; but perfect love casts out fear" (1 John 4:18). Fear and love are opposites. Dr. Jay Adams explains:

> The enemy of fear is love; the way to put off fear, then, is to put on love. . . .
>
> Love is self-giving, fear is self-protecting.
>
> Love moves towards others; fear shrinks away from them. But . . . love is the stronger since it is able to "cast out" fear. In dealing with fear, nothing else possesses the same expulsive power.[3]

3. Jay Adams, *The Christian Counselor's Manual* (Nutley, NJ: P&R Publishing, 1973), 414.

You know this from everyday life—a mother may be very afraid of water, but if she sees her baby drowning in a lake, that fear disappears and love takes over and compels her to dive right in.

This same principle applies to all of life. When your eyes are on yourself, you will be afraid. But when your eyes are on God and on others, that casts out fear.

If you are thinking about yourself, you might be scared to talk to new people. But if you get your eyes off yourself and start thinking about their needs, their good, that casts out the fear because you're not worried about what they will think of you. Instead you are thinking about how you can serve them.

Believers should be characterized by a spirit of love, not a spirit of selfishness. We should be marked by an awareness of God's love for us, a true and deep love for Him, and an overflowing love for others.

When you are in a frightening situation, you need to reflect on God's love for you. Remember that nothing—"neither death, nor life, nor angels, nor principalities, nor things present, nor things to come, nor powers, nor height, nor depth, nor any other created thing"— "will be able to separate us from the love of God, which is in Christ Jesus our Lord" (Rom. 8:38–39).

Thinking about God's love produces great courage. Why did Paul preach the gospel fearlessly? Why did he risk his life day after day? "The love of Christ controls us" (2 Cor. 5:14). He was a man controlled by the love of God.

Thinking about God's love should create in you a great love for Him. When you love God, you will stand up courageously for Him. If I were to see my wife being attacked by two very strong men, I wouldn't sit on the sidelines and wonder what I should do or if I should get involved. I wouldn't pretend like I didn't see it happening. No, love casts out fear. I wouldn't think about any of those concerns. My love for her would compel me to jump in to help her.

The true believer demonstrates love for God by loving others. The apostle John explained, "If you don't love you don't know God, for God is love" (1 John 4:8, author's paraphrase). In 2 Timothy 1:7 it's as if Paul were saying, "Remember, you are a Christian and the Spirit that resides in you is producing love. Don't respond to these trials like a worldly person. An unbeliever sees suffering coming and runs. That's because he's an unbeliever, and the person he is most concerned about is himself. You are not an unbeliever any longer. Remember who you are and what you are about. Stop being so concerned about yourself, start thinking about others, and boldly use the gifts God has given you. Your first concern in this difficult situation should be not your own safety but God's glory and His people's good. God has given us a spirit of love."

The Spirit of Sound Judgment

Fear produces confusion and chaos in the mind. That's where it does its most damaging work. It creates irrational thinking. When you talk to someone who is really afraid, what do you find? His or her thought life is all messed up.

Some people won't go on planes because one plane crashed, but they will drive a car even though many more people die each year as a result of car accidents. Some people won't go over a bridge because they are scared it won't support them, even though every day thousands of cars and trucks drive over that same bridge and it has never broken under the pressure. That is irrational thinking.

Some believers won't talk to others about Christ, about their eternal souls, because they're afraid of what those persons might think of them, even though they will probably never see each other again. Other people don't want to obey God because they are afraid they'll never be able to enjoy life again.

Christian, you are not to be controlled by irrational thinking. You have been given the Spirit of sound judgment. *Sound judgment* literally means to have "a secure and sound mind. It also carries the additional idea of a self-controlled, disciplined, and properly prioritized mind."[4] When God gives you sound judgment, you are able to think clearly about your life—the good, the bad, and the ugly. You apply godly wisdom to every area of your life.

4. John MacArthur, *2 Timothy* (Chicago: Moody, 1995), 19.

When you find yourself in frightening situations, you will be tempted to think irrationally. However, you need to stop and pray and work hard to think straight about things. My mother used to say, "Don't make a mountain out of a molehill. Don't allow your circumstances and feelings to dominate you. Instead live by truth." That's what the Spirit enables you to do—to stop being controlled by your circumstances and to be controlled instead by the Spirit. To stop being controlled by irrational thinking and instead be controlled by sound biblical thinking.

Paul's counsel to Timothy is very different from the world's counsel. The world says, "When you see a frightening situation coming, protect yourself at all cost! Compromise your relationship with Christ. Don't endure hardship for Christ. Run from the situation." But when people think this way, they create a prison for themselves. They are always thinking about their own protection. As a result they have no peace, and they are dominated by fear, worry, and anxiety. God says, "Remember the Spirit I have given you."

Don't be so eager to stay safe. Make pleasing and glorifying God your top priority regardless of what may come your way.

What happens to people who stop fearing the future and step out in faith? They find freedom. You can lock them up, you can beat them, but you can't take their joy and their courage away, because their joy and courage don't come from something changeable, like circumstances. Their joy comes from Someone who never changes, God Himself.

If your primary concern in life is protecting yourself, you are going to create a prison for yourself in your mind and throw away the key. But if your primary concern is glorifying God by His grace, by the enabling work of the Spirit who produces power, love, and a sound mind within you, then you've found the key to be free even if your body is locked up in a real prison.

Fear can be spiritually crippling, but it doesn't have to be. Fear has destroyed many lives. Yours does not need to be one of them.

This is a book about overcoming fear. But this entire book would be pointless if 2 Timothy 1:7 weren't true. Please take this to heart: You can be courageous. In fact, Paul says you *must* be courageous.

You don't have to be dominated by sinful fear, "for God has not given us a spirit of fear, but of power and of love and of a sound mind" (2 Tim. 1:7 NKJV).

QUESTIONS FOR DISCUSSION

1. How does fear cripple us? What are three specific ways fear has crippled you in your Christian life?

2. What concern did Paul have as he sat down to write 2 Timothy? What can we learn from this concern?

3. What kind of fear was Paul prohibiting? Why is it important to take note of that?

4. How could Paul expect us to be courageous when life is so frightening?

5. Who was Paul writing about in 2 Timothy 1:7? What difference does that make?

6. According to Dr. Martyn Lloyd-Jones, what is the miracle of redemption? Why is that truth so encouraging?

7. Without knowing your particular situation, how is it possible for us to tell you that you must throw your excuses for fear out the window?

8. What does this statement mean: "Your problem is that you are thinking of yourself as though you are still the same person you were before God saved you"?

9. What excuses do you tend to give for your fear?

10. What is biblical courage not based on? Why is that significant?

11. What is biblical courage based on?

12. How does knowing that the Holy Spirit is a Spirit of power help produce courage?

13. What is the ultimate proof that the Holy Spirit is powerful enough to help you in your time of weakness? What are some specific ways you can take this truth and implement it in your everyday life?

14. What is the danger of putting courageous people on pedestals? Have you done that in the past?

15. What can we learn from the weaknesses of Moses, Joshua, and Paul?

16. How is love the opposite of fear?

17. What does it indicate about us if we are controlled by fear, worry, and anxiety?

18. In what areas are you especially selfish? What are you going to do about it?

19. What should we do in frightening situations? How will that help us?

20. Where does fear do its most damaging work?

21. What are some examples of irrational thoughts with which you have struggled? Why are they irrational? (Support your answer with Scripture.)

22. What does it mean that we've been given the Spirit of sound judgment?

23. How is Paul's advice to Timothy different from what the world's advice would be?

24. What's the result of the world's advice? What's the result of God's advice?

2

GUARD YOUR HEART

THE CIRCUMSTANCES OF a believer's life are not all that different from an unbeliever's. Yet the believer's reactions to the circumstances of life must be completely different from the unbeliever's.

Believers and unbelievers both face circumstances that are frightening, challenging, confusing, and difficult. In that way, our lives are not all that different from the lives of unbelievers. The Bible doesn't try to hide the fact that the Christian life is difficult. When God saves you, He doesn't put a magic bubble around you to protect you from all the trials of life. In fact God promises us that "in the world you [will] have tribulation" (John 16:33).

Yet even so, our lives must be completely different from the unbelievers'. We too have problems. But the Christian's response to those problems should be completely different from the non-Christian's. Too often, however, our responses to the frightening circumstances that come into our lives are really not different from the responses of those around us.

When people say bad things about us, we get upset, and troubling thoughts flood our minds. We think about it and brood for days. We let it destroy us. When we have difficulties at work, we complain and get angry just like everyone else. When we are in a difficult financial situation, we are dominated by worry and fear. "What are we going to do? How are we going to survive? Life is coming to an end!" We respond to the problems of life just like an unbeliever.

Beloved, that should not be. We've already learned that the Christian's life ought to be characterized by courage, by steadiness, by a firm resolve to obey and glorify God despite all that is going on around us. We are to be immovable, always abounding in the work of the Lord, firm in the faith, brave, and strong (1 Cor. 15:58). We should be a strong, courageous, steadfast people. We're to respond to the troubles of life completely differently than the world.

Perhaps you're thinking, "I agree. Sounds great. But it's easier to say we're to respond to difficult times with courage than to actually do it. How in the world do I actually stand strong when life gets tough? How am I supposed to remain calm when life is frightening? How am I supposed to be bold when someone is out to get me? How can I be courageous when I get laid off at work? How am I supposed to avoid being overwhelmed with worry when finances are tight? How can I rejoice when I feel alone, as though my life is at a dead end? When someone treats me terribly? When my car breaks down? When a relationship ends? Sure, God wants me to respond differently than the world. Anyone can sit in church and nod in agreement when the pastor says to be courageous, but what does it actually take to do so? Exactly how do I rejoice when I am distressed? How do I remain calm in the midst of chaos? Where do I even start?"

These are good questions. And Jesus answers these very questions. In John 14:1–4, He teaches us a fundamental lesson in overcoming fear and developing courage. It's a lesson so important you won't be able to utilize the principles taught throughout the rest of this book unless you begin here.

Picture the scene. Jesus was about to die. He knew it. He was about to leave the men He had led and loved for the previous three years. This was difficult for Him. It was especially difficult for His disciples. When He had called His disciples, Jesus had told them, "Follow me!" And they had done so. They had left their homes, jobs, and families behind. For three years they had placed all their hopes in Jesus. They had taken up their crosses. They had denied themselves. They had sought after Christ. Others had turned back when they thought the cost had become too high, but not these disciples. Others had forsaken Christ when He explained that to be His disciples they must deny themselves, but not these men. They loved their Master and were committed to following after Him. But now they were confused because Jesus was making a number of troubling statements.

He told them that one of them would betray Him. We read in John 13:21, "When Jesus had said this, He became troubled in spirit, and testified and said, 'Truly, truly, I say to you, that one of you will betray Me.'"

Imagine their reaction. Someone was going to betray Christ? You can almost imagine a hush falling over the room. "A traitor! Who?" All the disciples looking at each other, at a loss to know about whom Jesus was speaking. One of us, Lord? No, it can't be!

But things got worse. Jesus started talking about leaving them. "Little children," He told them, "I am with you a little while longer. You will seek Me . . . [but] where I am going, you cannot come" (John 13:33).

Try to place yourself in the disciples' shoes and imagine how they felt when they finally understood what Jesus was telling them. Where was Jesus going? Why was He leaving them? Why couldn't they follow? They had left everything to follow Christ, and now He was leaving them? What would they do? How would they survive? They had no homes. No money. They didn't know what to do! What about the promised kingdom? Was this how it was all going to end?

You must admit, if anyone had a reason to be frightened, it was these disciples. All their hopes and dreams were being dashed right in front of them. Jesus knew they were confused and fearful. So He gently instructed them how they were to handle the difficult, confusing, challenging, frightening circumstances of life. He expected them to be courageous. He showed them what it was going to take. He taught them how to live completely differently than the unbelievers, when their lives were not that different from the unbelievers'. And in doing so, He showed us how to respond to the frightening circumstances of life in a way that pleases Him.

YOU MUST STOP

"Let not your heart be troubled" (John 14:1 NKJV).

If you are going to be calm in the midst of chaos, there's something you must stop doing. When life gets difficult, when it feels as though you are being squeezed by the pressures all around you, you must refuse to panic.

Jesus was not telling His disciples they were not allowed to be sad. He was not telling them it was wrong for them to be distressed in this particular situation. He was not telling them to ignore the pain and heartache they were experiencing.

There are certain situations in life that are frightening and troubling. Christians are not oblivious to their circumstances. When painful times come, we feel pain. When sorrowful times come, we feel sorrow. When frightening times come, we feel fear.

Jesus Himself experienced this. In John 12:27, we read that even Jesus was troubled as He contemplated what was going to occur. He cried out to God, "Now My soul is troubled, and what shall I say? 'Father, save Me from this hour'? But for this purpose I came to this hour" (NKJV). In 13:21 we read once again, "When Jesus had said these things, He was troubled in spirit" (NKJV).

Christ looked to the cross, and it disturbed Him. But you'll notice Jesus didn't allow His trouble to control Him. He still obeyed God despite His distress. He looked to God in the midst of His anguish. He actually sweated blood. He didn't accuse God, act selfishly, back away, or become paralyzed with fear. His distress didn't turn Him away from God. It didn't keep Him from doing what God wanted. Instead it actually drew Him closer to God. Jesus was troubled, but still He continued to walk in obedience to God in the midst of His anguish.

That's the distinction. It's not wrong to be distressed, to be troubled, to be frightened, or to have those emotions. It is wrong when those emotions control you. It's wrong when your anguish is not in keeping with the facts clearly given to you in Scripture. That's what Jesus was telling these disciples. Do not allow your distress to keep you from thinking biblically about your situation.

Christians are not to be controlled by their circumstances. God calls on us and gives us the power to rejoice when distressed, to be calm when all around us is chaos, and to be courageous, even when times are frightening. In John 14, Jesus commanded the disciples not to allow their distress, their trouble, their fear to control them.

Sometimes when you are going through difficult times, you might be tempted to think that you are the only one who has ever felt that way. You are not. When you are tempted to think, "Nobody knows . . ." or "I'm the only one who . . . ," remember, it is not true! Following Christ has been difficult since the beginning. Your particular situation may be very different from the disciples', but your reaction is not. You are troubled, and so were they.

Jesus wasn't telling the disciples, "Don't allow your hearts to become troubled." Rather, He was telling them, "Your hearts are already troubled, and this needs to stop." The disciples saw Jesus crying out in distress, they heard about the betrayal, and they finally understood that Jesus was leaving them. Their response? They started falling to pieces.

If you were looking for an easy ride when you became a Christian, you got on the wrong roller coaster. Don't be shocked when life gets tough. Situations will come into your life in which your faith is going to be tested. You will go through storms and trials. If you are living the Christian life thinking you will never have anything more to worry about, you are living in a fantasy world.

You are going to experience trouble. And you need to be aware that you will be tempted to respond as the disciples did—to fall to pieces.

If you are going to overcome your fear, you must be aware of that temptation and remember Jesus' prohibition. You will face frightening circumstances, you will experience normal human emotions such as fear and distress, but listen, believer, your situation is not hopeless. Don't act as if you have to be controlled by fear. You don't. A courageous response will not be easy. It may not even be natural. But it is possible.

Jesus was aware of the difficult situation the disciples were in. He knew the temptations they faced. Yet He didn't say, "Well, life is difficult, too bad. I guess there is no hope for you. I understand that you have to be controlled by fear and sorrow." No, instead He said, "Let not your heart be troubled." This was a command: stop giving your hearts permission to be controlled by fear.

The fact that Jesus commanded the disciples to stop allowing their hearts to become troubled means that the disciples had the strength to obey. Responsibility implies ability.

You have a responsibility, and therefore as a believer you have an ability, to refuse to panic. You have the responsibility, and therefore the ability to deal with the turmoil going on inside your heart. You have the responsibility, and therefore the ability, to refuse to allow your circumstances to control your response.

If you are a believer, you don't have to be broken by the hard times. You don't have to be dominated by fear. You don't have to be overwhelmed by worry. If you are a believer, you don't have to be dominated by fear and anxiety. If that's not true, then Jesus' statement is a cruel joke, because Jesus would have been commanding His disciples to do something they did not have the strength to do. You'll never be courageous until you understand that.

Too often, Christians give in right away. When you are troubled, do you allow yourself to be overwhelmed with fear and sorrow? Do you think, "What am I supposed to do? How could God let this happen to me? I can't handle this." Do you act and talk as if that were the only possible way you could ever respond to that difficult situation? It isn't.

As a believer, when you are distressed, you should look at your situation and say, "I recognize this is difficult and these circumstances are distressing. I am aware that I am being tempted to allow fear and sorrow to control me, but thank God, by His grace, I don't have to cave in. I am not going to be controlled by my fears and sorrows. Instead, by God's strength and power that is at work in me, I am going to control them!"

That's why Jesus can say, "Let not your heart be troubled."

When troubling times come into your life, remember that you are not the first to go through them. Understand that you are going to be tempted to become afraid and to be distressed. Realize that you are not going to respond correctly just by sitting back and doing what comes naturally. You can respond to these trials correctly. There is hope.

YOU MUST START

Now many worldly people would be willing to agree with us up to this point. But the problem is, the world's advice usually stops right there. When you are in the midst of a hard time, the world comes up to you and says, "Life is short. You're a nice person. You shouldn't be so upset. Don't worry, be happy."

The problem is, if you stop there, that's absolute nonsense. It won't hold up during the tough times. It's like telling a person who has been run over by a car, "Don't worry. Don't hurt. Life is too short to feel pain." That doesn't make sense. If you have a scratch on your knee, maybe you can keep telling yourself it doesn't hurt and fool yourself into believing it. If you've been run over by a car, you can tell yourself it doesn't hurt all you want, but it's still going to hurt. Likewise, if you have a minor problem and you tell yourself, "Don't worry about it, don't become troubled about it, be happy," you may be able to fool yourself into believing it. But anybody who has ever had a real trial knows that you can't stop your heart from becoming distressed just by telling yourself to smile because life is short. That's ridiculous.

One of the things I love so much about John 14 is that Jesus didn't just say, "Don't let your heart be troubled" and move on. He doesn't give us a little hug and encourage us, "Grin and bear it. Pretend like it doesn't hurt." No, His instruction for dealing with fear and anxiety was grounded in something substantial.

There was a substantial reason, a real reason the disciples shouldn't have been overwhelmed with worry and fear during this difficult time, and that was because of the character of Christ, which is the character of God.

Jesus was not telling them, "Let not your heart be troubled, put on a happy face, and pretend everything is okay." Instead Jesus was commanding them not to allow their hearts to be troubled because of what they knew about Him, and because of what they knew about God. He was telling them, "You need to exercise your faith! Because of what you know to be true about God and what you know about Me, you don't need to be afraid, you don't need to be worried." The reason you are becoming troubled is not because of your circumstances; it is because you are not exercising your faith. You are looking at your situation as if God does not exist. The problem is not just what you are doing (becoming troubled), it's also what you are not doing (believing God).

If the world does give you a reason for courage, it generally points you toward yourself. The world's counsel would be, "Let not your heart be troubled, believe in yourself."

Popular secular books on fear often tell you the root reason for your fear is your lack of self-esteem. In their "wisdom," these authors tell you that in order to overcome fear, you just need to feel better about yourself. If you're afraid, you overcome that fear by learning to believe in yourself. That's ridiculous advice because it calls you to put your faith in the wrong person. It tells you to close your eyes to reality.

Why would you put your faith in yourself? What good does that do? You're just a finite, limited person. You're not strong enough, you're not mighty enough, you're not that great. You're not in control of all things. You can't stop bad things from happening. Feeling good about yourself may help you control your fear, but it doesn't take away the reason to fear!

Do you understand that? If you are afraid of flying and you work really hard on feeling good about yourself so that you can get on a plane and not be afraid, what good does that do? Will feeling good about yourself keep the plane from crashing? No, you have no control over that. So really, feeling good about yourself doesn't have anything to do with the situation. It's like a child who carries around a blanket. When he has that blanket, he stays calm, but take away his blanket and he becomes frightened. Is that blanket going to be able to protect him from any harm? Of course not. But he trusts in it anyway. Trusting in yourself is like trusting in a security blanket. It may make you feel good, but it won't resolve your problem.

If you have a problem with fear, worry, or anxiety, it doesn't mean you have a problem with self-esteem. It means you have a problem with your faith! Improving your self-esteem, then, is not the answer. The real issue is where you put your faith. Don't put your faith in yourself. You can't do anything about the situation. You need to put your faith in Someone who really is in control.

Jesus put his finger on the disciples' problem: "Your hearts are troubled." Why? Their faith was weak. They needed to believe in God, and they needed to believe in Him.

How you respond to frightening circumstances reveals something about your faith in God. When you panic, when you are overwhelmed with fear, you are demonstrating a lack of faith, a lack of trust in God and in Jesus Christ.

Anyone can sit in church and say they believe in God, but when the tough times come, what they really believe becomes obvious.

A story in Luke 8:22–25 makes this clear:

> Now on one of those days Jesus and His disciples got into a boat, and He said to them, "Let us go over to the other side of the lake." So they launched out. But as they were sailing along He fell asleep; and a fierce gale of wind descended on the lake, and they began to be swamped and to be in danger. They came to Jesus and woke Him up, saying, "Master, Master, we are perishing!" And He got up and rebuked the wind and the surging waves, and they stopped, and it became calm. And He said to them, "Where is your faith?" They were fearful and amazed, saying to one another, "Who then is this, that He commands even the winds and the water, and they obey Him?"

The disciples were afraid. Jesus pinpointed the reason: they lacked faith.

It's easy for us to pick on the disciples, "Come on, boys, think about this. Why are you so afraid when Jesus is with you? God is in the boat with you. Why be afraid of a little storm?" But then again, isn't Jesus with us, too?

Why do we ever get fearful? Why are we overwhelmed with anxiety? Do we ever think of our fear and anxiety as a symptom of a lack of faith? When the storms of life are raging around us, why are we so frightened when God is on our side? We're not so different from the disciples after all, are we? We have the same reaction (fear and trembling), the same problem (lack of faith). But you argue, "This is too simplistic. I believe in God and I believe in Christ, but I'm still fearful. It's not helping."

You must understand something about the nature of faith. Faith is not something you had once a long time ago that covers you for every difficult time you are ever going to go through for the rest of your life. Faith is active. You must constantly, day in and day out, be putting your faith in God and in Christ. The disciples were believers. They had left everything to follow Christ. That took faith. But at this particular point they weren't exercising their faith. Jesus was telling them to do something. They had believed in Him, but now during this time of trial, they needed to exercise their faith in Him once again.

When Jesus was walking on the water in the storm (Matt. 14), Peter saw Him from the boat and acted in faith. He jumped out of the boat to run to Christ—on the water in the storm. Why would Peter do that? Faith. Peter trusted that Christ would be able to take care of him. But as Peter was walking along he took his eyes off Christ, and he started to look around him. He became afraid, and he started to sink. Why did Peter start to sink? Jesus told him, "You of little faith, why did you doubt?" (v. 31). Peter, you had faith, but then you started looking at your circumstances, took your eyes off Me, and you started to sink. That's what often happens to us. We start out well, we step out in faith, but then we start to look at our circumstances—things aren't going the way we think that they should. So we take our eyes off Christ, and we start to sink.

When you are sinking, when you are overwhelmed, recognize your problem—you've taken your eyes off Christ. Repent of your sin, and actively put your faith and trust in Him.

If you want to stand strong, to stop being so anxious, to be courageous, you have got to exercise faith. You've got to go back to the Scriptures, learn what is true about God, and apply it to your situation. You have to stop allowing your feelings to control you; you have to stop allowing what you see to control you. Instead, act in faith, trusting God's Word. You must tell yourself, "This is truth. I may not understand it, and I may not feel like it's true, but I believe it, and I am going to act on it—no matter what." Act in faith, trusting God's Word.

What does it take to be courageous when times are tough? "Don't let your heart be troubled." Recognize the temptation. Remember the prohibition. Stand guard at the door of your heart and wage war against all the doubt and anxiety that tries to enter. "Believe in God. Believe also in Jesus Christ." Actively seek to put your faith and trust in God. Rely on Him.

People of faith are people of courage. Isn't that what we see in Hebrews 11? How did Abraham leave his home, live in a tent in a foreign land, and prepare to offer up his son as a sacrifice to God? By faith! How did Moses choose to endure ill treatment rather than enjoy the riches of Egypt? By faith. How did Gideon, Barak, Samson, Jepthah, David, and Samuel conquer kingdoms, perform acts of righteousness, shut the mouths of lions, and endure great persecutions? By faith.

But Jesus didn't stop with commanding His disciples to put off doubt and put on faith. He continued by giving His disciples several specific faith-building promises. These are truths they needed to dwell on instead of the troubling thoughts they were thinking.

We should learn from that. When you are in the midst of a trial, go to Scripture to find out what God tells you about that situation. Hang on to that promise for dear life. Jesus didn't just tell the disciples to believe, He also reminded them why they should do so. He gave them specific promises to cling to.

Be careful. Don't just say you believe and then make something up to believe about God. Don't put your faith in words you put in God's mouth. Put your faith in promises that He has revealed to you through His Word. Those promises are your life preservers. Hold on to them and don't let go.

Don't know where to start? Study the promises Jesus gave His disciples.

Remember Heaven

When you are struggling with anxiety and fear about the things that are going on all around you, stop and think about heaven. Think about eternity. Think about what God is preparing for those who love Him.

Jesus told His disciples, "In My Father's house are many dwelling places" (John 14:2). In other words, Jesus told us, "Heaven is My Father's house. He's going to welcome you because He loves Me and I love you! Don't worry about your homes. Don't worry about your financial situation. Remember heaven; remember that heaven belongs to My Father, and that He has room for all of you."

Think about how wonderful heaven is going to be. Think about God's creativity and how beautiful a place that has never been marred by sin really is. Think about the fact that heaven belongs to your Father and that He has room for you. Start to put your problems in perspective. They don't seem quite as upsetting, do they?

Trust in My Character

When you start to wonder about what is going on in your life, fear may be starting to creep up on you and dominate your thoughts. Turn back to Jesus. Think about who He is and how He cares for you. Meditate on His promises. He isn't leading you on. He desires your best. He isn't playing a game with you. When you are frightened, remember Jesus loves you, and nothing can separate you from His love. You can trust Him.

Jesus explained, "If it were not so, I would have told you" (John 14:2). "Trust me," Jesus is saying. "Here you are all frightened. I would have let you know if things weren't going to turn out right in the end. I wouldn't deceive you. I wouldn't lead you on. There's not the slightest doubt about all this. I desire what is best for you. You need to stop worrying and trust in My character. If this weren't so, I would have let you know."

Understand Why I Am Leaving

When you are anxious and worried, remember that God has a purpose for all His actions. Things may look very dark, but God has a plan for even the darkest of times. From a human perspective, Christ's leaving the disciples looked like the worst thing that could possibly happen to them, but from God's perspective, it was the best.

Jesus reminded His disciples, "For I go to prepare a place for you" (John 14:2). In other words, "It's good for Me to leave you. Look a little deeper at what is happening here. You look at My leaving as if it is a terrible thing, but understand, I need to go to get heaven ready for you. This is why I have to go. I have to make My Father's house ready for you."

We serve an amazing God. From a human perspective, an event may look like the worst thing that could possibly happen to us, yet God uses it for our good. God has a purpose for all He does. We may not know it, we may not see it, but we can rest in Him.

It Won't Be Like This Forever

When life gets difficult, remember, Jesus is coming back. Now is not all there is. Jesus said, "If I go and prepare a place for you, I will come again and receive you to Myself, that where I am, there you may be also" (John 14:3). In other words, "I'm not leaving you forever. I'm coming back. If I go, you can be sure I will return. I'll take you home. And why am I doing all this? What's my purpose? That where I am, there you may be also."

Christ desires to be with His people. Think of that! I just hope that His people desire to be with Him. If Christ is your life, what have you to fear? He's preparing heaven so you can spend eternity with Him.

You Know the Way

When Jesus told the disciples that He had to leave them, they wanted to know where He was going. They didn't want to get stranded. They wanted to follow Him, and Jesus encouraged them, "You know the way where I am going" (John 14:4). You're not lost. You know how to get to where I am going.

Thomas didn't understand, so he asked, "Lord, we do not know where You are going, how do we know the way?" (v. 5). Poor Thomas, so clueless. Jesus said to him, "I am the way, and the truth, and the life; no one comes to the Father but through Me" (v. 6). The only way to heaven, the only way to partake of these great promises is through Jesus Christ. No one can have a right relationship with God the Father apart from Jesus Christ.

If you are not a believer, I beg you to run to Jesus Christ. You have every reason in the world to be afraid if you are not trusting in

Him. God is against you, you have no hope for heaven, and your life is empty. Jesus is the way, the truth, and the life. Repent of your sins and put your faith in Him. No Jesus, no peace. Know Jesus, know peace. The principles you'll learn in this book will be of no help to you if you don't belong to Jesus Christ.

If you are a believer, is your life different from the world's? Are you anxious, fearful, tense, and worried? Jesus says you need to put all that off. "Let not your heart be troubled." War against the anxiety that wars against you. Remember, you need to put something else in its place. "Believe in God, believe also in Jesus Christ." Actively put your faith in Christ. Repent of your lack of faith and cry out to God to increase your faith. Refocus by relying on the promises He has given in His Word. You can overcome fear. You can be a person of courage. You can remain calm in the midst of chaos. But you'll only be able to do so if you become a man or woman who actively exercises your faith.

There's a reason this chapter is at the beginning of the book. First, we want you to understand the importance of responding correctly to trials. Sinful fear is not an option. Second, the chapters that follow won't help you at all if you are not willing to start here: guard your heart and put your faith in God.

Before you move on, take a look back. Are you a true believer? Do you have a realistic perspective on life? Are you willing to work at overcoming fear? It's a matter of obedience.

QUESTIONS FOR DISCUSSION

1. How is the Christian's life different from the world's?

2. In one sentence, summarize what it takes to be courageous in fearful situations.

3. What were the external circumstances that could have tempted the disciples to be overwhelmed with fear?

4. How does knowing that you are not the only Christian who has been tempted to be overwhelmed with fear help you?

5. Is it wrong to feel distress and fear? Prove your answer biblically.

6. When do fear and distress become sinful?

7. Why does the fact that Jesus commands the disciples to stop being troubled give us hope?

8. What does it take to respond to trials correctly?

9. Why is it so important to understand this statement: "Courage and peace don't just come automatically because you are a Christian"?

10. Do we have to be overwhelmed with fear? Prove your answer biblically.

11. How did you respond the last time you were in a frightening situation? What did you do right? What did you do wrong?

12. How is Jesus' counsel to His disciples different from simply saying, "Don't worry, be happy"?

13. Why is the world's advice, "Life is short. You shouldn't get so upset. Don't worry. Just be happy," such nonsense?

14. In what did Jesus tell the disciples to put their faith? Why is that so much better than the world's wisdom to "put your faith in yourself"?

15. What does it mean to put your faith in God?

16. Finish this statement: If you have a fear problem, you have a problem . . .

17. What are you really saying when you are controlled by sinful fear?

18. Take a look at the last situation in which you became fearful and worried. What does your response tell you about what you believe about God?

19. What can you learn from Luke 8:22–25?

20. How would you respond to someone who says, "I believe in God, and I believe in Jesus Christ. But it's not helping. I'm still fearful!"?

21. What can you learn from the fact that Jesus didn't just tell His disciples to believe, He also told them why they ought to do so?

22. Why are these two chapters at the beginning of this book?

3

FACE TO FACE WITH FEAR

THE DAY BEFORE I turned twenty-five, I came down with mononucleosis. The problem was, I didn't know I had mono. I just knew I was sick. I'd never been sick like that before, and I never want to be sick like that again. It was four weeks of sheer misery. But the hardest part was not knowing what was wrong.

I went to the doctor, and he didn't know either. Still, he made a diagnosis and gave me a prescription. But his diagnosis was wrong, and the medicine he prescribed actually made me feel worse. After several frustrating trips to different doctors, one of them finally decided to do a blood test, and as a result he figured out why I was sick.

Knowing I had mono didn't make me better right away, but it surely did give me peace of mind, because at least I knew what I was up against. It's hard to solve a problem until you know what the problem is.

We've seen that as Christians we can be courageous, and in fact we must be courageous. We've also learned that courage doesn't come naturally. Life can be pretty frightening. If we are going to be courageous we have to exercise our faith. That's where change begins. Unfortunately, even though we can and should be courageous, we still struggle with fear. (That's probably why you are reading this book.) And that fear cripples us in our service to our King. It's a major problem.

Throughout this book we will look extensively at what the Scripture teaches about how to overcome fear. But before we do so, we must

49

answer an even more fundamental question: what is fear? If a doctor doesn't know what your problem is, he is unable to give you the correct prescription. And if you have not thought carefully about what the Bible says about this problem of fear, you are not going to understand its solution. You need to know what you are up against.

At first glance the question seems to be one we don't even need to answer. We all know when we're afraid. Why should we define it? Yet when you take a closer look at your fears, you'll find that they are not all the same. They are even a bit more complicated than you might have thought at first.

When we turn to Scripture, we quickly discover that there are as many different fears as there are people. Adam was afraid of God, Cain was afraid of physical harm, Jacob was afraid of losing his life, Moses was afraid of leadership, Job was frightened by bad dreams, Saul was afraid of David's popularity, Samuel was afraid of telling bad news to Eli, Peter feared people's opinions, Timothy feared persecution. But if we look a little more closely we discover that all these specific fears can be divided into three primary categories.

NATURAL FEAR

The Bible uses the term *fear* in different ways. There are times when God commands us not to fear, but there are almost as many times when God commands us to fear. In 1 Peter 3:2, Peter told wives that their behavior ought to be marked by chastity and fear. But then in verse 6 he said to do what is right without having any fear. Fear, but don't fear.

In Hebrews 13:6, we're told, "The Lord is my helper, I will not be afraid." Because God is with us, we don't need to fear. But in 1 Peter 1:17 God commands us, "Conduct yourselves in fear during the time of your stay upon earth."

Be afraid. Don't be afraid. Which is it?

Obviously if God commands us to not fear, and God also commands us to fear, there must be different types of fear. There's a fear God prohibits and a fear God commands. One we must avoid, and the other we must seek.

Our goal as Christians is not to become fearless. It's important to understand that. When we talk about overcoming fear, we are not talking about eliminating all fear. It's not good to be completely fearless. God gave us the emotion of fear for a specific reason. There are times when we should fear, and there are things we should fear.

If God commands His people not to fear, yet He also commands them to fear, obviously fear itself is not intrinsically evil. He doesn't command us not to commit adultery and also to commit adultery, or not to murder and also to murder. Murder and adultery are always wrong. Fear isn't.

There is a natural kind of fear that is not sinful; instead it's just part of being human. That natural emotion can become sinful, or it can become holy. It can either be destructive or productive, depending on whether it controls us or we control it.

David explained in Psalm 9:20: "Put them in fear, O LORD; let the nations know that they are but men." David was asking God to cause the wicked nations to fear. By doing that, what would God be reminding them? That they were just men. They had become proud and arrogant, they had forgotten about their weakness, and as a result they did not fear. If they hadn't had such a distorted view of themselves, they would have experienced fear.

In one sense, fear is an acknowledgment that you are just a human being, that you are not in control of everything, that there are things greater than you. So there is a type of fear that just goes along with being a creature and not the Creator.

Two words can help us understand this natural fear better. The first word is *prudence*. In Proverbs 22:3 we read, "The prudent [man] sees the evil and hides himself, but the naive go on, and are punished for it." The term *fear* is sometimes used in Scripture to describe just what the prudent man is doing in this proverb: seeing the evil, anticipating the danger, and taking steps to protect himself from that danger.

Isaiah 7:25 used the term *fear* in this sense: "As for all the hills which used to be cultivated with the hoe, you will not go there for fear of briars and thorns." Was Isaiah saying you will be terrified by briars and thorns, that the briars and thorns will control your life? No. He was just saying you will not want to go there, because you know that if you go there, it will hurt. That's natural fear.

Several years ago my wife and I went on a camping trip with a youth group. The students were excited about going rappelling. I'm not a big fan of heights, so that idea did not thrill me. But they desperately tried to get me to go along with them saying, "You've just got to overcome your fear."

Well, there's nothing wrong with being afraid of falling off a cliff! That's not a fear I want to overcome. I always want to be afraid of that. Eventually I did go rappelling, but not because I wanted to stop being afraid of falling off cliffs. That's just being prudent.

If you see a lion running at you, it's not a mark of extreme holiness to just stand there twiddling your thumbs. Christians are not unaware of danger; they feel those natural fears, and they make wise choices while paying attention to them.

Jesus Himself actually experienced this kind of natural fear. In Mark 14:32–33, we read the following:

> They came to a place named Gethsemane; and He said to His disciples, "Sit here until I have prayed." And He took with Him Peter and James and John, and began to be very distressed and troubled.

The Greek term translated here as *distressed* literally means to be amazed, to be alarmed, to be astounded, to be greatly disturbed. One Greek dictionary defines it as: "to throw into terror or amazement, to alarm thoroughly, to be struck with amazement, to be struck with terror."[1] Do you see what's happening? Christ looked to the future and felt a shuddering horror. Jesus was sinless, so this fear was not sinful—it was just a natural human reaction when considering a dangerous, difficult situation. He was a real man.

A second term that helps us understand this natural fear is the word *awe*. God has created us to be worshipers. We should experience awe before Him. And often throughout the Scripture the word for fear is

---

1. James Strong, *The New Strong's Complete Dictionary of Bible Words* (Nashville: Nelson, 1996), 611.

translated *awe* or *respect*. Awe is a combination of dread, veneration, and wonder. There are certain events, certain authorities, certain persons that deserve our respect. The greater the event, authority, or person, the more respect they should invoke. Sometimes these events or persons are so great that respect needs to explode into full-blown awe.

God has so ordered the world that there are authorities, and it is natural and right for us to respect and revere these authorities. Something is wrong if we don't.

Children are commanded to fear their parents, employees are told to fear their masters, and citizens are told to fear their government. We all are commanded to fear God. This type of fear ranges from respect to awe, and it is God-given.

God has given us this kind of natural fear for a productive purpose. It keeps us safe and prevents chaos in the world. Paul wrote in Romans 13:3–4 that God established government to produce fear in those who do wrong. "Do you want to have no fear of authority? Do what is good. . . . But if you do what is evil, be afraid; for it does not bear the sword for nothing; for it is a minister of God." Someone who is afraid because he has committed a crime and does not want to get caught is experiencing fear that is natural and right, because God says that if you do wrong you should be afraid. Something is wrong if you are not afraid in that situation, if you have no respect for the authorities God has placed in your life.

We'd be in great danger if men lost this natural fear. Many sins go uncommitted as a result of fear of the consequences. It's good that most people are afraid of going to prison. If not, many more crimes would be committed.

To lack this kind of natural fear or reverence for authorities is not a sign of courage or of holiness but of pride. There are things in this world that are greater than you, and it's right for you to have a reverence for them. Peter says that one of the ways false teachers prove how unrighteous they are is that they "despise authority. Daring, self-willed, they do not tremble when they revile angelic majesties" (2 Peter 2:10–11). Angels are greater and mightier than human beings are, but these false teachers are so corrupt that they have no respect for these authorities.

Instead they despise them, and they prove that they despise them by not being afraid or trembling when they revile them. It's natural and right to fear beings who are so much more powerful than you, but these men are so full of pride that they don't. Something's wrong.

God uses this kind of fear to stop us from sinning and to cause us to praise Him. In Acts 5 we learn that Ananias dropped dead in front of the whole church for lying to the Holy Spirit. Luke tells us the church responded with fear: "Great fear came over the whole church, and over all who heard of these things" (v. 11). That's the response God intended to produce. It wasn't sinful for them to be fearful; it was natural and it was right.

God enabled Paul to perform some extraordinary miracles. Luke wrote that unbelievers responded with fear: "Fear fell upon them all and the name of the Lord Jesus was being magnified" (Acts 19:17). The fear these people experienced was not sinful, or else Luke would not have written in the same sentence, "and the name of the Lord Jesus was being magnified." These were awesome events, they deserved the emotions of awe and respect, and God used these events to produce fear and to promote praise.

So you see, there is a natural kind of fear that is a God-given emotion. As Jay Adams explains, "Fear . . . is not wrong. God implanted all emotions in man. . . . Fear of dangers (e.g., falling over the cliff) that leads one to take necessary precautions is right and holy so long as it rests upon and grows out of a faith and trust in the providence of God."[2]

The problem is, our sinful nature takes this good, helpful emotion and twists, perverts, and distorts it. As a result, it's no longer productive but paralyzing, no longer natural but sinful.

SINFUL FEAR

At various times and in various ways throughout Scripture, God commands us, "Do not fear."

The fear of man brings a snare. (Prov. 29:25)

2. Jay Adams, *The Christian Counselor's Manual* (Nutley, NJ: P&R Publishing, 1973), 415.

Do not fear those who kill the body. (Matt. 10:28)

Be strong in the Lord. (Eph. 6:10)

Be anxious for nothing. (Phil. 4:6)

God has not given us a spirit of fear. (2 Tim. 1:7 NKJV)

Do not fear their intimidation, and do not be troubled. (1 Peter 3:14)

All are different ways of saying the same thing: there are certain kinds of fear that are sinful.

Biblical courage is not the absence of natural fear. It is the absence of sinful fear. If we are going to be courageous, we must carefully consider when fear becomes sinful.

Fear Is Sinful When It Keeps You from Obeying God's Commands

That's pretty obvious, isn't it? If God commands you to do something and you say no because you're afraid—that's obviously not holy fear; that's not the reason God gave you this emotion.

The root meaning of *phobo*, the Greek term for fear, is "flight." That's the nature of fear. Fear causes us to run away from things that frighten us. And fear becomes sinful when it causes us to run away from the things God has commanded us to do.

In 2 Timothy 1:7, Paul described this effect of sinful fear: "God has not given us a spirit of fear, but of power" (NKJV). Fear is the opposite of power and is synonymous with weakness. What is this weakness? Not using your gifts (v. 6). Being ashamed of Christ (v. 8). Christians are not to be characterized by the spirit of fear. What characterizes this sinful fear? Weakness. What is weakness? Not obeying God's commands and fulfilling your responsibilities.

You must understand that that's what sinful fear does. Fear is one of the greatest obstacles to obedience and to glorifying God. In Matthew 25:14–30, Jesus tells the parable of the talents. A master gave his servants some talents (money) to use while he was away. When he came back, he called each servant to give an account of how they had used their talents. Most of the servants used their talents to generate more talents, but one servant had just hidden his talent in the ground.

When his master called him to account for his actions and to explain why he had acted the way he had, the servant responded, "I was afraid, and went away and hid your talent in the ground" (v. 25). Fear kept him from making more of his talent. But that excuse didn't satisfy his master. His master rebuked him harshly saying, "You wicked, lazy slave" (v. 26). What was the lesson? When fear keeps us from using the gifts God has given us, we are sinning.

In Exodus 3–4 we read that God went to Moses and told him to go to Pharaoh and deliver Israel out of Egypt. How did Moses respond? "Who am I?" God answered and Moses responded, "Who am I going to tell them sent me?" God answered and Moses continued, "What if they don't believe me?" God answered and Moses still looked for a way out, "I am not eloquent, and I am not a good speaker." God responded, yet once again Moses begged God to send someone else.

You might understand Moses' fear. The last time he had stepped up, he'd had to flee Egypt and had been rejected by his people. He was just one insignificant individual, and God was telling him to command one of the most powerful men in the world, "Let God's people go!" That's a frightening prospect.

But from God's perspective, Moses' response wasn't understandable; it was sin. The Bible says that finally, after all Moses' excuses, "the anger of the LORD burned against Moses" (Ex. 4:14). Moses' fear was sinful because it was preventing him from stepping out in faith and obedience to God.

When fear causes you to start arguing with God, to be hesitant about obeying His commands, when it causes you to make excuses about doing what God wants you to do, it's sin.

When you are afraid, you need to ask yourself, "Is my fear stopping me from obeying God's commands?" Think specifically. Sometimes we ignore sin because we are dominated by sinful fear. God commands us to confront fellow Christians who are involved in sin. Many times fear keeps us from doing just that. Sometimes we fail to share the gospel because we are controlled by sinful fear. God has given us a message to proclaim, but we keep it to ourselves because we are afraid. Sometimes we neglect using our spiritual gifts because we're too afraid of what others might think. In 1 Peter 4:10, God told us, "As each one has received a special gift, employ it in serving one another as good stewards of the manifold grace of God." Often believers refuse to obey that command—using their gifts—because they are afraid. That's sin. As James 4:17 tells us, "To one who knows the right thing to do and does not do it, to him it is sin."

Fear Is Sinful When It Causes You to Disobey God's Commands

Fear can either stop you from doing the right thing, or it can cause you to do the wrong thing. In either case, it's sinful. Fear is a very powerful force. If you're not careful, it can cause you to do things you would never do otherwise.

That's why people make threats. Threats have the power of fear. People know that if they can make other people afraid, they can have great power over them.

An interesting story in Nehemiah 6 illustrates this point. Sanballat wanted to stop Nehemiah from doing God's work, so he sent Nehemiah a threatening letter.

One of Nehemiah's friends said, "Nehemiah, let's run. Let's go into the temple, close the door, and hide out so we can be safe, protected from the threats of these evil men."

Pay attention to how Nehemiah responded, "Should a man like me flee? And could one such as I go into the temple to save his life? I will not go in" (v. 11). Nehemiah thought about the situation and said:

> I perceived that surely God had not sent him, but he uttered his prophecy against me because Tobiah and Sanballat had hired him. He was hired for this reason, that I might become frightened and act accordingly and sin, so that they might have an evil report in order that they could reproach me. (vv. 12–13)

Why had Sanballat threatened Nehemiah? To get him to sin. He knew the nature of fear, that it can have a powerful effect on a person and cause him to do things he never would do otherwise. But Sanballat was wrong about Nehemiah. Nehemiah was too godly to let sinful fear control him.

In other places in Scripture, godly men didn't respond to fear nearly as well as Nehemiah did. Remember Isaac? We read in Genesis 26 that when Isaac settled in Gerar, he told everyone that his wife Rebekah was really his sister. She was beautiful and he was scared that they might kill him to get to her. So he lied.

Eventually the king spotted Isaac and Rebekah acting like more than a brother and sister, so he confronted them. "She's your wife. Why did you say she was your sister?" Isaac's response was, "I thought someone might kill me." Basically he said, "I lied because I was scared." A pagan had to confront Isaac, a believer, because Isaac had so allowed fear to control him that he had dishonored his wife and dishonored his God.

When you are afraid, ask yourself if your fear is causing you to disobey God's commands. Many times when we are frightened, we do just what Isaac did. We lie. That's an evidence of sinful fear. Other times we compromise in our actions. We cheat, we steal, we yell, we shrink back. We disobey God because we are afraid. That's sinful fear.

Fear Is Sinful When It Causes You to Think and Act Selfishly

As we saw in the previous chapter, sinful fear and biblical love are opposites. John asserts plainly, "There is no fear in love; but perfect love casts out fear" (1 John 4:18). John was telling us that when love comes in, it kicks out fear. The two can't coexist.

Biblical love puts the interests of others above its own interest, and as a result, it acts courageously. Love produces courage. Just look at Jesus. He did not allow His fear or distress to stop Him from going to the cross. Why? Because of the great love with which He loved us. Love kicked out His fear.

Paul is another godly example. Paul walked in Christ's footsteps. He poured himself out for the church. Why? One reason was Paul's love for God. Another was his love for others. Read through his letters and you'll find Paul continually putting the interests of others above his own.

Selfishness causes you to put your interests above the interests of others and, as a result, act cowardly. Selfishness produces fear. Think about Isaac. Who was Isaac thinking about when he lied about his wife? Was he thinking about his wife's needs? Was he thinking she might really want to end up married to one of those men? No! He was just thinking about himself.

When you are so dominated by fear that you become blind to the needs and concerns of others, you can be sure that fear is sinful. It's certainly not wrong to be concerned about your own safety, but it is wrong if you are so concerned about yourself that it stops you from serving others.

Would you call a man a coward just because he doesn't want to run into a burning building? Of course not. But what if he is a father whose child is trapped inside that building and no one else is there to help rescue the child? If he still chooses his own safety over rescuing his son or daughter, you probably would call him a coward. Why? Because he put his own interests above the interests of his child.

Fear springs from an intense focus on self. The more selfish we are, the more fearful we'll be. When we get trapped inside our heads and start wondering what people are thinking, what they are going to say about us, and what they are going to do to us, then fear begins to paralyze us. We get stuck and become continually timid and fearful.

The world would say your problem is self-esteem, that you are fearful because you lack self-confidence. But God's Word would say your problem is selfishness. You are fearful because you are more concerned about yourself than you are about others. When you are dominated by fear, ask yourself who or what you are primarily concerned about.

Fear Is Sinful When It Springs from Thinking Unbiblically

In Philippians 4:8, God told us the way we need to think: "Finally, brethren, whatever is true, whatever is honorable, whatever is right, whatever is pure, whatever is lovely, whatever is of good repute, if there is any excellence and if anything worthy of praise, dwell on these things."

If your fear is causing you to dwell on anything other than the qualities described in this verse, it is sinful fear. If it causes you to dwell on things that are not true, it is sinful.

Fear often comes from doing just that—thinking on things that are not true. Many people live in the land of "what if." What if they were thinking this? What if they said that? Their fear comes from dwelling on things that (1) they have no control over, and (2) most likely aren't true. Other people are expert mind readers—giving people thoughts and intentions they never even knew they had. Still others think completely irrationally. They have one thought and they run with it until it doesn't even resemble anything close to reality. All these people are dwelling on lies, and all those kinds of thoughts need to be banished.

The next time you are struggling with fear, ask yourself: "Is this thought true? Is this thought honorable? Is it lovely? Is this thought in keeping with the qualities Paul described in Philippians 4:8?"

God has not given us a spirit of fear but of a sound mind. A sound mind is a sensible mind. It is a mind that is under control. Self-controlled, rational, sensible, biblical thinking is the opposite of sinful fear.

Fear Is Sinful When It Flows Out of Unbelief

When you become afraid, you need to examine what is at the root of your fear. Sinful fear is produced by a lack of trust in God. Many times when you become frightened, if you would just look at the root cause of your fear, you would see that it is because you do not believe the promises and character of God. Scripture tells us "the people who know their God will display strength" (Dan. 11:32).

In John Bunyan's book *The Pilgrim's Progress*, when Christian begins his journey, he gets stuck early on in a place called the Slough of Despond. Bunyan says that there is a way out of that terrible slough, and the way out is through the promises of God. The same principle is true when we are stuck in the swamp of fear. The way out is the promises of God, but they are only helpful to us if we believe.

For example, take Romans 8:28: "We know that God causes all things to work together for good to those who love God, to those who are called according to His purpose." Ask yourself: are you fearful right now because you don't believe that God is going to work all this out for your good? After all, most people aren't afraid of good things. If God promises that He is going to work it all out for your good, what do you have to be afraid of?

Or read Romans 5:3–5: "We also exult in our tribulations, knowing that tribulation brings about perseverance; and perseverance, proven character; and proven character, hope; and hope does not disappoint, because the love of God has been poured out within our hearts." Ask yourself: are you afraid right now because you do not really believe that your trials and suffering have a purpose? God says that tribulations and trials produce spiritual good and that spiritual good is very valuable. So if God promises that He will use even your pain for your spiritual good, what are you afraid of?

When you become frightened, you should go through Scripture looking at promise after promise. And you should examine yourself for the root cause of your fears. If it's unbelief, it's sin.

The amazing thing about God is that He can even use our sinful fears for our good. He overrules sin and rebellion and uses it to accomplish His great plan. One way He uses fear is to punish those who continually rebel against Him. John Flavel notes, "If men will not fear God, they shall fear men," and as a result they will become a terror to themselves.

> It is a dreadful punishment for God to deliver a man up into the hands of his own fears. I think there is scarce a greater torment to be found in the world than for a man to be his own tormentor, and his mind an instrument of torture to his own body. What a dismal life do they live, who have no peace by day, nor rest by night. . . . The days of such men are terrible days, they wish for the night, hoping it may give them some rest, but their fears go to bed with them, their hearts pant and meditate terror, and then, Oh that it were day again.[3]

3. John Flavel, *The Works of John Flavel*, vol. 3 (London: Banner of Truth Trust, 1968), 255.

There is a natural kind of fear that we just accept; there's a sinful kind of fear that we must reject; and there is yet one more category of fear, one that we must seek after.

HOLY FEAR

God commands us to fear. In 1 Peter 1:17 we read: "If you address as Father the One who impartially judges according to each one's work, conduct yourselves in fear during the time of your stay on earth." If God commands us to fear, that means there is a kind of fear that is not sinful but that is holy and good. As John Flavel once said, "Natural fear is a normal passion of the soul, sinful fear is the normal passion of the soul corrupted and perverted, and holy fear is that normal passion sanctified and put to holy use."[4]

Without this kind of fear, we can't live godly lives. This kind of fear is good for us, a source of great spiritual benefit. According to Proverbs 1:7, it is the beginning of knowledge. Proverbs 14:27 tells us it is a fountain of life. And Psalm 31:19 says that God has stored up goodness to pour out on those who have this kind of fear.

Holy fear and sinful fear are opposites. Sinful fear destroys; holy fear enlivens. Sinful fear is a terrible affliction; holy fear is a great benefit. Sinful fear shortens our days; holy fear lengthens them. Sinful fear is a source of misery; holy fear is a spring of joy. Sinful fear leads men astray; holy fear puts men on the right path. The only way to overcome sinful fear is to replace it with holy fear.

What is this kind of fear? It's a fear of God. In the chapters that follow, we'll look at this fear of God in much greater detail. But for now, just realize that this fear of God produces fear of some other things.

Godly fear produces a fear of sin. That's what Peter tells us in 1 Peter 1:17. The fact that God is an impartial judge should cause us to take sin seriously, to live reverently, to refuse to play around with the things He hates. Paul wrote, "Work out your salvation with fear and trembling"

4. Ibid., 252.

(Phil. 2:12). Why does he say "with fear and trembling"? Because it is serious business. You can't play with sin, it's that dangerous. Jude put it like this:

> Have mercy on some, who are doubting; save others, snatching them out of the fire; and on some have mercy with fear, hating even the garment polluted by the flesh. (vv. 22–23)

Why should you have mercy with fear? God is such a holy judge that you don't want to be drawn into doing anything that might keep you away from Him. So you should have mercy, but with fear.

Godly fear produces a fear of God's Word. The psalmist wrote in Psalm 119:161, "My heart stands in awe of Your words." When God spoke to His people at Mount Sinai, they were afraid, because they saw that the One who was speaking was an awesome, mighty King. When we read His Word, we should have a proper kind of fear, not the fear of a slave of a terrifying master, nor a paralyzing fear, but an awe and a reverence for the Word, because of the greatness of the One who spoke it.

If natural fear has some positive results, and if God can use sinful fear for a good purpose, you can be certain that holy fear has many benefits. We'll study these benefits in great detail in later chapters. For now let's just note a few. Holy fear leads to knowledge and wisdom. "The fear of the LORD is the beginning of knowledge" (Prov. 1:7). "The fear of the LORD is the instruction for wisdom" (Prov. 15:33). The knowledge and wisdom about which these proverbs speak is the ability to use information and learning for living. If a person does not fear God, he will not even have the beginning of knowledge. He won't know how to honor God. He may know facts, but he doesn't understand how those facts fit into the great scheme of things, and as a result he doesn't have the beginning of wisdom. Holy fear keeps us from sin. "By the fear of the LORD one keeps away from evil" (Prov. 16:6). Sin is destructive. The wages of sin is death. But the fear of God keeps us from sinning. You sin because you don't fear God.

Joseph is a great example of how a regard for God produces holiness. He could have given every excuse in the book for sinning with Potiphar's wife. He was a slave. He was far away from home. He was being harassed. He would be thrown in jail if he didn't. But he still refused to give in, even under intense pressure. Why? Genesis 39:9 gives us the answer. Joseph said to her, "There is no one greater in this house than I, and he [Potiphar] has withheld nothing from me except you, because you are his wife. How then could I do this great evil and sin against God?" Joseph feared God, and as a result he stayed far away from evil.

The Hebrew midwives are another example of this principle. In the book of Exodus we see that Pharaoh told the midwives to kill all the sons of Israel. But they refused to do so, even though it could have meant their own deaths. Why? "The midwives feared God, and did not do as the king of Egypt had commanded them" (Ex. 1:17). Holy fear produces joy and contentment. Read Proverbs 15:16: "Better is a little with the fear of the LORD than great treasure and turmoil with it." The fear of the Lord helps you really enjoy life no matter what your circumstances. That's a great blessing. If you can enjoy life no matter what your circumstances, then you are a happy person! Holy fear makes you a person worthy of praise. Proverbs 31:30 says, "Charm is deceptive, and beauty is fleeting; but a woman who fears the LORD is to be praised" (NIV). The world is confused about true worth. The Bible isn't. It begins with the fear of the Lord.

In this chapter we've tried to give you a general biblical overview of the nature of fear. You can be courageous. You can overcome crippling fear. But you won't be able to solve your problem until you know what your problem is. To formulate the proper prescription, you need to begin by making the right diagnosis. You need to understand the nature of fear.

In the next several chapters we will get more specific. We'll start by looking at sinful fear. Since sinful fear comes in such varieties, instead of looking at every different type, we're going to zero in on one specific and very common example: the fear of man.

QUESTIONS FOR DISCUSSION

1. Why is the question "What is fear?" one we need to answer?

2. Explain what we mean by the term *natural fear*. Prove biblically that there is such a thing as natural fear.

3. What two words help us understand natural fear better? Explain in your own words what they mean.

4. Explain and defend this statement: "To not have this kind of natural fear or reverence for authorities is not a sign of courage or holiness but of pride."

5. How does God use natural fear for our good?

6. When is fear sinful?

When it keeps you from following God's commands.

7. How does the Greek term *phobo* help us better understand the nature of fear? *"Flight"*

8. Why is fear one of the greatest obstacles to obeying and glorifying God?

Steps from doing the right thing and makes you do the wrong one.
The end result will are disengaging from the Kingdom

9. What are some ways in which fear has prevented you from obeying God's commands?

Fear of rejection prevents me from getting more involved in doing things with other people.

10. Why do people make threats? What does that tell us about the nature of fear?

To gain power over another person.

11. Are there any ways in which fear is causing you to disobey God's commands?

I detest confrontation and would rather let hurtful things go.

12. How are fear and love opposite from one another?

Love produces courage
Fear produces terror

13. Where does our fear spring from?

Insecurity, sinfulness.

14. Are there specific ways in your life that fear is causing you to dwell on things other than the qualities described in Philippians 4:8? Be specific.

15. Are there specific ways you are living in the land of "what if"? Again, be specific.

16. How can God use sinful fear for our good?

17. What is holy fear?

18. What does holy fear produce?

19. What are some of the positive results of holy fear?

20. What have you learned from this chapter? How will the truths you have learned help you in your battle with fear?

4

TRAPPED!

SINFUL FEAR can ruin your life. If you want proof, just take a look at the life of King Saul. The book of 1 Samuel tells his tragic tale. When we first meet Saul, however, there is no indication that his life is going to end up a tragedy. In fact, we think we're in for a success story.

Saul had it all. According to the writer of 1 Samuel, Saul's father was a man of valor. Saul himself was choice and handsome, the most handsome man in all of Israel. He was a man destined for greatness.

The truth is, Saul's life did begin triumphantly. God chose Saul to be king over His people. Even the prophet Samuel was impressed by this man. He introduced Saul to the nation of Israel, "Do you see him whom the LORD has chosen? Surely there is no one like him among all the people" (1 Sam. 10:24).

But things turned sour very quickly. Just a short while after being chosen as king, Saul flagrantly disobeyed God's commands. God had enabled Saul to win a great victory for His people and then had commanded him to wait for Samuel, the priest, to arrive to lead the people in offering sacrifices and praise to God. Samuel didn't arrive immediately, and the people grew restless. Saul became afraid and took things into his own hands. As a result, he disobeyed God.

Samuel rebuked Saul for his fear and his compromise, but Saul didn't learn his lesson. Later we again find Saul blatantly disobeying God's command because of his fear of the people. This time he appeared to repent. But it becomes obvious as we read throughout 1 Samuel that he hadn't changed.

So God raised up David, who at first seemed to be Saul's opposite. When Samuel had looked at Saul he had said, "This is the one." When he looked at David he asked, "Is this the one?" But God gave David the strength to do what Saul should have done. David stood up for God's people by confronting the giant Goliath.

At first, David won Saul's favor. But that favor soon turned to anger. The nation rallied behind David. Women started singing songs about him: "Saul has slain his thousands, and David his ten thousands" (1 Sam 18:7). It made Saul incredibly angry: "They have ascribed to David ten thousands, but to me they have ascribed thousands. Now what more can he have but the kingdom?" (1 Sam. 18:8).

At the root of Saul's anger was fear. First Samuel 18:12 explains, "Saul was afraid of David, for the LORD was with him but had departed from Saul." And verse 15, "When Saul saw that [David] was prospering greatly, he dreaded him."

This fear took over Saul's life. He should have rejoiced that David was doing great things for Israel; instead he became afraid and began to act completely irrationally. Saul stopped thinking about how best to rule the nation and instead devoted his full attention to destroying David.

He began by making a plan to use his own daughter to ensnare David: "I will give her to him that she may become a snare to him, and that the hand of the Philistines may be against him" (v. 21). But it didn't work. Saul's daughter loved David. First Samuel 18:28–29 tells us that

> when Saul saw and knew that the LORD was with David, and that Michal, Saul's daughter, loved him, then Saul was even more afraid of David. Thus Saul was David's enemy continually.

Saul's son Jonathan also loved David. They were good friends, so Jonathan sought to protect David. This made Saul even angrier. First Samuel 20:30 tells us, "Then Saul's anger burned against Jonathan and he said to him, 'You son of a perverse, rebellious woman! Do I not know that you are choosing the son of Jesse to your own shame?'" Then Saul hurled his spear at his own son to kill him.

Saul made it his life mission to destroy David, but in the end Saul destroyed everything that mattered to himself, and not David. Saul and his sons were eventually slain, and the kingdom was handed over to David. Saul's is a story of great potential wasted, a man who had it all and lost it, because of a specific kind of sinful fear, the fear of man.

Saul's story is a classic illustration of Proverbs 29:25: "The fear of man brings a snare, but he who trusts in the LORD will be exalted." In the upcoming chapters we'll look at how to identify this type of sinful fear and how to overcome it. In this chapter, however, our goal is very simple: we want to forever cement in your mind the terrible consequences that result from sinful fear, specifically from the fear of man.

We've looked at how freeing it is to be a person of courage. Now we want you to see how enslaving it is to be controlled by fear. We want you to fear fearing man, because this type of sinful fear can ruin your life.

Solomon put it like this: "The fear of man brings a snare" (Prov. 29:25). You may not be a hunter, but you probably at least know this: a snare is not a good thing. To put it simply, a snare is a trap. It is something that is alluring. It is attractive but deceptive. It is something that is distracting. It keeps you from doing what you need to do. And it is destructive. The ultimate purpose of a snare is to destroy.

THE FEAR OF MAN IS DECEPTIVE

Some of you are thinking that you're not afraid of people, so this doesn't really apply to you. But before you give in to the temptation to skip over this section, please stop and reconsider. Remember, the fear of man is a snare, which means that it's deceptive.

Different people demonstrate fear in different ways. Some people become loud and obnoxious when they're frightened, others become quiet and shy.

In Luke 1, when the angel appeared to Mary, she was afraid and began to think and "ponder" (v. 29) what he was telling her. Peter had an opposite reaction to his fear. When Jesus was being taken away to be crucified, Peter became afraid and started talking, telling everybody he had nothing to do with Jesus Christ.

The same person may express fear differently in different situations. Sometimes when you are scared you run away; other times you hold your ground. First Samuel 13 tells us that when King Saul was frightened, he offered a sacrifice to appease the nation. Yet 1 Samuel 20 tells us that in a different situation he hurled a spear at his own son because of fear. The same person was experiencing fear in both situations, but he had two completely different reactions.

In a similar manner, the fear of man can be expressed differently in different people. That's one reason it's so deceptive. The fear of man is not simply shaking in your boots every time you meet someone new. The fear of man is a broad biblical category for many specific sins.

Dr. Ed Welch explains, " 'Fear' in the biblical sense is a much broader word [than merely being terrified by other people]. It includes being afraid of someone, but it extends to holding someone in awe, being controlled or mastered by people, worshipping other people, putting your trust in people."[1]

Some people don't do what's right because they are afraid of people. If you grew up in a non-Christian environment, you probably have a lot of non-Christian friends. You hear the gospel and you want to do what is right, but you don't because you are afraid of what those friends will think. Other people obey God and do what is right because of a fear of man. If you grew up in a Christian environment, you probably have a lot of Christian friends. Christianity is your culture. You don't want to publicly disobey God because you are afraid of what all your friends might think. This means you obey God not because you're concerned about what He will think, nor out of the desire of your heart, but from your desire to look good to others. It's the same basic sin, fear of man, but it manifests itself in very different ways.

Some people refuse to use their talents because of the fear of man. They are so afraid of what other people will think of them that they won't use the talents God has given them. This was a real battle for me. I hated speaking in front of people. And for a while, especially in high

1. Ed Welch, *When People Are Big and God Is Small* (Phillipsburg, NJ: P&R Publishing, 1997), 14.

school, I wouldn't do it. But other people overcommit themselves and won't say no to any service opportunity because of their fear of man. They so want to please people that they won't even say no when they know they should.

Some people close themselves up and run away from relationships because of their fear. They don't let anyone in, they refuse to communicate, and they hide in order to protect themselves because they are so afraid of what people might think of them. Others live their lives absolutely dependent on relationships because of their fear. They have to be in a romantic relationship, they've got to have friendships, they've got to be the center of attention—all because they are controlled by what others think of them.

Some people are very indecisive because of their fear. They hate making decisions because they are so worried about what others will think. When they do make a decision, they are always second-guessing that decision because they're controlled by the fear of man. Other people are very controlling because of their fear. They seem supremely self-confident, and they act very assertively, but it's really all just a show. They dominate others because they are afraid.

Some people feel empty. They feel purposeless because they are going nowhere in their lives and are controlled by the opinions of others; since others don't see them as "important" people, they feel like they're failures. Other people feel incredibly successful, very important. And the reason they feel so important is because they have made it; others do respect them. They derive their sense of worth from what others think of them—which means they are controlled by the fear of man.

Some people are always striving to conform because of their fear. They want to be invisible. They don't want to stand out. They wear the same kind of clothes everyone else does, dress like everybody else, because they're so afraid of what people might think. Others rebel against conformity because of their fear. They're dominated by a desire to stand out from the crowd. That's being dominated by a desire to have people look at you and notice you—which of course is the same as being dominated by the fear of man. So the fear of man is deceptive because it shows up in different forms.

Even more important, the fear of man is deceptive because it offers you something it can't possibly fulfill. Why do you fear man? Because you think you are going to receive some benefit. Why else would you do it? You think that in this specific situation it would be better for you to fear man than to put your trust in God.

Think about that. The Bible instructs you to confront your brother when he sins against you. God wants you to do that. But when you don't do it because you are afraid of what that person might think, what are your actions revealing? They reveal that you believe it is better for yourself not to confront that person. You must be thinking that, because if you really believed it was better for you to trust and obey God, you would obey.

Are you constantly seeking other people's approval? Are you always trying to get people to like you? Why? You are thinking there's profit in that. You think it's going to make you feel good. You think that if everybody is happy with you, then your life will be great. You think that in order to be happy you need people to like you. You think it's profitable to fear other people. Otherwise you wouldn't do it.

When you fear other people, you are acting as if God alone is not capable of making you happy and keeping you secure. In reality, you are making other human beings your idol. You have set your heart on their approval. You are motivated by what they think of you. Their opinions and their desires master and rule you. You serve them, not God. And that's idolatry.

When you depend on people in the place of God, those people have become your idol. For example, when you think that your life would be successful if you could just get people to respect you, and you believe your life is empty and you consider yourself a failure when you don't accomplish this, then you are an idolater. If you think being fulfilled involves getting others to like you, and you are tremendously bothered and discouraged by criticism, you are involved in idolatry. You are setting yourself up for misery and unhappiness. Your idol promises you happiness and fulfillment, but it actually leads you to sorrow and pain. That's the nature of idolatry. Idols always lie.

Dr. David Powlison explains that each of our idols "makes false promises and gives false warnings: 'if only . . . then . . .'" He continues:

Because both the promises and warnings are lies, service to each idol results in a hangover of misery and accursedness. Idols lie, enslave, and murder. They are continually insinuated by the one who was a liar, slave master and murderer from the beginning. They are under the immediate wrath of God who frequently does not allow such things to work well in His world.[2]

It's foolish to look to people for something they can't possibly provide. It's like trying to get candy out of a soda machine. You can put your quarters in all day long, you can bang on the machine, but you're not going to get any candy out of it because there's no candy in the machine. Because mere human beings aren't God, they can't possibly fulfill your hopes. True justice cannot come from people; it comes from God. Safety and security ultimately don't come from people; they come from God.

Putting your trust in an idol always has negative consequences. That's why Solomon says, "The fear of man brings a snare" (Prov. 29:25). We mistakenly think that if we put our trust in people we will be kept safe, we will be free. Instead, when we use people to meet our desires, we end up enslaved to them.

THE FEAR OF MAN IS DISTRACTING

Remember, a snare is defined as something that lures a person away from his or her real purpose. That's exactly what the fear of man does—it distracts you from your real purpose. If you are dominated by the fear of man, you can be certain that you are not fulfilling the purpose God has for you.

It Distracts You from Doing What You Are Designed to Do, Which Is to Glorify God

You can't serve two masters. Jesus tells us, "No one can serve two masters; for either he will hate the one and love the other, or he will

2. David Powlison, "Idols of the Heart and Vanity Fair," *Journal of Biblical Counseling* 13, no. 2 (Winter 1995): 37.

be devoted to one and despise the other" (Matt. 6:24). In that context, Jesus was talking about God and money, but the principle holds true. If the fear of man is your master, you won't be serving God. Paul put it like this in Galatians 1:10: "Am I now seeking the favor of men, or of God? Or am I striving to please men? If I were still trying to please men, I would not be a bond-servant of Christ."

It's impossible to be a bond servant of Christ if you are a slave to man's opinions and man's desires. If your main priority in life is getting people to like you or think well of you, you won't be able to live all out for God.

Haven't you seen this principle demonstrated in your own life? Haven't you ever gone to church so concerned about what everybody else was thinking about you that you forgot that the purpose of going to church is actually to worship and glorify God? Haven't you ever gone to work so focused on everybody else that you couldn't do your job to the glory of God? It's a snare.

It Distracts You from Thinking about What God Wants to Happen in a Particular Situation

When you are concerned about what you want, you don't stop to think about what God wants to happen.

That's exactly what happened to Peter. Paul told us the story in Galatians 2. Paul and Peter were spending time with the church at Antioch. For a while Peter was including everyone in the fellowship; he was eating with the Jewish and the Gentile believers, setting a good example of the unity that is ours in Christ. Then, because of the fear of man, he made a complete U-turn.

Paul wrote in Galatians 2:11–13:

> When [Peter] came to Antioch, I opposed him to his face, because he stood condemned. For prior to the coming of certain men from James, he used to eat with the Gentiles; but when they came, he began to withdraw and hold himself aloof, fearing the party of the circumcision. The rest of the Jews joined him in hypocrisy, with the result that even Barnabas was carried away by their hypocrisy.

Peter was there in Antioch to minister to God's people, to be a light for Christ, but what happened? Peter withdrew from certain people and became aloof. He was distracted from God's purpose for his life because he was afraid of what other people thought. He was so concerned about what they thought that he stopped being concerned about what God thought.

Once again, you know the truth of this from personal experience. You get caught up in a situation. You are on the go. You are making decisions, doing things. And you never once stop to consider what God might want you to do in that situation. The fear of man sucks you into its trap.

The Fear of Man Distracts You from Considering the Needs of Others

God wants you to be sincerely interested in the needs of others. Read Philippians 2:3–4:

> Do nothing from selfishness or empty conceit, but with humility of mind regard one another as more important than yourselves; do not merely look out for your own personal interests, but also for the interests of others.

And Romans 12:10: "Be devoted to one another in brotherly love; give preference to one another in honor." It's hard to obey those commands when you are consumed with your own concerns.

If you are constantly wondering what people are thinking of you, whether they like you, why they are looking at you a certain way, or why they said what they said to you, you're going to be so blinded by those thoughts that you won't be able to even see the needs of the person who is right in front of you. When you fear others, your ultimate idol is yourself. That's why you're afraid—because you are totally wrapped up in yourself. It's all about you.

Sometimes the fear of man produces actions that look like service for others. If you do things for other people because you want something from them, that is just selfish service. If you're someone's friend because of the way they make you feel, or if you're nice to someone so they will be nice to you, that's selfishness. <u>Once again, when you are afraid of people, you are making an idol out of yourself.</u> As a result, you are distracted from truly and sincerely looking out for the needs of others.

THE FEAR OF MAN IS DESTRUCTIVE

A snare is something that lures people away from their real purpose in order to destroy them. You need to realize this is a serious issue. <u>The fear of man will ultimately ruin your life.</u>

Fear of man produces grumbling and complaining. It literally sucks the joy out of life. What happened during the exodus? God delivered Israel from slavery to Egypt in an amazing way. He proved that He was God and that He cared about His people. Exodus 13 tells us that God Himself literally led His people out of Egypt.

The Israelites should have been jumping up and down for joy. They had been freed from slavery; God was their leader and protector. It couldn't have gotten any better than that. But in Exodus 14:11–12, we find them grumbling and complaining. "Is it because there were no graves in Egypt that you have taken us away to die in the wilderness? Why have you dealt with us in this way, bringing us out of Egypt? Is this not the word that we spoke to you in Egypt, saying, 'Leave us alone that we may serve the Egyptians'?" They should have been rejoicing, but instead they were saying, "Oh, I wish we were still slaves in Egypt!" Why? Because Pharaoh was pursuing them, and the people of Israel "became very frightened" (v. 10).

Some people literally live their entire lives complaining. They wear a permanent frown on their faces. If that's true of you, if you are constantly grumbling, you ought to ask yourself, "Do I have this attitude because of the fear of man?"

It Creates Trouble in Your Heart

<u>The fear of man is like a tornado in your soul, wreaking havoc on your inner man.</u> Throughout Scripture, many kinds of negative attitudes are associated with the fear of man. In Deuteronomy 1:21 it's linked with discouragement; in Deuteronomy 20:3 with panic and a

trembling, fainting heart. In Joshua 10 we read that it's the opposite of strength and courage, so it is synonymous with weakness and cowardice. In 1 Kings 19 it is linked with depression, and in Psalm 46 it is associated with excruciating anguish. Are you dismayed, discouraged, fainthearted, about to give up, acting irrationally, trembling, weak, jealous, or troubled? Check your heart. The fear of man could be at work.

It Leads to Compromise

Think about Abraham. He was traveling with his beautiful wife. He was afraid that the Egyptians were going to do something to him in order to get his wife. So what did he do? He lied. He said, "She's not my wife; she's my sister." The fear of man had Abraham so ensnared that he lied and dishonored God, and totally shamed his wife. He even allowed his wife to get married to another man because he was afraid. But that's what the fear of man does. It deceives you. You think you're protecting yourself, when in reality you are destroying yourself and your family.

Abraham's not alone, is he? You probably can think of times in your life when you have done what you knew was wrong because you were afraid of what other people might think. That's a dangerous path. Disobedience always has consequences.

It Produces Hypocrisy and Sometimes Even Apostasy

Remember Peter in Galatians 2? He knew what God wanted him to do, but he acted in a completely different way. Why? He was afraid of what people might think. The fear of man caused him to act like a hypocrite.

This kind of thing happens all the time in churches. We know what the Bible says about sin and about how we need to encourage each other in the faith, but we are so afraid of others that we are not willing to be real, to admit that we have problems. We put on a front—we've got to have everybody think we have it all together. We can't have anybody thinking that we actually have problems with sin. We're stuck in this quicksand, getting drawn in deeper and deeper. There are people all around who are willing to help us get out, but we don't cry out for help. We just pretend as though everything is all right, putting on a brave face for Sunday, and then being suffocated by our sin all week, ensnared by the fear of man.

Sometimes the fear of man has even more tragic results, such as apostasy. Think about Aaron. Aaron was a man of God, a leader of the nation of Israel. God chose him to help Moses. But think about how far he fell. Moses went up on the mountain to meet with God. While he was up there, the people got restless. They forgot all about Moses. They gathered around Aaron and commanded him to make them a god, but Aaron knew better. He should have rebuked them; after all God had just miraculously delivered them from Egypt and told them not to worship any other gods. But what did Aaron do? He told them to bring him all their gold so he could make them an idol. When Moses came down from the mountain, he became furious. He asked Aaron, "Why did you do this?" Aaron's response? "Don't look at me; look at them." The fear of man caused him to shipwreck his faith.

It Stirs Up Jealousy, Can Create Irrational Thinking, and Can Even End Up Destroying Relationships

Do you remember King Saul? Saul feared David and ended up lashing out at those closest to him. His actions made no sense. He threw spears at David, who was helping him. He even tried to throw a spear at his own son Jonathan. He forced his own daughter to marry David because he wanted her to be a snare to him. Think about how the fear of man ensnared Saul. It ruined his rule, it turned him against his family, it destroyed his life.

Sadly, it is still doing the same thing today. The fear of man causes people to act in all sorts of irrational ways. It causes them to do all sorts of things that hurt them and cause harm to the ones they love. Proverbs 29:25: "The fear of man brings a snare."

I am convinced that the fear of man is one of the most common problems in the Christian life, as well as one of the most devastating. It's a crippler. If you don't deal with this fear of man, it will hinder you from being who God wants you to be and from living the way God wants you to live. Guaranteed!

We've seen that the fear of man is dangerous. It's a snare. But knowing that won't do you much good if you don't know how to get out of its clutches! In the next few chapters we will look at God's way of escape. But before you can ever think of escaping, you must realize first you are ensnared by the fear of man, and second, that God wants you to be free!

QUESTIONS FOR DISCUSSION

In what ways does the fear of man ensnare you? Don't know where to start? A good place to begin is by examining your actions.

1. Are you different on the outside than you are on the inside? Do you denounce sin publicly but indulge in it privately (Matt. 23)? Be very specific. In what ways are you different when you are around others than you are when you are alone?

2. Are you doing something you know is wrong because of what others might think? Perhaps this takes place at work or even in your role as a parent (1 Sam. 13).

3. Are you doing something right because of what others might think? Are you "practicing your righteousness before men to be noticed by them" (Matt. 6:1)? In what ways is this occurring in your life?

4. Are you the same person at home that you are at work, at church, or with your friends? Are you a different person depending on what friends you are with (James 3:17)? Ask someone close to you to help you evaluate yourself in this area.

5. Do you get upset when others don't notice the good deeds you do (Rom. 12:9)? When was the last time you served someone else and your service went unrecognized? How did you respond?

6. Do you judge the motives of other people (1 Cor. 13:4–7; Phil. 4:8)? Do you spend much time wondering what other people are thinking?

7. Do you worry about what people are thinking of you (Phil. 2:3–4)? Be honest and specific. About whom do you worry and why?

8. When you have conversations with others, are you constantly thinking about yourself (Phil. 2:3–4)? Think about the last conversation you had with someone who mattered to you. What were you thinking about during that conversation?

9. Do you tell outright lies? Do you shade the truth (Gen. 20; 26; Gal. 1)? When was the last time you lied? What was the reason for your lie?

10. Do you always have to be right? Do you become defensive when you are rebuked (Prov. 3:5–6; 14:12; 16:2; 17:10; 18:1–2)? When was the last time you were rebuked? How did you respond? Why?

11. Are you jealous (1 Sam. 18:10)? Of whom are you jealous? Why are you jealous of them?

12. Do you feel empty on the inside? If so, describe this feeling further.

    yes, I do. Since Jim died I do not seem to be able to find my place in the world. Feeling displaced is the scariest feeling I have ever had.

13. When do you feel the happiest? When do you feel the saddest? Think about the last time you were really happy. What caused your happiness?

    I am happiest when I am with my family, cooking for them, taking care of their needs, cooking with them. I love to feel that I am a part of their lives. It gives me a sense of belonging and a certain level of fulfillment

14. Are you afraid to talk to others? To whom do you get nervous about speaking? Why do you experience this nervousness?

15. Do you feel crushed when you are criticized? Do you get upset when others are praised and you are not?

    Yes, I definitely feel crushed. For some reason the criticism feels very much like a rejection.

16. Are you afraid to tell others about Christ because of what they might think or what they might do? How did you react the last time you were given an opportunity to be a witness for Christ?

17. When in trouble, where do you turn? In what do you put your hope (Isa. 7–8)?

If you answered these questions honestly, they should help expose some symptoms of the fear of man—and identifying the symptoms is a good place to start. You wouldn't go to a doctor unless you knew you were sick.

You need to know if you are caught in the snare of the fear of man. But you must not stop with merely exposing the symptoms. If a doctor only treats the symptoms, he'll never cure the real problem. To overcome the fear of man, you must go deeper than mere symptoms. You must identify the root causes.

5

GETTING TO THE HEART OF THE PROBLEM

THERE'S NO DOUBT that the fear of man is a problem. It's impossible to argue with Solomon when he calls it a snare. This land of sinful fear truly is a type of bondage. It robs you of many of the comforts and pleasures of life, and steals much of the joy and peace you should have in God and His Word.

It's an especially serious problem because it is a sin that affects every area of your life. The fear of man will seep in and corrupt everything you do. It will complicate your life in all sorts of different ways and cause a multitude of problems. The fear of man ensnares us, and then it controls us.

Since the fear of man produces so many complicating problems, many of us have struggled to overcome it. We may not have realized that what we were battling was the fear of man, but we all have certainly struggled with the symptoms of this root problem. Unfortunately, all too often we fail to defeat it. One of the reasons for this constant failure is that we are merely trying to change the external aspects of the situation. We start doing this or that differently, thinking that a few surface changes will fix the problem. For example, we say, "I won't struggle so much with peer pressure if I just keep telling myself that what other people think doesn't matter." Or, "If someone calls asking me to do something, I'll just tell them my spouse won't let me do it." When we deal that way with the problems that the fear of man produces, it's like putting a bandage on a cancer patient.

If you are going to overcome the fear of man, you must not merely deal with the externals. You need to deal with the root. You'll never effectively deal with the underlying problems the fear of man produces until God helps you deal with what is in your heart, because biblically speaking, behavior problems are heart problems. That's exactly what Jesus explained in Matthew 15:19–20, "Out of the heart come evil thoughts, murders, adulteries, fornications, thefts, false witness, slanders. These are the things which defile the man." You say, "Why do I do what I do?" Jesus says, "Because of what is going on in your heart."

Paul Tripp uses an illustration of an apple tree to help us picture this principle. Imagine an apple tree that produces rotten apples year after year. Finally the owner gets so fed up with the tree that he decides to do something about it. He wants people to know that he has a good tree. So he goes to the store and buys a bunch of really nice apples, the best apples in the grocery store, and he staples them to the tree. Now the tree looks pretty good! But did he fix the problem? Of course not. To do that, the owner would have to deal with the root. All he has done is make the tree look a little nicer.[1]

Unfortunately that's what too many of us do with our lives. We have problems, bad fruit, and in an effort to clean up our act, we staple some good fruit on our tree. But always remember: if you never deal with the root, you'll never fix the problem. Before there can be change on the outside, you must first deal with the inside. To deal with the *what*, you must first deal with the *why*. To deal with actions, you must first deal with the heart. And to deal with your fear of man, you can't just try to change your behavior; you must go deeper. You must first deal with what is going on in your heart.

THE HEART OF THE PROBLEM

The Bible gives many different reasons for why we fear man. Examine your heart with care. What is it that causes your fear?

1. Paul David Tripp, *Instruments in the Redeemer's Hands: People in Need of Change Helping People in Need of Change* (Phillipsburg, NJ: P&R Publishing, 2002), 63.

A Guilty Conscience

Do you have a guilty conscience? Solomon wrote, "The wicked flee when no one is pursuing, but the righteous are bold as a lion" (Prov. 28:1). One person flees for no good reason; the other doesn't. One person has a fear of man; the other doesn't. What's the difference between the two? The one has a guilty conscience; the other doesn't. Quite simply, one of the reasons people are dominated by fear is because they are in sin.

I once counseled a man who was infuriated because someone had dared to question his integrity. A friend had written him a note asking how he was doing spiritually, and that enraged him. "How could he ask that?" he asked me. "He has problems in his own life! How dare he question me?" After he finished his tirade, I responded, "Okay, I understand you are upset, but how are you doing spiritually?" He replied, "Not good, but he doesn't know that. He just assumed that about me." The reason he was so bothered that his friend had asked the question was because there was something wrong. If he had been doing well spiritually, it wouldn't have bothered him at all. If you are experiencing fear of man, ask yourself: am I knowingly disobeying God's Word?

Don't rush by that question too quickly. After Adam's sin in the garden, God asked him, "Adam, why are you hiding?" Adam replied, "Because I am naked." But Adam had been naked before and hadn't felt the need to hide. What had changed? He was hiding because he was in sin. His sin had created fear in his heart.

Sometimes, just like Adam, we deceive ourselves. We rationalize our sin. We're not willing to admit the reason that we are afraid is because we are living in unrepentant sin. Your fear of man will not change until you have dealt with your sin.

The Wrong Value System

When you become overwhelmed with the fear of man and what others think of you, you are more concerned about your life here on earth than your heavenly destination.[2]

---

2. Richard Baxter, "Directions against Sinful Fear," *Fire and Ice: Puritan and Reformed Writings*, http://www.puritansermons.com/baxter/baxter23.htm.

Do you become afraid because you're concerned that people are somehow going to take away your treasure in heaven? Do you become afraid because you think they are going to somehow hinder your relationship with God? Are you frightened that they are going to cause God to stop loving you? Are you afraid that they are going to come between you and Christ? Are you afraid that they are going to stop God from hearing your prayers?

No, when you fear people, you aren't thinking about Christ, you aren't thinking about your heavenly treasures; you're concerned with things of earth. You're afraid you are going to be hurt financially, or they're going to tell others bad things about you here on earth, or you're worried that they're going to do something to you physically. The fear of man reveals your values. It reveals those things you think of as most important.

Consider the apostle Paul as he wrote the book of Philippians. He was in prison, yet he was rejoicing and praising God. Even while he was in prison, people were attacking him. He wrote in Philippians 1:15: "Some, to be sure, are preaching Christ even from envy and strife, but some also from good will." Yet how did Paul respond? He was experiencing physical punishment—he was in prison, and it would have been natural to fear what others were thinking of him—because people were intentionally trying to make him look bad. Look at verse 18: "What then? Only that in every way, whether in pretense or in truth, Christ is proclaimed; and in this I rejoice. Yes, and I will rejoice." Then verse 20: "According to my earnest expectation and hope, that I will not be put to shame in anything, but that with all boldness, Christ will even now, as always, be exalted in my body, whether by life or by death." You wonder why Paul wasn't afraid? He had the right value system. His goal was to see Christ exalted, and because he had his priorities straight, he could rejoice.

In 2 Corinthians 4:16–18, Paul gave another insight into why he didn't fear man:

> We do not lose heart, but though our outer man is decaying, yet our inner man is being renewed day by day. For momentary, light affliction is producing for us an eternal weight of glory far beyond

all comparison, while we look not at the things which are seen, but at the things which are not seen, for the things which are seen are temporal, but the things which are not seen are eternal.

Paul lived life with an eternal perspective. He valued the things of heaven more than the things of earth.

In chapter 5:7–8 he wrote:

We walk by faith, not by sight—we are of good courage, I say, and prefer rather to be absent from the body and to be at home with the Lord.

We fear man because we value comfort and life on this earth more than we value heaven. The more we love heaven, the less we'll fear bad things happening on earth. God has given believers all sorts of wonderful promises concerning our eternal future. We won't fear man if we bank on His promises.

If so be that we suffer with him, that we may be also glorified together. For I reckon that the sufferings of this present time are not worthy to be compared with the glory which shall be revealed in us. (Rom. 8:17–18 KJV)

In no way alarmed by your opponents—which is a sign of destruction for them, but of salvation for you, and that too, from God. For to you it has been granted for Christ's sake, not only to believe in Him, but also to suffer for His sake. (Phil. 1:28–30)

Therefore we both labour and suffer reproach, because we trust in the living God. (1 Tim. 4:10 KJV)

I also suffer these things: nevertheless I am not ashamed: for I know whom I have believed, and am persuaded that he is able to keep that which I have committed unto him against that day. (2 Tim. 1:12 KJV)

Fear none of those things which thou shalt suffer: behold, the devil shall cast some of you into prison, that ye may be tried; and ye shall have tribulation ten days: be thou faithful unto death, and I will give thee a crown of life. (Rev. 2:10 KJV)

Check your heart. Do you fear man because you are living by a worldly value system that places your own glory, your own comfort, and your own sinful pleasures above Christ's glory?

Unbelief

Proverbs 29:25 teaches us: "The fear of man brings a snare, but he who trusts in the LORD will be exalted." Do you see the contrast between the two? One person fears man. The other person trusts in the Lord. The person who fears man does not trust the Lord, and the person who trusts the Lord does not fear man.

Some people don't trust God because they are ignorant of who He is. In Matthew 10, Jesus told His disciples not to fear men because men can kill only the body; rather we are to fear God because He can destroy both body and soul. In other words, when you truly know God, you will lose your fear of men. But if you are ignorant about who God is, you are more likely to be frightened by man.

Ignorance is like darkness in your mind. When it's dark outside, everything is scarier. You can't see very well, so the bushes look like bears, and everything seems worse than it actually is. When morning comes and it becomes light, you look at what you were scared of in the dark and realize how foolish you were. Why would you ever be scared of something like that?

Many believers are frightened by man simply because they don't know God well enough. They need God's Word to turn on the light so they can see how silly their fears actually are. Seeing God for who He is will put everything in perspective. For example, when the psalmist considered the wicked and began to become discouraged, he wrote:

When I pondered to understand this,
It was troublesome in my sight
Until I came into the sanctuary of God;
Then I perceived their end. (Ps. 73:16–17)

He was bothered and troubled because he had forgotten who God is and what God will do.

John Flavel explained that when we fear man it is because "either we know not, or at least do not duly consider his Almighty power, vigilant care, unspotted faithfulness, and how they are all engaged, by covenant, for his people."[3] We aren't thinking about how God is at work as He promised for our good. If we understood how much God could do, how much God loved us, and how committed God was to keeping His promise, there's nothing that could cause us to be truly afraid. Our courage would be up, and our fears would be down.

Some people don't trust God because they have a distorted view of who He is. Their view of God is unbiblical. Instead they have made a god in their own image. God rebuked His people for doing just this:

> Because this people draw near with their words
> And honor Me with their lip service,
> But they remove their hearts far from Me,
> And their reverence for Me consists of tradition learned by rote,
> Therefore behold, I will once again deal marvelously with this people,
>   wondrously marvelous;
> And the wisdom of their wise men will perish,
> And the discernment of their discerning men will be concealed."
>
> Woe to those who deeply hide their plans from the LORD,
> And whose deeds are done in a dark place,
> And they say, "Who sees us?" or "Who knows us?"
> You turn things around!
> Shall the potter be considered as equal with the clay,
> That what is made would say to its maker, "He did not make me";
> Or what is formed say to him who formed it, "He has no understanding"?
>   (Isa. 29:13–16)

"You think you know Me, but you don't," God said to them. "You don't know what I am like. You don't know My character. You don't know Me."

---

3. John Flavel, *The Works of John Flavel*, vol. 3 (London: Banner of Truth Trust, 1968), 258.

People do the same thing today. They attend church, and might have done so for years, but they are unconcerned about what the Bible says about God. They just make up what they want to believe about God, or they get their ideas about God from other people instead of personally searching Scripture—where God has revealed Himself—and submitting to His Word. Thus they don't put their trust in God, because the god they have created in their minds is not worthy of being trusted.

Many people think of God as the ultimate good guy. He's the nice man up there in heaven who wants to do good but who is not really capable of taking action. He wants what is best, but He can't do anything to bring it about. If that's your view of God, you are not going to put your trust in Him. What good would it do? He can't help you anyway.

Other people think of God as a mean old man who is playing with their lives. They don't understand His love and grace. So, of course, they don't put their trust in Him. Who would put their trust in somebody who wants to do them harm? You are not going to put your trust in God if you have an incorrect or invalid view of who He is.

Many people just blatantly, sinfully, rebelliously refuse to put their trust and faith in God. They've sat in a good church, they've heard the truth, but they still refuse to believe. Hebrews 3:12 warns, "Take care, brethren, that there not be in any one of you an evil, unbelieving heart that falls away from the living God." Like the Israelites in the Old Testament, they stiffen their necks, harden their hearts, and suppress the truth. They simply refuse to put their trust in God.

Isaiah illustrated this attitude:

For thus the Lord GOD, the Holy One of Israel, has said,
"In repentance and rest you will be saved,
In quietness and trust is your strength."
But you were not willing,
And you said, "No, for we will flee on horses,"
Therefore you shall flee! (Isa. 30:15–16)

They were not willing. Simple, straight-out unbelief. They wanted what they wanted, and they didn't want God getting in their way.

So if you are lying, compromising, feeling empty, and fearing man, you ought to begin to make a change by taking a look at your heart. Do you fear man because you refuse to believe God? Are you failing to put your trust in God because you don't know Him very well, because you have a distorted, unbiblical view of Him, or because you are just rebelliously refusing to place your confidence in Him? To overcome the fear of man you must put your trust in God. You've got to deal with your unbelief.

Idolatry

When you fear man you aren't trusting God. And if you don't trust God, you are trusting someone else. That's called idolatry. You fear man because you have put your trust in man.

We normally think of these two words, *fear* and *trust*, as opposites, and at times they are. But it's important to see that these two words are also inextricably linked. You fear what you trust, and you trust what you fear. If you fear man, it's because you are trusting in man, and if you fear God, it's because you are trusting in God.

That might seem confusing, so let me explain. If you put your hope in people, if you place your confidence in people, if you rely completely on people, then you are going to fear them because everything they do will affect you in some way. If you look to people for deliverance, then you are going to end up being afraid of them. But if you trust God, rely on Him, and place your confidence in Him, then you are going to fear Him.

Look again at Proverbs 29:25: "The fear of man brings a snare, but he who trusts in the LORD will be exalted." Do you see the contrast between fearing man and trusting the Lord? In Psalm 33:16–21, the writer was making a similar point, but he just flipped the concepts:

> The king is not saved by a mighty army;
> A warrior is not delivered by great strength.
> A horse is a false hope for victory;
> Nor does it deliver anyone by its great strength.

Behold, the eye of the LORD is on those who fear Him,
On those who hope for His lovingkindness,
To deliver their soul from death
And to keep them alive in famine.
Our soul waits for the LORD;
He is our help and our shield.
For our heart rejoices in Him,
Because we trust in His holy name.

The writer of Proverbs made the contrast between fearing man and trusting in the Lord; the psalmist made the contrast between trusting in man and fearing God. Don't trust in man: "the king is not saved by [his] mighty army." Instead, fear the Lord: "the eye of the LORD is on those who fear Him." The point is that these two concepts are interchangeable. Trust and fear are inextricably linked. Solomon could have just as easily said, "Trusting in man brings a snare, but he who fears the Lord will be exalted," because trusting in God produces holy fear, and trusting in man produces sinful fear.

Think about this. If I say, "I am going to place my life savings in the stock market, I'm putting all my eggs in that basket, I'm completely relying on the stock market for my retirement because I am confident that the stock market is going to yield great dividends," when the stock market goes up I am going to be delighted. But when the stock market goes down, I am going to be upset; I'm going to become afraid. Why? Because that's where I have placed my confidence. I am relying on it, I'm trusting in it. And since the stock market is volatile, I'm going to be happy or frightened depending on how it performs.

But if I don't have any money or trust in the stock market, and it drops, then it's not going to bother me. I'm not going to care, because that's not where my hope is. I have placed my hope and confidence in something else.

If you place your confidence in people, then when they are happy with you, you are going to feel great, but when they are upset with you or against you, you are going to become frightened. Your life is going to be controlled by people, because that's where your hope is. You are turning to people for your strength, and that's why you are afraid.

The fear of man really reveals that you've lost perspective in life. You are living in a fantasyland. You are putting human beings in the place of God. You are looking to people for something that only God can provide. You are making human beings your "god."

There are a number of ways to do this. We'll look at just two. Sometimes we credit men with having power that only God has. Throughout the Scripture, and still today, fear of physical harm is one of the greatest fears people experience.

When we become frightened about how other people might hurt us, or what they might do to us, what are we really saying? We're saying that people can do things to us that God has no power to stop, that people are stronger than God. We're giving them power that only belongs to God.

Throughout the Old Testament, God had to keep reminding the Israelites, "Look, I'm God! Those nations are just people. I'm in control. Don't fear them—fear Me!"

Get some perspective. Fearing man is really useless, because people can't do anything to you apart from the will of God. People are just instruments in the hand of God. If you walk into your kitchen and see a knife on the table, are you going to be scared of that knife? Are you going to say, "I'm frightened. That knife is going to get me!"? No. You know that knife can't do anything on its own. Neither can the most powerful of men without God's approval.

Psalm 62:11 explains that "power belongs to God." Daniel 4:35 says that "all the inhabitants of the earth are accounted as nothing, but He does according to His will in the host of heaven and among the inhabitants of earth; and no one can ward off His hand or say to Him, 'What have you done?'" The result is that even the most powerful and mighty of men are just instruments in God's hands. He illustrated this for Isaiah by telling him that the great nation of Assyria was "the rod of My anger and the staff in whose hands is My indignation, I send it against a godless nation and commission it against the people of My jury" (Isa. 10:5–6).

Yes, men do sin and rebel against God. Yes, they are totally responsible for their actions. God does not force them to sin. But He is so awesome, powerful, and wise that He is able to take that sin and rebellion and use it to accomplish His purpose. And according to Romans 8:28, God's purpose is always His people's good. So if you are a believer, there is nothing men can do to you that God will not ultimately turn in your favor. It might feel bad at the moment, you might not understand why it is happening, but God promises to work it all out for your benefit. If you are truly afraid of what people can do to you, it's because you believe that God is neither telling you the truth nor has the power to do what He says. You've lost perspective because in your mind you have given mere humans power that only God has.

Sometimes we act like the opinions of people are more important than God's opinions. Most of us don't waste time worrying about whether someone is going to do us physical harm, but many of us do worry about what other people think about us, that they might say something bad about us, reject us, or be disappointed in us.

There have been times in my life when I have been crushed by what someone else said about me. But then I stop and think: why does their opinion bother me so much? God has saved me and forgiven me. I know that I have peace with God for all eternity. There is no condemnation for those in Christ Jesus, He loves me, I'm going to heaven, I am one of His chosen people. Why, then, am I so bothered about what someone else thinks about me? The answer, of course, is that in practice I am valuing their opinion more than God's.

John described a group of people like this. He wrote that many of the rulers of Jesus' day believed in Jesus but "were not confessing Him, for fear that they would be put out of the synagogue; for they loved the approval of men rather than the approval of God" (John 12:42–43). They put human beings in God's place. They acted as though the approval of these other people were more important than God's approval.

When your life on earth has ended and you stand before God, it's not going to matter whether you had a fan club here on earth, or if there is a website in your honor. It won't be important that people cheered when you entered the room, you got stopped on the sidewalk for autographs, or if you were person of the year. The only thing that is going to matter is what God thinks of you, what His opinion is. That's why Paul could write in 1 Corinthians 4:3–4:

To me it is a very small thing that I may be examined by you, or by any human court; in fact, I do not even examine myself. For I am conscious of nothing against myself, yet I am not by this acquitted; but the one who examines me is the Lord.

Paul was telling these people: "You have all your opinions about me, but it doesn't really bother me. In the end, what you think of me is a small thing, because you are not my judge."

What matters is what God thinks. When you allow man's opinion of you to control your actions, you are indicating that what people think is more important than what God thinks—and you are in a dangerous place!

Don't put anyone in the place of God. No one else deserves the position of Lord in your life. Don't fear people. Fear God. God alone is worthy of your trust. He alone is worthy of being worshiped. Put your confidence in Him, and you will be safe. People are just people. People are not God, and they are not worthy of being treated as if they are. If you keep putting them in God's place, you are going to ruin your life and your relationships. The fear of man is a trap.

Have you ever felt trapped physically? It's a terrible experience. I can still vividly remember feeling trapped while playing hide-and-seek with my elementary school friends. We were playing inside another child's house, and they had an old cedar chest. For some reason, the rule was that the person who did the counting had to be in that old chest while everyone else ran off to hide. When it was my turn, I knew I didn't want to get in that box, but I had to. So, smart boy that I was, I told my friends, "Whatever you do, don't sit on top!"

Of course, as soon as I climbed in the chest, they piled on top!

I'd never been so scared. It seemed as though the walls were closing in on me. I was sure I was going to die by suffocation. Every once in a while, they opened the lid a bit, let some light in, listened to my screams, and then slammed it shut before I could push my way out. I was only trapped inside that box for a short period of time, but it felt like hours. When I finally did get out, I was ready to give up on the game of hide-and-seek forever.

If you have ever felt physically trapped, you know it's no fun. But what is even worse is being trapped spiritually—feeling desperate, hopeless, knowing you have problems you can't possibly overcome and that they are destroying you, but feeling powerless to do anything about them yourself.

You may be feeling a bit like that after reading this chapter. You feel trapped. Perhaps you had never before realized you had a problem with the sinful fear of man. Perhaps you are beginning to realize just how pervasive this sinful attitude is in your life.

You've taken a good look at Proverbs 29:25: "The fear of man brings a snare." You now understand that the problem is putting other people in the place of God, and you understand how destructive the problem is: it cripples you, steals your joy, and dishonors God. But now that you see what the problem is, you still need to know how to overcome it. You want out!

There is hope. If you are a believer, you don't have to live your life ensnared by the fear of man. God's not playing games with you. First Corinthians 10:13 is a promise: "No temptation has overtaken you but such as is common to man; and God is faithful, who will not allow you to be tempted beyond what you are able." If God says the fear of man brings a snare, you can be confident He makes a way to escape that snare and, even better, a plan to avoid being ensnared at all. You don't have to be trapped forever!

Understand this: the only way you'll be able to use these instructions to your advantage is if you are a believer. If you are an unbeliever, you have bigger problems than just the fear of man. You need to repent of your sins and turn to Christ. Only in Him will you discover the resources to deal with the fear of man.

But even if you are a believer, you must understand that, although God has given you all the resources you need, overcoming the fear of man will require effort on your part. You won't magically get rid of sinful fear simply by reading the rest of this book. You must discipline yourself for the purpose of godliness. In the next several chapters we will learn the Bible's solution to sinful fear. Realize that the process won't be easy. It's natural to try to change by just working on the externals.

It's not natural for us to try to change from the inside out. But that's the only way true change will take place. If you are going to truly overcome the fear of man, by God's grace, you must stop dealing with externals alone, and start dealing with what is going on in your heart.

QUESTIONS FOR DISCUSSION

1. What are some examples of the problems the fear of man produces? What problems has it created in your life? Give specific illustrations.

2. What reason does this chapter give for our frequent failures to overcome the fear of man?

3. What was the point of Dr. Tripp's apple tree illustration? What are some of the ways in which you have lived out this illustration in your life?

4. Give an example of how a guilty conscience can produce fear.

5. What does fear reveal about the things you treasure?

6. How does understanding that principle help you overcome fear?

7. How was Paul able to be courageous in the midst of the most difficult situations? Give scriptural support for your answer.

8. What are some reasons people don't trust God?

9. How can a distorted view of God produce fear?

10. Are there ways in which you have become sinfully afraid as a result of unbelief? Be specific.

11. Explain why fear and trust are "inextricably linked." Give scriptural support for your answer, and explain why an understanding of this can help you overcome fear.

12. How does the fear of man reveal that you've lost a correct perspective?

13. What are some of the ways in which you put people in God's place? Give specific examples of ways that you have done this.

14. Explain why you can be certain there is hope for overcoming sinful fear.

15. What will it require for you to overcome sinful fear?

16. What do you need to change as a result of the truths contained in this chapter?

17. What specific steps are you going to take to accomplish that change?

6

THROW OFF
THE COVERS

PERHAPS YOU'VE HEARD the story passed around the Internet about the man who had an accident at work and was asked by his insurance company for more information. He sent the following letter:

Dear Sir,

I'm writing in response to your request for additional information in Block #3 of the accident reporting form. I put "Poor Planning" as the cause of my accident. You asked for a fuller explanation, and I trust the following details will be sufficient.

I am a bricklayer by trade. On the day of the accident, I was working alone on the roof of a new six-story building. When I completed my work, I found I had some bricks left over, which when weighed later were found to weigh 240 lbs. Rather than carry the bricks down by hand, I decided to lower them in a barrel by using a pulley, which was attached to the side of the building at the sixth floor.

Securing the rope at ground level, I went up to the roof, swung the barrel out, and loaded the bricks into it. Then I went down and untied the rope, holding it tightly to insure a slow descent of the 240 lbs. of bricks. You will note on the accident reporting form that my weight is 135 lbs.

Due to my surprise at being jerked off the ground so suddenly, I lost my presence of mind and forgot to let go of the rope. Needless to say, I proceeded at a rapid rate up the side of the building.

In the vicinity of the third floor, I met the barrel, which was now proceeding downward at an equally impressive speed. This explains the fractured skull, minor abrasions, and the broken collarbone, as listed in Section 3 of the accident reporting form.

Slowed only slightly, I continued my rapid ascent, not stopping until the fingers of my right hand were two knuckles deep into the pulley that I mentioned in paragraph 2 of this correspondence. Fortunately, by this time I had regained my presence of mind and was able to hold tightly to the rope despite the excruciating pain I was now beginning to experience.

At approximately the same time, however, the barrel of bricks hit the ground—and the bottom fell out of the barrel. Now devoid of the weight of the bricks, the barrel weighed approximately 50 lbs. I refer you again to my weight. As you might imagine, I began a rapid descent down the side of the building. In the vicinity of the third floor, I met the barrel coming up. This accounts for the two fractured ankles, broken tooth, and severe lacerations of my legs and lower body.

Here my luck began to change slightly. The encounter with the barrel seemed to slow me enough to lessen my injuries when I fell into the pile of bricks, and fortunately only three vertebrae were cracked. I am sorry to report, however, as I lay there on the pile of bricks, in pain, unable to move, and watching the empty barrel six stories above me, I again lost my composure and presence of mind and let go of the rope.

We can laugh at that story because it didn't really happen. It's an urban legend. But it does provide a fitting illustration of what happens when many people attempt to deal with their sin on their own. This man had a problem. He tried to fix it but kept making choices that only made his problem worse. In many ways that's the story of mankind's spiritual life. Only this time it's not funny, because it's not fiction, it's reality, and the consequences are much more serious.

COVERING UP

Mankind has a problem; the Bible calls it sin. Man tries to fix his problem himself, but in doing so keeps making choices that only make the problem worse. Specifically when people are left to their own resources to try to deal with their problem of sin, they create a worse problem by covering it up. God understands our nature so well that He even made a promise about this. It's found in Proverbs 28:13: "He who conceals his transgressions will not prosper." Trying to cover up your sin only makes it worse.

Hiding from God

What did Adam do after he sinned? He hid from God. "They heard the sound of the LORD God walking in the garden in the cool of the day, and the man and his wife hid themselves from the presence of the LORD God among the trees of the garden" (Gen. 3:8). Why did they hide? They were trying to cover up their sin.

Some people hide from God by staying far away from His Word. Hebrews 4:12 tells us, "The word of God is living and active and sharper than any two-edged sword, and piercing as far as the division of soul and spirit, of both joints and marrow, and able to judge the thoughts and intentions of the heart." The Word of God is like a spotlight because it exposes the sin in our hearts. This makes many people uncomfortable, so they don't study the Word and they refuse to listen to it. They attend churches that don't teach the Word so they can say they go to church but avoid being convicted of their sin.

Others hide from God by refusing to develop close friendships with godly people. Many professing believers keep others at a distance. They refuse to allow other Christians to get too close because they don't want to expose their sinful heart attitudes. Instead they gather friends who flatter them and who don't know the Word. They don't want to become uncomfortable or have anyone uncover the sin in their lives. Although at the time they may feel comfortable, in the long run they are doing themselves great harm. The writer of Hebrews admonishes, "Encourage one another day after day, as long as it is still called 'Today,' so that none of you will be hardened by the deceitfulness of sin" (3:13). We must have Christian friends who will tell us the truth and who will encourage us in God. Otherwise, we are in grave danger of falling away from the faith!

Some people hide from God by keeping a full schedule and staying very busy. They fill their lives with activity and allow no time for self-examination. They never stop and think about what is going on in their souls because they have pushed the problem to the back of their minds. That way they are able to convince themselves that everything really is fine.

If all you had to do were change a few outward behaviors, Christianity would be easy. But God wants us to deal with our hearts. That's difficult because our hearts are full of sin, and when we examine them closely we'll discover much we don't like. Most of us have pretty pictures of ourselves in our minds. The problem is, they're a fantasy. But because we don't want anything to contradict these imaginary pictures we have of ourselves, we refuse to do any self-examination, and we cover our sin.

Passing the Blame

When God confronted Adam with his sin in the garden of Eden, Adam quickly responded by passing the blame—"It's that woman you gave me!" Although many things have changed since that day in the garden, unfortunately when it comes to dealing with sin, mankind has stayed the same. Today, thousands of years later, when confronted with their sin, men and women still respond just like Adam, though they may word it differently: "If so-and-so weren't so mean, then I wouldn't be mean in return." "If my husband weren't so rude, I wouldn't feel the need to constantly defend myself." "If people paid more attention to me, I wouldn't sin in the ways that I do." "If my family loved me more, I wouldn't feel so insecure." Each is trying to do the same thing—make excuses for sin, cover it up.

Telling Lies

Cain murdered his brother, God confronted him, and Cain responded, "Am I my brother's keeper?" (Gen. 4:9). In other words Cain was saying, "I don't know where Abel is, so get off my back!" He lied to God.

It's a stupid idea to lie to God, because He is everywhere and He knows all things. But we still do it anyway. We lie to God, to others, and sometimes even to ourselves. We can be very subtle in the ways we lie about our sin. We might obey part of God's law and then pretend we've obeyed the whole thing. Take, for example, what happened when Samuel confronted Saul (1 Sam. 15). God had told Saul to kill everything when he defeated Amalek, but Saul only partially obeyed. Yet when Samuel confronted Saul about it, Saul said, "We've completely obeyed." But when Samuel heard some sheep bleating in the distance, Saul quickly backpedaled: "Well, almost completely."

We do that. We obey God in the externals while we are disobeying Him in our hearts. We are hypocrites. We go to church and say all the right words, but we live a totally different life on the inside. We profess to worship God, and we say that we desire His glory more than anything, but then we go out and live our lives entirely for our own glory and to meet our own desires. That's lying to God. It's an attempt to cover our sin. It doesn't work.

Ignoring Sin

One of the most popular ways of concealing sin in our day is to simply refuse to acknowledge it as sin. There's not a lot of talk in our culture about repentance and confession, because there is not a lot of talk about sin. Our society has declared war on the word *sin*. Unfortunately many in the church have joined the battle.

The truth is, most people are willing to admit that the fear of man is a problem. It's hard to deny. The problem is, most people are not willing to admit it is sin. Instead they make excuses. If you go to your local bookstore, you'll find numerous books about low self-esteem, overcoming shyness, dealing with anxiety, and helping your kids overcome peer pressure—to name just a few. As we've learned in previous chapters, all those terms are just pseudonyms for what the Bible labels the fear of man.

If you are going to overcome the fear of man, you must refuse to hide it. That's the place to start. Stop hiding from God, stop passing the blame, stop attempting to deceive yourself and others! Instead, recognize the fear of man for what it is: sin. Throw off the covers and come out of hiding.

THE FEAR OF MAN IS SIN

The fear of man is a moral evil. It is not merely a mistake, not just a weakness, not simply a character fault; it is a sin against God. The main issue is not how the fear of man makes you feel, or the problems it brings into your life. The main issue is that it is a sin against God.

It Is Direct Disobedience to God

The fear of man is sin because it is direct disobedience to God's commands. Let's consider the different commands you are disobeying when you fear man.

The fear of man is disobedience to God's command not to worry. Philippians 4:6 tells us, "Be anxious for nothing, but in everything by prayer and supplication with thanksgiving let your requests be made known to God." When you fear man, you are troubled. You are worried, either about what man will do to you or what man will think of you. God makes it very clear that we are to be anxious for nothing. That includes being anxious about what people might do to us, say about us, or think about us.

Being afraid of people is disobedience to God's command to do nothing out of selfishness. When you don't reach out to encourage someone because you are afraid of what they will think, about whom are you most concerned? Yourself. When you are wondering throughout an entire conversation what the other person is thinking of you or what their opinion is of you, about whom are you most concerned? Yourself.

When you become jealous of what someone else has, who is your greatest concern? Yourself. When you constantly do things to gain the approval of others, to get them to like you, about whom are you most concerned? Yourself. When you do good things to seem spiritual, about whom are you most concerned? Yourself. The fear of man springs from selfishness. Paul told us in Philippians 2:3–4:

> Do nothing from selfishness or empty conceit, but with humility of mind regard one another as more important than yourselves; do not merely look out for your own personal interests, but also for the interests of others.

About whom are you most concerned when you fear man? You are not more concerned about the interests of others, about their good, or about the glory of God. You are being completely self-centered. And that's sin.

The fear of man is disobedience to God's many commands to be sensible. The word *sensible* means "sober-minded." It means to think biblically about life, and to be controlled by truth. When you fear man you are not thinking biblically, and you are not thinking sensibly. You are acting as if this world will last forever and heaven is nonexistent, as if this body is all you've got and death is the end. Your mind is out of control, thinking completely irrationally. You're not being sensible.

The fear of man is disobedience to the two great commandments: "Love the Lord your God with all your heart, and with all your soul, and with all your mind"; and "You shall love your neighbor as yourself" (Matt 22:37, 39). When you fear man, you are not loving God with all you have, and you aren't loving your neighbor as yourself.

The fear of man is disobedience to God's many commands not to fear. Jesus said, "Do not fear those who kill the body but are unable to kill the soul; but rather fear Him who is able to destroy both soul and body in hell" (Matt. 10:28). Paul wrote in Romans 8:15, "You have not received a spirit of slavery leading to fear again, but you have received a spirit of adoption as sons by which we cry out, 'Abba! Father!'" He rebuked Timothy, "God has not given us a spirit of timidity, but of power and love and discipline" (2 Tim. 1:7). The spirit of fear or cowardice is not from God, which means, of course, that it's sin!

The fear of man is a root sin that produces all sorts of other sins. Scripture tells us that it produces lies, jealousy, threats, anger, hate, worry, attempts at murder and genocide, betrayal, distrust, compromise, and hypocrisy.

It Is a Direct Assault on God's Character

Perhaps even more significantly, the fear of man is a direct assault on the character of God. Throughout Scripture, God commands us to put our complete trust in Him. He bases those commands on His character.

Those who know Your name will put their trust in You,
For You, O LORD, have not forsaken those who seek You. (Ps. 9:10)

> Trust in the LORD forever,
> For in GOD the LORD, we have an everlasting Rock. (Isa. 26:4)

> Command those who are rich in this present age not to be haughty,
> nor to trust in uncertain riches but in the living God, who gives us
> richly all things to enjoy. (1 Tim. 6:17 NKJV)

> Cast all your anxiety on him because he cares for you. (1 Peter 5:7 NIV)

We don't place our trust in God irrationally. When we place our trust in God, we are making a statement about the character of God; we are placing our trust in Him because He's worthy of it.

Whether you realize it or not, when you fear man, you are making a statement about the character of God. You are saying that you don't think He is worthy of your trust. When you are overwhelmed with the fear of man, you are saying one of at least three things about God:

God's promises aren't true. God said, "All things work for good for those who love God" (Rom. 8:28, author's paraphrase). We say, "No, it doesn't. This can't work out for good. God, You are lying." If we really believed it worked out for good, we wouldn't be afraid. God said, "No temptation has overtaken you but such as is common to man; and God is faithful" (1 Cor. 10:13). We say, "No, He's not. This temptation is too much; I can't handle it. I've got to give in."

God doesn't love me. He's not concerned about me. He's just playing games with me. Paul wrote,

> I am convinced that neither death, nor life, nor angels, nor principali-
> ties, nor things present, nor things to come, nor powers, nor height,
> nor depth, nor any other created thing, will be able to separate us from
> the love of God, which is in Christ Jesus our Lord. (Rom. 8:38–39)

And we say, "Oh, yes, they can. God's forgotten about me. He doesn't care."

God isn't powerful enough to do anything about this situation. God's good, and He loves me, but He can't take care of me. He's not powerful enough to take care of me in this situation. The psalmist wrote, "Power belongs to God; and lovingkindness is Yours, O LORD" (Ps. 62:11–12). But when we fear man, we say, "No, it doesn't. Man is much more powerful than You in this situation, God."

You fear man because you refuse to put your trust in God. Scripture tells us, "The Lord is my helper, I will not be afraid, what will man do to me?" (Heb. 13:6). By being courageous, he was making a statement about God: "I don't fear man, because I know God." But by your fear, you are also making a statement about God. You are saying, "The Lord is my helper, but I don't care. I'm still afraid, because man can do all sorts of terrible things to me."

Because of all the ways that God has taken care of you throughout your life, it's especially sad when you, as a believer, fear man and don't put your trust in God.

He sent His Son to die for you, He saved you, He has promised you heaven, He has always taken care of you. But now when you are in a difficult circumstance, you throw all that out the window, and you say, "Nope, this time God's not going to take care of me."

It's very sad when you turn your back on God. God is perfect. He never does anything wrong. So you are turning your back and refusing to trust Him on the basis of absolutely nothing but your own fears and misunderstandings.

There's an interesting story in Numbers 14 that provides a powerful illustration of just this attitude. The people of Israel were on the verge of entering the Promised Land. But before they did, they sent in some spies to check things out. Ten of the spies came back with a bad report: "The people are huge; we'll never defeat them. We're dead! Run for Egypt!" But two of the spies stood up and said, "God is big. He's protected us so far. By His power we can do this!"

The people of Israel listened to the ten, not the two. In Numbers 14:1 we read, "All the congregation lifted up their voices and cried, and the people wept that night." Joshua and Caleb, the two spies, rebuked the people: "Do not rebel against the LORD; and do not fear the people of the land" (v. 9). But the people became angry and wanted to stone Joshua and Caleb for speaking the truth (v. 10).

You might say their fear is understandable. After all, in the previous chapter we read, "The land through which we have gone, in spying it out, is a land that devours its inhabitants; and all the people whom we saw in it are men of great size. There also we saw the Nephilim . . . and we became like grasshoppers in our own sight, and so we were in their sight" (13:32–33). The people were huge. They were great warriors. "We are going to be destroyed," the people cried out.

It made sense to be scared, right? Wrong. Look at what God had to say: "The LORD said to Moses, 'How long will this people spurn Me? And how long will they not believe in Me, despite all the signs which I have performed in their midst?'" (14:11). God had promised the Israelites that He would protect them, and He had proved that He could, time and time again. But every time a difficulty came up, the people of Israel refused to put their trust in Him. God always keeps His promises. So when the Israelites feared man, they were calling God a liar, saying that He was unable to take care of them. That's sin.

That's exactly what you do when you allow yourself to be controlled by your fear of man. A difficulty comes into your life, and you begin to become fearful. Your mind starts running, and you start complaining, and before you know it, you are dominated by fear. You are in a difficult spot, and you refuse to stop and praise Him for all the ways He has taken care of you in the past. Instead, on the basis of one problem that you don't understand, you refuse to trust Him.

When my wife taught kindergarten, she had to wait with the children after school for their parents to pick them up. She had one little boy in her class who was usually the last one to be picked up. His mom always came after most of the other children had gone home. Every day, almost without fail, this little boy would start weeping and wailing. "Mom's not going to pick me up. She forgot about me. She doesn't love me. What am I going to do?" And every day my wife had to remind this little boy, "Your mom has never forgotten about you. She always comes and picks you up. Trust her. You don't need to get so upset."

Many times we're just like that little boy. God has never forgotten about us, but we cry and wail, so afraid that He will, and as a result we refuse to put our trust in Him. When you fear man, God is small in your eyes. You are refusing to put your trust in Him. And that's a serious sin.

Perhaps you are wondering what this chapter has to do with overcoming the fear of man. Have you ever noticed that many people are willing to admit they have problems, but few are willing to call those problems what they really are? Sin. That's sad, because they think they are doing themselves a favor, when in reality they are doing themselves great harm.

You've seen that the fear of man is a problem, you've taken a look at what is at the heart of the problem; now write it down. It's sin. It won't do you any good to try to excuse it. Hiding your sin, rationalizing it, and covering it up, will only make your problems worse. It's time to throw off the covers, because as we'll see in the next chapter, you won't truly change until you truly repent.

QUESTIONS FOR DISCUSSION

1. How does the promise of Proverbs 28:13 apply to dealing with fear? *"He who conceals his transgressions will not prosper.*

2. What do you think are some reasons people conceal their sin?

3. What are some of the specific ways you have concealed your sin in the past?

4. What are some ways in which people hide from God? What are some of the ways in which you have hidden from God?

5. Do you have anyone in your life who will confront you when you sin? If so, who is that person? If not, why not?

6. How do people lie about their sin? What lies do you use to cover up your sin?

7. Why is it so important to stop concealing the fear of man?

8. Why is it absolutely essential to recognize that the fear of man is sin?

9. How is the fear of man selfishness? Give a specific example from your life when the fear of man caused you to be selfish.

10. Explain how the fear of man is not sensible.

11. In what ways is the fear of man an assault on the character of God?

12. What are you saying about God when you are controlled by sinful fear? Be specific.

13. Why is it so sad for you as a believer not to trust God?

14. What can you learn from Numbers 14 about trusting God?

15. What does this chapter have to do with overcoming the fear of man?

16. What are the top three truths you learned from this chapter? How are you going to change as a result of what you learned?

7

THE WAY UP
IS DOWN

KING DAVID had a problem. The nation was at war, and he was back at the palace with too much time on his hands.

One night he couldn't sleep, so he decided to go for a walk on his roof. Picture him pacing on the rooftop, looking across his kingdom, perhaps thinking about all his accomplishments as a king. Suddenly he saw a beautiful woman, unclothed, bathing. He lingered, looked, lusted, and acted, sending his men to her home to bring her over to the palace. David sinned. And soon Bathsheba sent a simple message back to him: "I'm pregnant."

No doubt David knew who the father was. Bathsheba's husband, Uriah, was away at war. David had a scandal on his hands. So not unlike many modern-day politicians, David devised a plan to cover it up. He called Uriah back from the battlefield and tried to convince him to spend the night with his wife. But being an honorable man, Uriah refused. His country was at war, he was a soldier, and he refused to go home while his fellow soldiers suffered in the field. So David wrote a letter and gave it to Uriah to take back to the head of the army. Little did Uriah know he was delivering his own death sentence. David had ordered that Uriah be sent to the front lines.

David's strategy worked. Uriah died. Bathsheba mourned. David waited, and after a discretionary period of a few months, he married Uriah's wife. Problem solved, right? Wrong.

"The thing that David had done was evil in the sight of the LORD" (2 Sam. 11:27). God sent the prophet Nathan with a message for the king. Nathan told David a story: There are two men in one city. One is rich; the other is poor. The rich man stole everything the poor man had. What should be done?

David's anger burned. He condemned the rich man, calling for his death: "Surely the man who has done this deserves to die" (2 Sam. 12:5).

Now Nathan had David right where he wanted him. You can almost picture the prophet pointing his finger at David, declaring loudly, "You are the man!" (v. 7). David crumbled in humility and repentance. God had broken through; David's hard heart was softened, and he cried out, "I have sinned against the LORD" (v. 13).

Later, when David wrote a psalm about his experience, the story he told illustrated an absolutely fundamental principle for dealing with sin:

> When I kept silent about my sin, my body wasted away
> Through my groaning all day long.
> For day and night Your hand was heavy upon me;
> My vitality was drained away as with the fever heat of summer. . . .
> I acknowledged my sin to You,
> And my iniquity I did not hide;
> I said, "I will confess my transgressions to the LORD";
> And You forgave the guilt of my sin. (Ps. 32:3–5)

THE FIRST STEP TO OVERCOMING FEAR

David's story is a perfect illustration of the first step to overcoming sinful fear, particularly the fear of man. Perhaps after reading the past few chapters you realize that you are stuck in sin. You are humbled by the ways in which you have fallen and have placed your trust in man rather than in God. You want to overcome. You want your relationship with God to be restored. The first step to accomplishing this is genuine, biblical repentance.

There are two strategies for dealing with sin, which have both been around since the beginning. They are illustrated in the story of King David and explained by his son Solomon in Proverbs 28:13: "He who conceals his transgressions will not prosper, but he who confesses and forsakes them will find compassion."

This proverb tells us of two men, both of whom had sinned. The difference between these two men was not the fact of their sin, but rather what they did with it. The one concealed it: he hid it, minimized it, rationalized it, and excused it. The other confessed it: he acknowledged it and forsook it. These two strategies had very different results. The one who covered up his sin didn't prosper, but the one who confessed and forsook his sin found compassion.

In a previous chapter you were encouraged to stop covering up your fear of man, to stop making excuses, to see it as sin. In this chapter we are calling on you to repent of it. To overcome the fear of man, you must stop hiding and start repenting. That's the first step to biblical change. Whatever you cover, God Himself will uncover. What you uncover, God will cover. You need to repent.

You can find evidence of this throughout the Scriptures.

Moses preached repentance. He told the people of God that if they continued in their sin they would be punished.

> But if they confess their iniquity and the iniquity of their fathers, with their unfaithfulness in which they were unfaithful to Me, and that they also have walked contrary to Me, and that I also have walked contrary to them and have brought them into the land of their enemies; if their uncircumcised hearts are humbled, and they accept their guilt—then I will remember My covenant with Jacob, and My covenant with Isaac and My covenant with Abraham I will remember. (Lev. 26:40–42 NKJV)

Cover your sin and suffer; repent and find compassion.

The prophets went to the people of God time and time again to make this same basic plea: "Repent and be forgiven; rebel and be judged." God told Jeremiah,

> Go and proclaim these words toward the north and say,
>
> "Return, faithless Israel," declares the LORD;
> "I will not look upon you in anger.
> For I am gracious," declares the LORD;

"I will not be angry forever.
Only acknowledge your iniquity,
That you have transgressed against the LORD your God
And have scattered your favors to the strangers under every green tree,
And you have not obeyed My voice," declares the LORD.
"Return, O faithless sons," declares the LORD;
"For I am a master to you,
And I will take you one from a city and two from a family,
And I will bring you to Zion."

Then I will give you shepherds after My own heart, who will feed
you on knowledge and understanding. (Jer. 3:12–15)

God told Ezekiel,

Now as for you, son of man, say to the house of Israel, "Thus you have
spoken, saying, 'Surely our transgressions and our sins are upon us, and
we are rotting away in them; how then can we survive?'" Say to them,
"As I live!" declares the Lord GOD, "I take no pleasure in the death of
the wicked, but rather that the wicked turn from his way and live. Turn
back, turn back from your evil ways! Why then will you die, O house of
Israel?" . . . When the wicked turns from his wickedness and practices
justice and righteousness, he will live by them. (Ezek. 33:10–11, 19)

That's Proverbs 28:13: Cover your sin and you will suffer. Repent
and you will find compassion.

No matter how many steps you have taken away from God, it's
only one step back. Isaiah 1:2–6 makes this crystal clear. "Listen, O
heavens, and hear, O earth; for the LORD speaks, 'Sons I have reared
and brought up, but they have revolted against Me'" (v. 2). The people
of God were like rebellious children. "An ox knows its owner, and a
donkey its master's manger, but Israel does not know, My people do not
understand" (v. 3). They had less understanding than an ox or a donkey.

Alas, sinful nation,
People weighed down with iniquity,

Offspring of evildoers,
Sons who act corruptly!
They have abandoned the LORD,
They have despised the Holy One of Israel,
They have turned away from Him.

Where will you be stricken again,
As you continue in your rebellion?
The whole head is sick
And the whole heart is faint.
From the sole of the foot even to the head
There is nothing sound in it. (vv. 4–6)

Rebellious sons, a people without understanding, a sinful nation weighed down with iniquity. What do you expect from God? Judgment!

Yet notice God's invitation in verses 16–20:

"Wash yourselves, make yourselves clean;
Remove the evil of your deeds from My sight.
Cease to do evil,
Learn to do good;
Seek justice,
Reprove the ruthless,
Defend the orphan,
Plead for the widow.

"Come now, and let us reason together,"
Says the LORD,
"Though your sins are as scarlet,
They will be as white as snow;
Though they are red like crimson,
They will be like wool.
If you consent and obey,
You will eat the best of the land;
But if you refuse and rebel,
You will be devoured by the sword."

What you cover, God will uncover, and what you uncover, God will cover.

The apostles proclaimed this same life-changing message in the New Testament. God loves to save sinners. First Timothy 1:15 tells us that "Christ Jesus came into the world to save sinners," but He only saves repentant sinners. As Jesus explained, "Unless you repent, you will . . . likewise perish" (Luke 13:5). The apostles made this a central theme whenever they preached the gospel:

> Now when they heard this, they were pierced to the heart, and said to Peter and the rest of the apostles, "Brethren, what shall we do?" Peter said to them, "Repent, and each of you be baptized in the name of Jesus Christ for the forgiveness of your sins; and you will receive the gift of the Holy Spirit." (Acts 2:37–38)

> Therefore repent and return, so that your sins may be wiped away, in order that times of refreshing may come from the presence of the Lord. (Acts 3:19)

> Therefore having overlooked the times of ignorance, God is now declaring to men that all people everywhere should repent. (Acts 17:30)

> I did not shrink from declaring to you anything that was profitable, and teaching you publicly and from house to house, solemnly testifying to both Jews and Greeks of repentance toward God and faith in our Lord Jesus Christ. (Acts 20:20–21)

> The Lord is not slow about His promise, as some count slowness, but is patient toward you, not wishing for any to perish but for all to come to repentance. (2 Peter 3:9)

You can't be saved unless you repent.

REPENTANCE IS A LIFESTYLE

Sometimes people think of repentance as a one-time act, something they did way back when they were first saved and never have to do again. But nothing could be further from the truth. Our lives as believers should be ones of continual repentance. We sin daily, and so we should repent, confess, and forsake sin daily.

That's why Jesus commanded us to pray,

> Give us this day our daily bread.
> And forgive us our debts, as we also have forgiven our debtors.
> (Matt. 6:11–12)

Just as we ought to express our dependence on God for our daily bread, we ought to be repenting and crying out to God for forgiveness on a daily basis. Thomas Watson notes: "They whose sins are forgiven must not omit praying for forgiveness. . . . Believers who are pardoned must be continual suitors for pardon. . . . Sin, after pardon, rebels. Like Samson's hair, though it be cut, it will grow again. We sin daily, and must ask for daily pardon as well as for daily bread."[1] Jim Elliff explains, "The believer in Christ is a lifelong repenter. He begins with repentance and continues in repentance."[2] Or as Martin Luther put it, "When our Lord and Master, Jesus Christ, said 'Repent,' He called for the entire life of believers to be one of repentance."[3] John Murray writes,

> Just as faith is not only a momentary act but an abiding attitude of trust and confidence directed toward the Savior, so also repentance results in constant contrition. The broken spirit and the contrite heart are abiding marks of the soul. As long as sin remains there must be the consciousness of it and this conviction of our sinfulness will constrain self-abhorrence, confession and the plea of forgiveness and cleansing. Christ's blood is the laver of initial cleansing but it is also the fountain to which the believer must continually repair. . . . The way of sanctification is the way of contrition for sins past and present.[4]

1. Thomas Watson, "The Fifth Petition in the Lord's Prayer," *The Lord's Prayer*, *The Thomas Watson Reading Room*, accessed November 20, 2013, http://www.fivesolas.com/watson/lp_5.htm.

2. Jim Elliff, "The Unrepenting Repenter," *Christian Communicators Worldwide* (blog), accessed November 20, 2013, http://www.ccwtoday.org/article/the-unrepenting-repenter/.

3. Martin Luther, "The 95 Theses," *A Mighty Fortress Is Our God: Martin Luther*, accessed November 20, 2013, http://www.luther.de/en/95thesen.html.

4. John Murray, *Redemption Accomplished and Applied* (Grand Rapids: Eerdmans, 1955), 116.

In 1 John 1:8–9, the apostle John contrasted believers and unbelievers. He wrote that unbelievers deny they are sinners, concealing their
transgressions, but true believers are marked by continual confession
of sin. He wrote in verse 9, "If we confess our sins, He is faithful and
righteous to forgive us our sins and to cleanse us from all unrighteousness." Confessing your sin is an indicator that you truly are a Christian.
An unbeliever lies and covers over his sin. He's not willing to repent
of it. But true believers acknowledge their sin and run to Christ for
forgiveness.

If you love God, you are not going to hate sin just when you first
get saved. You are going to hate sin throughout your whole life! In his
classic work on repentance, John Colquhoun writes,

> The waters of godly sorrow for sin in the renewed heart will con-
> tinue to spring up there while sin is there, though they may, through
> remaining hardness of heart, be obstructed for a time. After the heart
> at the sinner's first conversion was smitten with evangelical repen-
> tance, the wound still bleeds and will continue more or less to bleed
> until the hand of glory be put about it in the holy place on high. If
> therefore a man regards repentance only as the first stage on the way
> to heaven and instead of renewing daily his exercise of it satisfies
> himself with concluding that he has passed the first stage, the truth
> of his repentance is very questionable. The man who does not see his
> need of exercising repentance daily may have a counterfeit, but he
> cannot have a true repentance. He may have a superficial sorrow for
> his sins . . . and yet be a total stranger to that evangelical repentance
> which is both a saving grace and an abiding principle.[5]

Genuine biblical change always begins with repentance. Paul made
this very clear in his second letter to the believers in Corinth.

> I now rejoice, not that you were made sorrowful, but that you
> were made sorrowful to the point of repentance; for you were
> made sorrowful according to the will of God, so that you might

5. John Colquhoun, *Repentance* (London: Banner of Truth Trust, 1965), 27–28.

not suffer loss in anything through us. For the sorrow that is according to the will of God produces a repentance without regret. (2 Cor. 7:9–10)

Paul was writing believers, telling them, "I said what I said in order to lead you to repentance." He was not talking about the initial act of repentance at the beginning of the Christian life; he meant repentance as believers. Paul knew that if the Corinthians were going to change, first they had to repent. These Christians needed to get "their thinking turned around so that their living also might be inverted."[6]

Many believers are stuck in the fear of man simply because they are not repenting of it. Proverbs 28:13 is true for you as a believer: "He who conceals his transgressions will not prosper, but he who confesses and forsakes them will find compassion." If you are going to overcome the fear of man, you must repent.

WHAT TRUE REPENTANCE LOOKS LIKE

The problem is, many people don't know what it means to truly repent. Some don't understand it all. Others understand it in a very superficial way. As a result, many professing Christians neglect this vital step.

In Proverbs 28:13, Solomon helps us understand the nature of true repentance by describing two of its fruits: "He who confesses and forsakes [his sins] will find compassion." True repentance produces confession and is followed by change. Understanding these two words helps us understand what it means to repent.

The word Solomon used for *confess* basically means to acknowledge, to agree, to openly admit. It's used throughout the Old Testament in two ways: (1) to give praise to God, and (2) to confess one's sins to God. When you praise God, what are you doing? You are making a statement about Him. And at a very basic level, that is what you are doing when you confess your sin. You are making a statement about your sin. You acknowledge and openly admit it.

6. Jay Adams, *2 Corinthians* (Hackettstown, NJ: Timeless Texts, 1994), 148–49.

Origen once explained that confession is the vomit of the soul.[7] It's bringing up all that rotten stuff that's hidden within your soul and getting it out. When you confess your sin, you are making a conscious decision to stop hiding your sin and start pointing it out to God. You are humbly bringing your sins out into the open.

David helped us understand what confession means. In Psalm 32 he wrote, "When I kept silent about my sin, my body wasted away" (v. 3). There was a time when David was silent about his sin. That's the opposite of confession. You could say that confessing your sin is breaking the silence. David continued: "I acknowledged my sin to You, and my iniquity I did not hide; I said, 'I will confess my transgressions to the LORD'; and You forgave the guilt of my sin" (v. 5).

Do you see the positive and negative sides to confession? Positively, confession is openly admitting your sin. Negatively, it's refusing to hide it any longer (v. 5). He was logically saying, "When I confessed my sin, I stopped covering and concealing it."

The New Testament gives a little more color to our definition. The apostle John wrote, "If we confess our sins [literally, keep on confessing our sins], He is faithful and righteous to forgive us our sins and to cleanse us from all unrighteousness" (1 John 1:9). The word translated here as *confess* means to say the same thing as another or to agree with another.

Jay Adams explains that this word *confess* was used in the ancient world in legal and business transactions.

> There, it regularly means "agreement." When two or more parties agree to do something, the contract drawn up is called an agreement. . . . So too a confession of faith is an agreement by those who subscribe to it that they hold those truths. . . . Confession then is an acknowledgement on our part that we agree with God in what He has said about our sin in His Word. We stand on His side—the side of the one offended—and acknowledge that He is right in holding us guilty of an offense. Confession is a formal acknowledgment of

---

7. Thomas Case, *The Morning Exercise Methodized; or Certain Chief Heads and Points of the Christian Religion Opened and Improved in Divers Sermons* (London: printed by E.M. for Ralph Smith, 1660), 524, https://archive.org/details/morni00case.

the fact. It involves a personal, on the record admission of guilt. The confessee says, "I have sinned, I am liable."[8]

Kenneth Wuest explains,

The English word "confess" means to admit the truth of an accusation, to own up to the fact that one is guilty of having committed the sin, but the Greek word means far more than that.... Confession of sin on the part of the believer means therefore to say the same thing that God does about that sin, to agree with God as to all the implications of that sin as it relates to the Christian who committed it and to a holy God against whom it is committed. That includes the saint's hatred of that sin, his sense of guilt because of it, his contrition because of it, the determination to put it out of his life and never to do that thing again.[9]

Think carefully about those definitions. They reveal several different aspects of true confession.

To Confess Your Sin You Must First See Your Sin

Imagine taking your car to a mechanic. He takes a look under the hood and says, "Yep, something's wrong." Well, what is it? "I don't know, but something's really wrong under there." Could you be a bit more specific? "You either have a problem with your engine, your transmission, or it could be something else." He's not going to be much help, is he? You can't fix what's wrong unless you know some specifics.

Unfortunately, when it comes to confessing our sin, many of us are a lot like that mechanic. What are you confessing? Sin. Well, what specifically? Fear. Well, how do you show fear? I act fearful, and I think fearful thoughts. What do you mean? I get scared and I act frightened. Do you want to talk about something else?

It's very hard to repent if you don't have any idea what sins you are repenting of. "I'm really sorry about my sin." Well, in what ways are

8. Jay Adams, *A Theology of Christian Counseling* (Grand Rapids: Zondervan, 1979), 216.
9. Kenneth Wuest, *In These Last Days* (Grand Rapids: Eerdmans, 1963), 104.

you sinning? "I don't know . . ." You need to think more deeply than that. You won't overcome fear if you are content with fuzzy generalities. You need to get specific. You need to see your sin.

Your Confession of Sin Must Flow from Godly Sorrow

True repentance begins with an acknowledgment of sin and flows out of genuine godly sorrow over it. Author Thomas Watson explains that sorrow must be in true repentance: "A woman may as well expect to have a child without pangs as one can have repentance without sorrow. He that can believe without doubting, suspect his faith; and he that can repent without sorrowing, suspect his repentance."[10]

You sorrow over your sin because you begin to understand just how disgusting sin really is. It's sin that steals man's happiness. Communion with God is the best thing man could ever have, and it is sin that has separated man from God. You sorrow over sin because it's sin that brought all pain and destruction into the world. Sin produced death. You sorrow over your sin because it is our sin that caused Christ's suffering and death. If something you did were the reason someone you loved had to die, you would sorrow over it. You sorrow over your sin because you know your precious and glorious Savior died for your own sin. And you sorrow over sin because you love God. As John Colquhoun explains, "The true penitent loves God supremely and therefore his sins are a heavy burden to him. He loathes himself because he has walked contrary to the holy Lord God and thereby insulted, reproached and provoked Him."[11] Your greatest desire in life is His glory. You realize that sin is anti-God. When you sin, you are opposing God Himself, and that breaks your heart. Joseph, when tempted, cried out, "How then can I do this great wickedness, and sin against God?" (Gen. 39:9 NKJV). He hated the thought of sinning against such a great God, such a glorious, gracious, majestic, loving King. He refused to even think of doing so. When you confess your sins, you are wounded and pierced to the heart that you would ever

---

10. Thomas Watson, *The Doctrine of Repentance* (Edinburgh: Banner of Truth Trust, 1987), 19.
11. John Colquhoun, *Repentance*, 17.

have even thought of treating such a good and holy God so poorly. Your heart breaks not just because of what sin did to you but because of what your sin did to God.[12] You sorrow over your sin because you know forgiveness. God's been so good to you, He's died for you, and you grieve because you are still sinning against a God who forgives you after all you've done to Him.

You see, when you sorrow the way that God wants you to sorrow over your sin, you are not just sorry about the consequences. You are not just sorry because you got caught. That's the kind of sorrow King Saul had, but that's not godly sorrow. With godly sorrow, you are sorry because you love God with everything you've got. You are sorry because you desire Christ, and you realize that your sin is against Him. The kind of repentance that results in true confession always flows out of godly sorrow over sin. Not just sorrow over the consequences of sin, but over the sin itself. When you repent, it means you have changed your mind about your sin. You now see it as God sees it. You now hate it as God hates it. You love God, so you hate sin and you grieve over it.

To overcome the fear of man, you need to see your fear as sin, and you need to sorrow over it. If you are not sorrowing over this sin as you should, begin to practice each of the following:

Cry out to God for help. The apostle James says, "Every good thing given and every perfect gift is from above, coming down from the Father of lights" (James 1:17). Confession is a good thing, and we are unable to even confess our sins the way God desires unless He's at work in us. We serve a Father who loves to give good gifts to His children, so if we earnestly and sincerely ask for His help in this endeavor, we can be sure that He won't deny us. Don't trust in yourself; instead cry out to God, "I want to sorrow over my sin. I want my sins to be brought to my attention so that I can confess them. Oh God, have mercy on me! Please help me to repent!"

12. For more on this thought, see Samuel Davies, "The Nature and Necessity of True Repentance," *Bible Bulletin Board*, accessed November 20, 2013, http://www.biblebb.com /files/davies/repentance.htm.

Get to know God. Do you know what happens in the Bible when people get a right view of God? They cry out over their sins. Think of Isaiah. He was in the throne room of God, with the cherubim surrounding the throne crying out, "Holy, Holy, Holy" (Isa. 6:3). What did Isaiah say? "Woe is me, for I am ruined! Because I am a man of unclean lips, and I live among a people of unclean lips; For my eyes have seen the King, the LORD of hosts" (6:5).

If you are going to truly follow God, your life's goal has to be to know God and to commune with Him. Meditate on His sovereignty. When you sin, you are rebelling against the King of the universe. Meditate on His kindness. Think about all the ways that God has shown love to believers, and specifically all the ways that He has shown love to you. Remember that when you sin, you are sinning against a God who loves you.

Study His Word. In 2 Timothy 3:16–17 we learn that one of the reasons God gave us His Word was to reprove us—to show us our sins. Hebrews 4:12 explains that God's Word is "living and active and sharper than any two-edged sword, and piercing as far as the division of soul and spirit, of both joints and marrow, and able to judge the thoughts and intentions of the heart." The Word of God exposes our sin. Stop allowing your mind to be conformed to the pattern of this world. Instead get into the Scriptures so the Holy Spirit can transform you by the renewing of your mind. Study the Bible, not just to fill your mind with Bible trivia but to know God and to know what He wants for your life. Commune with the living Word by studying the written Word.

Think about your Savior. The more you realize just how good Christ is, the more you will feel convicted of and sorrow over your sin. When I hear that someone I don't know is bothered by my behavior, it doesn't upset me all that much, because I don't know them. But when I hear that my wife doesn't like something I am doing, that grieves me, because I know my wife and I love her. Frankly, the reason many of us aren't concerned about our sin, and don't grieve over it, is because we don't know our Savior. We are not in love with Him.

When You Confess Your Sin, Stop Passing the Blame and Get Specific

Our culture has declared war on guilt. Read almost any pop-psychology book, and it will tell you that if you have guilt feelings, you need to get rid of them as quickly as possible, usually by excusing, rationalizing, or shifting the blame for whatever caused the guilt. The Bible makes it clear, however, that the answer to those guilt feelings is not to deny them, but to acknowledge that you have sinned and that you are guilty. Stop excusing yourself, stop rationalizing away your guilt, and stop blaming others for your sin. As Jay Adams explains, "Confession is the opposite of all such behavior. It begins with repentance—rethinking all such attitudes—and ends with owning up to one's sins before God."[13]

Don't try to play games with God. When you truly are repentant of your sins, when you seek to truly confess them, you are concerned about God's glory. You are focused on God. You are not there to make yourself look good. You are standing there before God because you want to glorify Him. You want to make Him look good. So you acknowledge that He is right in His judgment of you. You glorify Him by specifically confessing your sins.

When you confess your sin, you are not coming before God vaguely saying, "God, I am a sinner." No, you have stopped hiding your sin. "I acknowledged my sin, my iniquities I did not hide." You get specific about your sins when you bring them before God because you are making a formal acknowledgement of them. You are going on the record, admitting your guilt. You are not coming before God just confessing some of your sins, and hiding the ones you really enjoy; no, you are confessing them all. You want to glorify Him by bringing them out into the open and laying them out before Him.

That's what John meant in 1 John 1:9 when he wrote that believers should confess their sins. He was referring to a regular, specific, particular confession of sin. "If we confess our sins, He is faithful and righteous to forgive us our sins." Author D. Edmond Hiebert explains:

13. Adams, *A Theology of Christian Counseling*, 144–45.

A confession is more than a general acknowledgement that we all are sinners by nature, such a confession costs little and does not meet the need. We must honestly confront and frankly confess the sins that we are guilty of without defending ourselves or excusing our sinful deeds. The plural "sins" demands that specific sins be named and confessed. It is a humbling experience and guarantee of our sincerity. The present tense underlines that such confession is to be our standing practice whenever sins do occur.[14]

In true repentance, you see your sin, sorrow over it, stop passing the blame, and go on record, specifically acknowledging your sins before God.

But repentance doesn't stop there. Remember Proverbs 28:13. It is the person who both confesses and forsakes his sin who will find compassion. True repentance produces confession and is followed by change. Isn't that obvious? If you see your sin for what it is, if you are truly grieved by it, if you acknowledge your guilt and if you specifically confess it to God, you're not going to continue to wallow in it. You are going to work on turning away from that sin with everything you've got.

Do you want to overcome the fear of man? Do you want to overcome any kind of sinful fear? This is where victory begins. "He who confesses and forsakes [his sins] will find compassion." That's a promise.

When was the last time you actually repented of your sins? When's the last time you actually humbled yourself before God, cried out for His mercy, pointed out your sins, acknowledged your guilt, and laid yourself bare before Him?

Our God is a great, compassionate, wonderful God who loves to show mercy to sinners. But He only shows compassion to sinners who repent! If you are going to overcome the fear of man, you need to stop covering your sins, start confessing them, and commit to forsaking them.

All true change begins with putting off—repenting and forsaking. But that's not where it ends. You must also learn what to put on in its place. That's exactly what we're going to look at in the next several chapters.

14. D. Edmond Hiebert, *The Epistles of John* (Greenville, SC: Bob Jones University Press, 1991), 66.

QUESTIONS FOR DISCUSSION

1. What principle does David's story illustrate?

2. What are two strategies for dealing with sin?

3. What's the difference between the two men described in Proverbs 28:13?

4. What must you do if you are going to overcome the fear of man? Why?

5. What would you tell someone who came to you and asked, "Why should I repent?" Support your answer biblically.

6. Is repentance a one-time act? Prove your answer scripturally.

7. What do we learn from 2 Corinthians 7:9–10? Apply this to your situation.

8. What is one reason many believers are stuck in their sin?

9. What are some possible reasons people don't repent?

10. What does it mean to confess your sin?

11. What do we learn from Psalm 32 and 1 John 1:9 about confession?

12. Why is it difficult to see your own sin?

13. From what does true confession flow?

14. Why should you be sorry over your sin? Be specific.

15. What is godly sorrow over sin? How does it differ from worldly sorrow?

16. What should you do if you don't feel sorrowful over sin the way you should?

17. What are some ways you pass the blame for your sin?

18. What's the result of true repentance?

19. When was the last time you truly repented of your sin?

8

GOD'S GAME PLAN

NOBODY CAN DENY that we live in a frightening world. You may enjoy wearing a T-shirt that says, "No Fear," but you know as well as we do that, apart from God, many things in this world are pretty terrifying. Although you may feel safe and secure right now, soon enough you can be certain that something will come into your life that will confront you with the harsh reality that you are not nearly as safe and secure as you like to pretend.

Every one of us will be tempted to fear. That's life. In the past several chapters we've taken a good look at one of the most common and difficult of the temptations you'll ever face—the temptation to fear man. We've sought to understand the fear of man and why it's so important for you to overcome it. In upcoming chapters, we're going to study what God wants for you to put in its place. Understand how to overcome this sinful fear, and you'll understand how to overcome all other sinful fears.

In this chapter we want to take a step back and present God's basic game plan for dealing with the temptation of fear. Before we look at the specifics, we need to understand God's overall strategy for living courageously in a frightening world. It's summarized for us in Isaiah 8:11–14:

> For thus the LORD spoke to me with mighty power and instructed me not to walk in the way of this people, saying,
>
> "You are not to say, 'It is a conspiracy!'
> In regard to all that this people call a conspiracy,

And you are not to fear what they fear or be in dread of it.
It is the LORD of hosts whom you should regard as holy.
And He shall be your fear,
And He shall be your dread.
Then He shall become a sanctuary."

THE WRONG WAY TO RESPOND IN TIMES OF TROUBLE

God granted Isaiah great spiritual privileges. He called Isaiah and set him apart as a prophet. Isaiah saw things most men have never seen. He actually visited the throne room of God and saw the King of Kings in all His glory.

God gave Isaiah a message to proclaim, but He never promised Isaiah that his ministry would be easy. In fact, God told him that the people of Judah would refuse to listen to him and would reject his message. Yet Isaiah didn't back down. He stepped up and faithfully proclaimed God's Word. He's a hero of the faith.

Despite all his great spiritual privileges, Isaiah was a man just like us. When difficult times came, he was tempted to become fearful, and that's what we find happening in Isaiah 8.

Judah was at war. They were barely a speck of a nation, not great and powerful but rather weak and insignificant. Israel, their closest neighbor, was set on their destruction. We read in Isaiah 7:1 that "in the days of Ahaz . . . Rezin the king of Aram and Pekah the son of Remaliah, king of Israel, went up to Jerusalem to wage war against it." Israel was so committed to defeating Judah that they even made a pact with another powerful nation to do so, making it two against one.

The people of Judah were terrified. "When it was reported to the house of David, saying, 'The Arameans have camped in Ephraim,' his heart and the hearts of his people shook as the trees of the forest shake with the wind" (7:2). These people were scared.

But believe it or not, Isaiah had it worse than the rest of Judah. They didn't know whether they would win or lose. At least they had some hope; Isaiah didn't. He knew that Judah was going to be defeated. They weren't going to lose to Israel or Aram; instead they were going to be destroyed by the very nation they turned to for help, Assyria.

God made it clear to Isaiah that Judah was going to be humiliated: "The Lord will shave with a razor, hired from regions beyond the Euphrates, (that is, with the king of Assyria), the head and the hair of the legs; and it will also remove the beard" (7:20). Judah was going to be impoverished:

> It shall be in that day
> That a man will keep alive a young cow and two sheep;
> So it shall be, from the abundance of milk they give,
> That he will eat curds;
> For curds and honey everyone will eat who is left in the land.
> (7:21–22 NKJV)

And Judah was going to be devastated: "It shall happen in that day, that wherever there could be a thousand vines worth a thousand shekels of silver, it will be for briers and thorns" (7:23 NKJV).

Isaiah wasn't Superman. You can imagine that when he stood up and said, "Assyria is going to totally destroy us," he would have been tempted to be afraid. He was a part of Judah. He wasn't prophesying from some remote satellite hookup far away from where the action would take place; he was at ground zero in Jerusalem where all this devastation would occur.

And Isaiah was having struggles. This news wasn't easy for him to take. This was his home, his family, his nation about which he was prophesying, and as a result he was tempted to respond like everyone else. He was becoming afraid. God knew that, so He came to give Isaiah special instruction on how to handle those frightening times: "Thus the LORD spoke to me with mighty power and instructed me not to walk in the way of this people" (8:11). The word translated here as *instructed* means "corrected or disciplined for the purpose of education." Even Isaiah had to be "educated" on how to be courageous in a frightening world.

God's basic charge to Isaiah was very simple: when times of trouble come, your response should be very different from the world's. He told Isaiah "not to walk in the way of this people." The world reacts to trouble one way and you, Isaiah, are to react very differently. "Don't respond like everyone else!"

Don't Compromise

"You are not to say, 'It is a conspiracy!' in regard to all that this people call a conspiracy" (v. 12). God exhorted Isaiah not to compromise.

This term *conspiracy* could be translated "confederacy," meaning "alliance." We know from 2 Kings and 1 Chronicles that King Ahaz was attempting to save Judah, and his own neck, by making an alliance with the Assyrians. Trouble came, and he looked to men for help rather than God. God hates that kind of response. He says in Jeremiah, "Cursed is the man who trusts in mankind and makes flesh his strength, and whose heart turns away from the LORD" (Jer. 17:5).

In Isaiah 8, we see that He rebuked Israel for doing just that: "Inasmuch as these people refused the waters of Shiloah that flow softly, and rejoice in Rezin and Remaliah's son" (8:6 NKJV). The northern nation of Israel had refused to depend on God and had instead looked to man for strength, and now the king of Judah was doing the same.

God could have been saying to Isaiah, "Don't say the word *alliance* like this is a positive thing." "Don't encourage this alliance." "Don't agree with everybody else and look to man for help when you should be looking to Me!" "Don't compromise by responding to fearful times just like the world, who look to the creature for strength rather than to the Creator."

Sometimes we do that, don't we? When times get difficult, we put our confidence in anyone and everyone except God. We'll never be courageous until we stop compromising by trusting in people. "Cursed is the man who trusts in mankind and makes flesh his strength, and whose heart turns away from the LORD. . . . Blessed is the man who trusts in the LORD and whose trust is the LORD" (Jer. 17:5, 7).

More likely, however, when God said, "You are not to say, 'It is a conspiracy,'" He wasn't talking about a confederacy, but a more treasonous alliance. The word *conspiracy* is used most often in the Old Testament to describe people binding themselves together for the purpose of committing treason. The people of Judah may have been calling Isaiah a traitor.

Imagine a pastor in our day standing up and saying that God was going to use a terrorist to destroy the United States. That pastor wouldn't be very well liked. He'd be called all sorts of names, hated as a traitor, and vilified by the press.

Yet that's basically the message God gave Isaiah to proclaim: "God is going to use Assyria, a very evil nation, to destroy us, His people."

You can imagine the nation's response: "What are you talking about, Isaiah? We're looking to Assyria for help, and you're telling us they're going to defeat us? Do you want us to die at the hands of the Israelites and Arameans? You're betraying your own country, Isaiah. You're telling us to trust God and not turn to Assyria? You are a traitor!"

That's exactly what they accused the prophet Jeremiah of doing. We read in Jeremiah 37 that Jeremiah stood up and said,

> Thus says the LORD, "Do not deceive yourselves saying, 'The Chaldeans will surely go away from us,' for they will not go. For even if you had defeated the entire army of Chaldeans who were fighting against you, and there were only wounded men left among them, each man in his tent, they would rise up and burn this city with fire." (vv. 37:9–10)

The Jewish people didn't like to hear that message. So how did they respond? They attacked the messenger! We read that as Jeremiah was leaving Jerusalem to take care of some business and "was at the Gate of Benjamin, a captain of the guard whose name was Irijah . . . was there; and he arrested Jeremiah . . . saying, 'You are going over to the Chaldeans!'" (v. 13). (In other words, "You are a traitor.") "But Jeremiah said, 'A lie! I am not going over to the Chaldeans'; yet he would not listen to him. So Irijah arrested Jeremiah and brought him to the officials" (v. 14). The officials beat Jeremiah and threw him into prison for treason.

That same thing could well be what was occurring in Isaiah. We don't know for certain, but it wouldn't be surprising. The people didn't like Isaiah's message, so they were attacking him, saying he was a traitor, a part of a conspiracy, plotting their downfall. So God came to Isaiah and exhorted him, "Don't compromise. Don't change the message just because people don't like to hear it. Don't say what they want you to say just so they will like you better. I've given you this message to proclaim; proclaim it!" (Isa. 8:12, author's paraphrase).

In the end, whether God was saying, "Don't agree with the world and encourage this alliance with Assyria," or "Don't agree with the world and call what you are doing a conspiracy," His point was the same: "I've given you truth. Don't believe the world's lies. Don't falter, don't compromise, don't think like the world. Stand strong!"

When you are frightened, you will be tempted to compromise. You will be tempted to look to other people for help, or you will be tempted to distort God's Word. You will be tempted to go the way of the world rather than stick to the path God has laid out for you. Perhaps you are in a situation in which the right path is clear. But you think, "This way is too hard. The world's way looks easier," so you are tempted to make up excuses and follow the world's path. Maybe it is a financial situation. You are in a tight spot and you know what the Bible says about giving, but you don't know how you could possibly obey God and still survive. Maybe it is a parenting situation. You know what God wants you to do with your children, but it seems too difficult. Maybe it is in a friendship. You've read the Bible and understand what kind of friends you are supposed to have, but you look at the people around you and think, "If I follow God's path, I am going to be lonely." Whatever the particular situation you are in, when you are in a frightening situation, you are going to be tempted to compromise.

God's Word to you is this: Don't do it. Don't respond to trouble the way the world does. Stand strong. The person who compromises always loses in the end.

Don't Cave In

God continued speaking to Isaiah, "You are not to fear what they fear or be in dread of it" (v. 12). The world is in chaos, but you must remain calm.

That's quite a command. From a human perspective, the Jewish people had a great deal of which to be frightened. They were at war. They were going to be destroyed. They were in the midst of a national crisis. They were looking death and destruction in the eye, and they were scared. It seemed normal.

But God told Isaiah, "I know the people are afraid of all this, but you shouldn't be." This was an emphatic negative command, which is a fancy way of saying, "Whatever you do, don't do this! Isaiah, you should be completely different from the world around you. They are afraid of this great enemy. You shouldn't be. They are afraid of death. You shouldn't be. They are afraid of destruction. You shouldn't be. Don't fear the things they fear."

"Good for Isaiah," you might be thinking. "I'm glad I'm not in his shoes." But you are. God has given each one of us a similar command. Peter quoted this very verse in 1 Peter 3:14–15. He wrote that when you are being persecuted for righteousness, when the world is against you, when people want to destroy you, when you are suffering for the gospel, you shouldn't be afraid. Don't fear what they fear, and don't be intimidated by their threats.

Christians should be marked by courage in the midst of life's most difficult situations. That's not optional, that's biblical. Our response to the troubling circumstances of life should be completely different from the response of the world around us. The world responds to difficulties by caving in; we must respond by standing strong.

"But," you say, "how is that possible? How can God command me not to fear someone who wants to persecute me? How can He ask me not to fear physical torment? How can I overcome fear when I am walking through the valley of the shadow of death? If life is so challenging, how can I be courageous?"

Isaiah probably asked the same questions. "Sounds great. 'Don't fear!' Easy for You to say. But how in the world can You expect me not to fear or dread the Assyrians coming into my country and breaking us to pieces? That's frightening! How can I be fearless when things are so frightening?"

THE RIGHT WAY TO RESPOND TO TIMES OF TROUBLE

In Isaiah 8:13, God revealed the path to overcoming worldly fears: "It is the LORD of hosts whom you should regard as holy. And He shall be your fear, and He shall be your dread."

Set God Apart in Your Heart

One translation words this verse as follows: "The LORD of hosts, Him shall you hallow" (NKJV). To *hallow* means to make holy, to have great respect or reverence for. When times of trouble come, we often get so overwhelmed by our circumstances that we forget to hallow our Creator. When that happens, we need to stop and remember who God is. We need to make a conscious choice and a deliberate decision to set Him apart in our hearts.

The term translated *to hallow* is also translated *sanctify*. *Sanctify* means "to set apart as holy." There are places in the Old Testament where you'll read that certain items were sanctified unto God. That means the people of Israel took those items and separated them from their everyday things for a holy purpose.

They said, "These items are to have a distinct use. They are to be for God—totally separate from our other common, everyday things." Other times, we read of people being sanctified. For example, Moses' brother, Aaron, was sanctified. What did that mean? God chose Aaron and set him apart from the rest of the men of Israel to serve a special purpose.

When you sanctify something or someone, you are placing them in a unique position. To sanctify God is to give Him an absolutely unique position in your heart and life.

Too often we think that God is just like us. That's why we become afraid. God rebuked Judah for doing just this:

Woe to those who deeply hide their plans from the LORD,
And whose deeds are done in a dark place,
And they say, "Who sees us?" or "Who knows us?"
You turn things around!

Shall the potter be considered as equal with the clay,
That what is made would say to its maker, "He did not make me";
Or what is formed say to him who formed it, "He has no understanding"?
    (Isa. 29:15–16)

That's what it means to not hallow God. When you think of God in ordinary terms, you are not hallowing Him. You are not setting Him apart when you treat Him like He is just another creature. You are not hallowing God when you think He is just like you!

To sanctify God means to set Him apart in your heart from absolutely everything and everyone else. It means that you are no longer going to think and act as though God is ordinary, just like everybody else. Instead you will purposefully exalt Him to the place in your life that no one else has and no one else deserves. You are hallowing God when you stand in awe of Him, give Him glory, worship Him as the Creator, and understand that He is the potter and you are the clay.

The reason we struggle so intensely with the fear of man (the creature) is because we haven't set apart the Creator. That's the root of all our sinful fears. We're weak because we don't really understand who God is. Our thoughts of God are too small, and our thoughts of men are too big. John Flavel explains that fear often comes from ignorance: ignorance of God and ignorance of men.

Either we know not or at least do not consider His Almighty Power, vigilant care, unspotted faithfulness, and how they are all engaged by covenant for his people.... Were it once thoroughly understood and believed, what power there is in God's hand to defend us, what tenderness in his bowels to commiserate us, what faithfulness in all the promises, in which they are made over to us, O how quiet and calm would our hearts be! Our courage would quickly be up, and our fears down.... We fear [men] because we do not know them; if we understood them better we would fear them less; we over-value them and then fright at them. They say the lion is painted more fierce than he is; I am sure our fancy paints out man more dreadful than indeed he is; if wicked men, especially multitudes of wicked men be confederated against us, our hearts fail, and presently apprehend inevitable ruin. "The floods of the ungodly made me afraid," saith David, i.e. the multitudes of them which he thought, like a flood or mighty torrent of water, must needs sweep away such a straw, such a feather, as he was, before them; but, in the mean time, we know or consider not that they have no power against us, but what is given them from above, and that it is usual with God to cramp their hands, and clap on the bands of restraint upon them, when their hearts are fully set in them to do mischief: did we see and consider them as they are in the hand of our God, we should not tremble at them as we do.[1]

To overcome fear, we must stop giving the creature more honor and more power than he really has, and we must stop thinking of God as less glorious and less powerful than He really is.

It's a great sin to fear men because it means we aren't thinking properly about God. The next time you are tempted to become frightened, stop. Get your mind in order. Remember how powerful God is. Remember how glorious God is. Remember how faithful God is. Acknowledge Him as God. Don't just give Him praise with your lips; worship Him sincerely, from the bottom of your heart.

Train your mind to think specifically about God and His character. God tells Isaiah to sanctify Him as the "LORD of hosts." He knows the particular fear with which Isaiah is struggling, so He reminds Isaiah of a facet of His character that would comfort him during this particular trial.

The title "Lord of hosts" has military overtones. It literally means "Lord of armies." God was reminding Isaiah that He alone is the ruler over every power in the universe. He alone is the Commander in Chief. Instead of fearing the army of Assyria, God was saying Isaiah should fear the true Ruler of the army. Assyria was just the "rod of My anger and the staff in whose hands is My indignation" (10:5). In other words, Assyria was just a tool in God's hands. They may not have even known it, but God was using them for His sovereign purposes. What an awesome God we serve!

As John Newton commented:

1. John Flavel, *The Works of John Flavel*, vol. 3 (London: Banner of Truth Trust, 1968), 258–59.

The kings of the earth are continually disturbing the world with their schemes of ambition. They expect to carry every thing before them, and have seldom any higher end in view than the gratification of their passions. But in all they do they are but servants of this great King and Lord, and fulfill his purposes, as the instruments he employs to inflict prescribed punishment upon transgressors against him, or to open a way for the spread of his Gospel. . . . They had one thing in view, he had another.[2]

The great nations of the earth don't have any power in and of themselves. Their power is in God. He can raise them up and destroy them in an instant. God was reminding Isaiah, "This situation is not out of control. Remember who I am. I am the Lord of hosts."

God alone is King, exalted over all, and His power and strength are limitless. Amos 9:5–6 expresses this thought beautifully:

> The Lord GOD of hosts,
> The One who touches the land so that it melts,
> And all those who dwell in it mourn . . .
> The One who builds His upper chambers in the heavens
> And has founded His vaulted dome over the earth,
> He who calls for the waters of the sea
> And pours them out on the face of the earth,
> The LORD is His name.

God is not small, God is not weak, He is the great Ruler of the universe and does whatever He pleases. In times of trouble, stop focusing on your circumstances, and start focusing on the One who rules over your circumstances.

Fear God

"He shall be your fear, and He shall be your dread" (Isa. 8:13). God is not asking us to be fearless, just to fear the right Person. Don't fear the creature—fear the Creator. Let Him be your fear, let Him be your dread!

2. Cited in Jerry Bridges, *Trusting God* (Colorado Springs: NavPress, 1988), 79.

One old Puritan saying explains, "The fear of God will swallow up the fear of man, a reverential awe and dread of God will extinguish the slavish fear of the creature."[3]

We're going to look in greater detail at the fear of God in upcoming chapters. But take note for now: if you want to be a person of courage, you need to first become a person who fears.

The key to overcoming sinful fear is to replace it with holy fear. Heroes of the past weren't courageous because they were fearless, but rather because they were full of the right kind of fear. R. C. Sproul Jr. makes this point by using the courage of early Christian martyrs as an illustration and a challenge to us today. He argues that while these martyrs were no doubt strengthened by God to face death, they were most likely also strengthened by a fear that was "properly directed.... Courage for the Christian, like wisdom, begins with the fear of God."[4] In the end he concludes that "we must not allow the petty but visible things which cause us to fear cloak that which is truly fearful."[5]

In Isaiah 8:14 we see that God gave Isaiah a powerful encouragement to do so. If you fear God, "then He shall become a sanctuary." In the Hebrew this is a play on words: "*Kadesh* the Lord of hosts, and He will become your *mikadesh*." Set apart God as holy, and He will become your holy place.

The term *mikadesh* refers to a special place where God dwells. In the Old Testament it is often used to describe the temple. Here it is used metaphorically to describe how God chooses to dwell with and protect a person who places their trust in Him alone.

"If you fear Me, Isaiah, if you depend on Me in times of trouble, I will dwell in a special way with you. I will be your safe place, I will be your refuge. Don't fear man and turn to him for safety. Fear me, and I will protect you!"

Are you frightened or overwhelmed with fear? Turn to God. He alone is worthy of your trust. Place your hope and confidence in Him. As you look at the difficulties in your life, the circumstances

---

3. Flavel, *The Works of John Flavel*, 244.
4. R. C. Sproul Jr., "Coram Deo," *Tabletalk* 20, no. 10 (October 1996): 2.
5. Ibid.

that are bringing you fear, remember who God is. Think about His character. Don't allow your circumstances and your feelings to cloud your thinking. Stop and think correctly. Set God apart from everyone and everything else in your life. Remember His promises. The psalmist wrote,

> He who dwells in the shelter of the Most High
> Will abide in the shadow of the Almighty.
> I will say to the LORD, "My refuge and my fortress,
> My God, in whom I trust!" (Ps. 91:1–2)

If God is our refuge, of what are we afraid?

> God is our refuge and strength,
> A very present help in trouble.
> Therefore we will not fear, though the earth should change
> And though the mountains slip into the heart of the sea;
> Though its waters roar and foam,
> Though the mountains quake at its swelling pride. (Ps. 46:1–3)

Spurgeon explains it this way:

> Why, it matters not what God has given us to do, if he helps us we can do it. Give me God to help me, and I will split the world in halves and shiver it till it shall be smaller than the dust of the threshing floor; ay, if God be with me, this breath could blow whole worlds about, as the child bloweth a bubble. There is no saying what man can do when God is with him. . . . There is no fear of a man who has got God with him, he is all-sufficient; there is nothing beyond his power.[6]

Or as the apostle Paul wrote, "If God is for us, who is against us?" (Rom. 8:31). Fear God, and you need fear no one else! When you are tempted to become afraid, when you are tempted to give in to sinful

---

6. C. H. Spurgeon, "Fear Not" (sermon, Music Hall, Royal Surrey Gardens, London, October 4, 1857), *The Reformed Reader*, http://www.reformedreader.org/spurgeon/1857-28.htm.

fear, realize this: there's a right way and a wrong way to respond. And to respond successfully, first and foremost you need to be a person who is pursuing the fear of God.

This concept is so fundamental to overcoming fear that we're going to take the next several chapters to examine it. We need to know: Exactly why should I fear God? What does it mean to fear God? And how do I develop this healthy fear of God?

QUESTIONS FOR DISCUSSION

1. What is the purpose of this chapter?

2. What was happening in Isaiah 8? Why was Isaiah in a difficult position? What reasons could he have given for becoming afraid?

3. What was God's basic charge to Isaiah? What can we learn from it?

4. What was God saying to Isaiah in verse 12?

5. What are some of the ways you tend to compromise when you are placed in frightening situations?

6. How does the world usually respond to frightening situations? Give examples. Is it all right for believers to respond to frightening situations just like the world would? Explain biblically.

7. What is the path to overcoming your fears? Defend your answer with Scripture.

Is 46

8. What does it mean to sanctify God?

9. What would it look like for you to sanctify God? How could you
   go about doing this? Be practical. What specific steps can you take
   this week to sanctify God in your heart?

   meditate on the things we know about God.

10. What is one reason this chapter gives that we struggle so intensely
    with the fear of the creature rather than the Creator?

11. How does fear spring from ignorance? Relate this to your own
    situation. In what ways has your own fear come from ignorance?

12. What can you learn from the fact that God is the Lord of hosts?

13. What is God's basic game plan for becoming a person of courage?

14. As a result of what you've learned from this chapter, what will you do differently the next time you are tempted to fear?

9

BE AFRAID—
BE VERY AFRAID

IF YOU ARE SEARCHING for one key principle to help you in your struggle with fear, here it is. In order not to fear, you must begin to fear.

If you think you've read that before, you have. We've made it a point to repeat that basic principle throughout this book, because quite frankly it's a concept you won't hear many other places. You certainly won't hear it from the world, and unfortunately you won't hear it from most Christians. But the Scripture is clear: the only way to overcome sinful fear is to develop holy fear. Develop a holy fear of God, and you won't be plagued by a sinful fear of man or anything else.

That's not a very popular statement, because the fear of God is not a very popular subject. In fact, there are many professing Christians who actively oppose it. They don't promote the fear of God; instead they attempt to stifle it. They are convinced that all fear is sin. "Doesn't 2 Timothy 1:7 tell us that believers have not been given the spirit of fear?" they will ask. "Wasn't it Paul who said in Romans 8:15 that believers have not been given the spirit of bondage to fear? Didn't the apostle John write that perfect love casts out fear? Fear is demeaning, destructive, disheartening, and unworthy of a Christian." For these professing believers, that's proof enough that it is time to start talking about something other than the fear of God. Sadly, they couldn't be more wrong.

Jerry Bridges described an encounter he had with a certain Christian leader to whom he spoke about the joy of fearing God. He said the man looked at him with a puzzled expression and said, "That's an interesting combination of words." He explained he suspected from the man's confused look that this man was really thinking, "How can anyone enjoy fearing God?" Bridges went on to point out that the man's response was telling: "The fact that a Christian leader would respond to the concept in this way tells us something about the current state of Christianity."[1] We couldn't agree more. To many Christians the idea of "fearing God" sounds like an outdated, antiquated concept that may have had its place in the days of Bunyan and Edwards but by now has certainly outlived its usefulness. Therefore, they assert, any discussion of fearing God is a step backward not forward.

Our goal in this chapter is very simple: we want to show you how reasonable it is to fear God, and then challenge you to develop and sustain a healthy, wholesome fear of God, making it a top priority in your life.

Without a healthy fear of God you won't overcome sinful fear and, what's more, you won't be able to live a life that honors God. Scripture places a tremendous emphasis on the fear of God. The fear of God is not a minor issue—it's a major theme.

You'll find references to the fear of God from the first book of the Bible to the last. You'll find many passages throughout the books of Psalms and Proverbs, the Major and Minor Prophets, the Gospels, Acts, and the Epistles that emphasize the importance of fearing God. Time and time again, God makes it clear: you ignore and neglect the fear of God to your own destruction.

IT IS AN ABSOLUTE REQUIREMENT

When I was teaching at the Master's College, I sometimes gave my students optional assignments they could complete for extra credit. Other assignments I gave them were not optional; they were requirements. If students didn't fulfill those assignments, they didn't pass the course.

The fear of God is not an optional assignment. It's an absolute requirement. Moses asked Israel, "Now, Israel, what does the LORD your God require [of] you?" (Deut. 10:12). It's a simple question for which

1. Jerry Bridges, *The Joy of Fearing God* (Colorado Springs: WaterBrook Press, 1997), 1.

there is a clear answer: "fear the LORD your God," "walk in all His ways and love Him," "serve the LORD your God with all your heart and . . . soul," and "keep the LORD's commandments and His statutes which I am commanding you today for your good" (vv. 12–13). In the New Testament, you will find in Matthew 10:28 that Jesus commanded His disciples to do the same thing: "Do not fear those who kill the body but are unable to kill the soul; but rather fear Him who is able to destroy both soul and body in hell." Peter made a similar point in 1 Peter 1:17: "Conduct yourselves in fear during the time of your stay on earth." If you do not fear God, you are sinning.

In fact, you could say that a lack of the fear of God is at the root of all sin. In Romans 3:10–18, Paul gave a description of the human condition apart from God. It's not a pretty picture. He explained in verses 10–17 that we are all under sin. There is none righteous, not even one. There is none who understands, none who seeks after God. Sin has affected our speech: our throats have become an open grave, our tongues continue to deceive. Sin has affected our integrity: the poison of asps is under our lips. Sin has affected our behavior: our mouths are full of cursing and bitterness, our feet are swift to shed blood, destruction and misery are in our path, and the path of peace we have not known.

In verse 18 Paul came to the climax of his argument. Why do we sin in this way? "There is no fear of God before their eyes." We sin because we don't fear God. We need to develop a healthy fear of God. If we don't, we sin, and we open ourselves to all sorts of other kinds of sins.

IT IS ONLY REASONABLE

It makes sense to fear God. Unfortunately many professing Christians don't understand that. Their view of God is much too small. Author David Wells explains that all too often the church has

> turned to a God that we can use rather than to a God we must obey;
> we have turned to a God who will fulfill our needs rather than to a
> God before whom we must surrender our rights to ourselves. He is a
> God for us, for our satisfaction—not because we have learned to think
> of him in this way through Christ but because we have learned to

think of him this way through the marketplace. In the marketplace, everything is for us, for our pleasure, for our satisfaction, and we have come to assume that it must be so in the church as well. And so we transform the God of mercy into the God who is at our mercy. . . . If the sunshine of his benign grace fails to warm us as we expect, if he fails to shower prosperity and success on us, we will find ourselves unable to believe in him anymore.[2]

God does not fit in any of our little boxes. We must not worship the God we make up. Instead we must worship the true and living God. Although the God of our imaginations may be less awesome and more comfortable, He isn't real and therefore isn't a source of true strength or hope. The psalmist explained,

> Our God is in heaven;
> He does whatever He pleases.
> Their idols are silver and gold,
> The work of men's hands.
> They have mouths, but they do not speak;
> Eyes they have, but they do not see;
> They have ears, but they do not hear;
> Noses they have, but they do not smell;
> They have hands, but they do not handle;
> Feet they have, but they do not walk;
> Nor do they mutter through their throat.
> Those who make them are like them;
> So is everyone who trusts in them. (Ps. 115:3–8 NKJV)

We need to see God for who He is. When we do that, when we stop trying to make God into our own image, we'll understand just how extremely appropriate it is to be awestruck and stunned in the presence of a holy and awesome God.

Do you want proof? Just read the biblical accounts of how the men who truly experienced God's presence reacted. They feared Him. John

---

2. David Wells, *God in the Wasteland* (Grand Rapids: Eerdmans, 1994), 114.

wrote in Revelation 1:17: "When I saw Him, I fell at His feet as dead" (NKJV). Isaiah cried out, "Woe is me, for I am undone! Because I am a man of unclean lips, and I dwell in the midst of a people of unclean lips" (Isa. 6:5 NKJV). John Bunyan pointed out that even when God comes to bestow mercy, His presence produces fear.

> When God comes to bring a soul news of mercy and salvation, even that visit, that presence of God is fearful. When Jacob went from Beersheba towards Haran, he met with God in the way by a dream, in which he apprehended a ladder set upon the earth, whose top reached to heaven; now in this dream, from the top of this ladder he saw the Lord, and heard him speak unto him not threateningly, not as having his fury come up into his face, but in the most sweet and gracious manner, saluting him with promise of goodness after promise of goodness, to the number of eight or nine. . . . Yet I say, when he awoke, all the grace that discovered itself in this heavenly vision to him could not keep him from dread and fear of God's majesty. "And Jacob awoke out of his sleep, and said, 'Surely the Lord was in this place and I knew it not'; and he was afraid and said, 'How dreadful is this place; this is none other but the house of God; and this is the gate of heaven.'"[3]

The point is: you are not worshiping the true God if you are worshiping a God you don't fear. The fear of God is not irrational. It's not a relic from a bygone era. It is entirely reasonable.

Edward Payson explains,

> With what profound veneration does it become us to enter the presence and to receive the favors of the awful Majesty of heaven and earth. . . . Suppose that the sun, whose brightness even at this distance, you cannot gaze upon without shrinking, were an animated, intelligent body; and that, with a design to do you good, he should leave his place in the heavens and gradually approach you. As he drew more and more near, his apparent magnitude would increase;

3. John Bunyan, *Complete Works of Bunyan*, vol. 2 (Marshallton, DE: National Foundation for Christian Education, 1968), 404.

he would occupy a larger and larger portion of the heavens, until at length all other objects would be lost, and yourselves swallowed up in one insufferably dazzling, overpowering flood of light. Would you not, in such circumstances, feel the strongest emotions of awe, of something like fear? . . . What, then, ought to be the feelings of a sinful worm of the dust, when the Father of lights, the eternal Sun of the universe, who dwells in the high and holy place, and in the contrite heart, stoops from his awful throne, to visit him, to smile upon him, to pardon him, to purify him from his moral defilement, to adopt him as a child, to make him an heir of heaven, to take possession of his heart as his earthly habitation.[4]

We should fear God because He is awesome. In our day we use the word *awesome* very lightly. We have an ice cream sundae, and we say, "That was an awesome sundae"; or we hear a great musician and say, "That guy is an awesome musician"; or we read a beautiful piece of poetry and we comment, "That poem was awesome."

When I think of what it means to be awesome, I think of what happened to my wife and me in January of 1994, while we were living in California. We went to bed one night, and shortly after 2:00 a.m. something awoke us. We heard a tremendous roar, and suddenly the little house in which we were living began to shake. It was as though a huge giant had picked up our house and was shaking it, just as he might shake a rag doll. We were in a waterbed, and it was as though we were experiencing a tidal wave. The television sitting on top of our dresser flew across the room; other things flew all over the place. When I got out of bed, I kept bumping into things that had been moved by the earthquake. I was unable to open our bedroom door because objects had been slammed up against it. I was scared. Others were too. As a result, for a long time after the earthquake many people wouldn't sleep in their bedrooms; they slept out in their cars. People were so afraid that they kept their lights on at night. They were scared to death of that earthquake and its many aftershocks. I vividly

4. Edward Payson, *Legacy of a Legend* (Vestavia Hills, AL: Solid Ground Christian Books, 2001), 5.

remember teaching a class and seeing what happened to my college students sitting in front of me when a strong aftershock occurred. As the building began to shake, tears began to stream down many of the students' cheeks. Prior to that January night in California, I had read of earthquakes, I had heard of earthquakes, but I had never experienced one. It was awesome!

When you read that God is *awesome*, don't think ice-cream sundae awesome, think earthquake awesome. You should be afraid. You should literally tremble before Him. He is awe inspiring. He is not a small, insignificant little god that you can control. He is the King. Psalm 97:2–5 paints a graphic picture of God our King:

> Clouds and thick darkness surround Him;
> Righteousness and justice are the foundation of His throne.
> Fire goes before Him
> And burns up His adversaries round about.
> His lightnings lit up the world;
> The earth saw and trembled.
> The mountains melted like wax at the presence of the LORD,
> At the presence of the Lord of the whole earth.

If the mountains melt like wax in His presence, how much more should we? We can't even begin to imagine how great, mighty, and majestic God is. If we could just catch a glimpse of Him, we'd be knocked flat on our face in awe. There is no one who is equal with God. There is no one or no thing that we should fear in the way that we fear God, because nothing can compare to Him.

You should fear God because He is the Creator of all men and the Creator of all things.

> Know ye that the LORD he is God: it is he that hath made us, and not we ourselves. (Ps. 100:3 KJV)

> All things were made by him; and without him was not any thing made that was made. (John 1:3 KJV)

For by Him all things were created, both in the heavens and on earth, visible and invisible, whether thrones or dominions or rulers or authorities—all things have been created through Him and for Him. (Col. 1:16)

You should fear God because He is the Sustainer of all things.

In Him we live and move and exist. (Acts 17:28)

In Him do all things consist and in Him all things hold together. (Col. 1:17, author's paraphrase)

If God would cease to exist, we'd cease to exist.
You should fear God because He's the Sovereign over all men.

The earth is the LORD's, and all it contains,
The world, and those who dwell in it. (Ps. 24:1)

The LORD has established His throne in the heavens,
And His sovereignty rules over all. (Ps. 103:19)

All the inhabitants of the earth are accounted as nothing,
But He does according to His will in the host of heaven
And among the inhabitants of earth;
And no one can ward off His hand
Or say to Him, "What have You done?" (Dan. 4:35)

You should fear God because He is the Judge of all men.

He has appointed a day on which He will judge the world in righteousness by the Man whom He has ordained. (Acts 17:31 NKJV).

Each one of us will give an account of himself to God. (Rom. 14:12)

It is appointed for men to die once and after this comes judgment. (Heb. 9:27)

We will all die, and then face the judgment of God.

You should fear God because He is the only Redeemer of men.

> He who believes in the Son has everlasting life; and he who does not believe the Son shall not see life, but the wrath of God abides on him. (John 3:36 NKJV)

> There is salvation in no one else; for there is no other name under heaven that has been given among men by which we must be saved. (Acts 4:12)

> There is one God, and one mediator also between God and men, the man Christ Jesus. (1 Tim. 2:5)

You should fear God because He is infinitely superior to anyone and anything. He is beyond comparing. He is infinitely transcendent.

> Who is like You among the gods, O LORD?
> Who is like You, majestic in holiness,
> Awesome in praises, working wonders? (Ex. 15:11)

> The LORD your God is in your midst, a great and awesome God. (Deut. 7:21)

You can see why Isaiah asked, "To whom then will you liken God? Or what likeness will you compare with Him?" (Isa. 40:18). God is beyond comparison.

Isaiah wanted us to see just how great God is, so he asked in 40:12, "Who has measured the waters in the hollow of His hand?" At least two-thirds of the earth is covered by water. Isaiah says God is so huge and so awesome, He's got a hand that is so big that He can hold all the water in the world, in one of His hands. That is how big God is!

"[He] marked off the heavens by the span" (v. 12). Do you know what that means? It means that He is so big he can hold the earth and the heavens in his hand. Scientists tell us that the heavens go on and on. We are still discovering new universes out there, new galaxies. God is so huge that He can put His thumb on one place in all the universes and reach around the whole of all these universes and still touch His thumb with his little finger. My hand is rather small; it is six inches from my little finger to the tip of my thumb. I can just about measure my Bible in the span of my hand. But God is so awesome that He can put His thumb on one part of the universe and span the whole universe with that hand. He is awesome! That is a big hand!

And more than that, Isaiah informed us that He calculates the dust of the earth by the measure (v. 12). God knows how much the dust in this earth weighs. He has put the hills on a pair of scales (v. 12). Isaiah said God could tell you how much the hills or the mountains weigh. Isaiah said that to God "the nations are like a drop from a bucket" (v. 15). Think about that. The nations are like a drop from a bucket, not even like they were poured out in gallon form, but just a teensy little drop that falls out of a bucket. You wouldn't even notice if you lost a drop from the bucket. Well, that is what the nations are in comparison to God. They are "regarded as a speck of dust on the scales."

Years ago people used balancing scales. You put a certain amount of weight on one end of the scale and then you put your product on the other end. By doing that you assessed how much the product weighed. If, for example, you were going into a store to buy something and the store owner put the product on one end of the scale and you noticed that there was a speck of dust on the other end of the scale and you didn't want to be cheated, a speck of dust would be so insignificant that you wouldn't even say to the store owner, "Hey, wipe that speck of dust off there before you weigh my product." No, a speck of dust is nothing! The Bible tells us that on God's scales all the nations of the world are like a speck of dust.

Still further, Isaiah told us "He lifts up the islands like fine dust" (v. 15). The picture is that of someone coming to a pile of dust and picking up that pile and letting it run through his fingers. That would be easy for anyone to do. It wouldn't require much strength. Well, God is so strong that He does that with the islands. He can easily pick them up.

Continuing his description of God's awesomeness, Isaiah wrote,

Even Lebanon is not enough to burn,
Nor its beasts enough for a burnt offering.
All the nations are as nothing before Him,
They are regarded by Him as less than nothing. (40:16–17)

In fact, the nations are not just nothing: "they are regarded by Him as less than nothing and meaningless" (v. 17). God is greater than the nations, He's greater than all the rulers of the world. In verses 23–24 we learn it is God "who reduces rulers to nothing, [He] makes the judges of the earth [the most powerful, significant people in the world] meaningless."

"Scarcely have they been planted, scarcely have they been sown, scarcely has their stock taken root in the earth, but He merely blows on them, and they wither" (v. 24). Isn't that amazing? God blows on them, and they are gone. That is how powerful He is. He just blows on them, and they are gone; they are withered. "And the storm carries them away like stubble" (v. 24). Our God is greater than all the rulers of the earth, He's greater than all the kings, and He's greater than all other gods. In verses 18–20 Isaiah wrote,

To whom then will you liken God?
Or what likeness will you compare with Him?
As for the idol, a craftsman casts it,
A goldsmith plates it with gold,
And a silversmith fashions chains of silver.
He who is too impoverished for such an offering
Selects a tree that does not rot;
He seeks out for himself a skillful craftsman
To prepare an idol that will not totter.

All the supposed gods of this world that people worship are nothing in comparison to God. He is greater than all the dignitaries in this world.

Isaiah continued in verse 26: "Lift up your eyes on high and see who has created these stars. The One who leads forth their host by number, He calls them all by name." God is so great that He has named and knows the name of every star. Jerry Bridges writes that when he once asked an astrophysicist how many stars there are in the universe, the reply staggered him. "He said there are about one hundred billion galaxies, each one containing about one hundred billion stars. A hundred billion times a hundred billion."[5] Yet the Bible says, "He counts the number of the stars, and He calls them all by name" (Ps. 147:4, author's paraphrase). Isaiah says that not only does God know how many stars there are, He has actually named them all.

A few years ago I traveled back to my hometown, Carlisle, Pennsylvania. The church at which I was preaching had run an advertisement in the town paper saying a "Carlisle [n]ative" would preach on Sunday morning and evening. The article went on to describe my education and my ministry, and mentioned some of the books I had written. Some of the people who had known me when I was a little boy and then a teenager, and some of the fellows with whom I had played football, came out to see this thing that had come to pass.

One man walked up to me after the service, stuck out his hand, and said, "You remember me, don't you?" Now I hadn't seen him for forty-five years, and he'd changed a little bit during that time. Did I remember him? No. And I certainly didn't remember his name. Remembering names is somewhat problematic for us, but not for God! He is so great and He has such an incredible memory that He knows the names of all the galaxies and all the hundreds of billions and billions and billions and billions of stars.

Even a cursory reflection on the character and nature of God as depicted in the Bible should lead us to cry out with Jeremiah,

> There is none like You, O LORD;
> You are great, and great is Your name in might.
> Who would not fear You, O King of the nations?
> Indeed it is Your due!
> For among all the wise men of the nations
> And in all their kingdoms,
> There is none like You. (Jer. 10:6–7)

Do you get the point? God is worthy of our fear. The fear of God is not demeaning and not unworthy of a Christian. The truth is, fear-

---

5. Bridges, *The Joy of Fearing God*, 56.

ing God is completely reasonable. God has not changed. We may live thousands of years after Isaiah and Jeremiah, but we worship the same God. We should fear Him, because given who and what God is, it's totally insane, absolutely absurd, not to!

QUESTIONS FOR DISCUSSION

1. What's the one key principle this chapter gives for overcoming fear? Explain what that principle means, and support your answer with Scripture. *To start fearing rightly*

2. Why do many professing Christians minimize the importance and value of fearing God? *They believe it is an old fashioned principle.*

3. How would you respond to someone who says it is not biblical to fear God? *Psalm 112 Blessed is the man who fears the Lord.*

4. Give some reasons it is so important to fear God. Support your
   answer with Scripture. *Psalm 112.*
   Is 46

5. Why can it be said that a lack of the fear of God is at the root of
   all sin? *Romans 3:18*

6. What is David Wells' point when he writes that all too often the
   church has "turned to a God that we can use rather than to a God
   we must obey; we have turned to a God who will fulfill our needs
   rather than to a God before whom we must surrender our rights
   to ourselves"?

7. What, according to Psalm 115, happens to you when you worship
   a God of your imagination?

8. Give ten reasons why it is reasonable to fear God. Explain each
reason in your own words.

Without Him we will cease to
exist
We will account ourselves to
Him when we die.
He is the only Redeemer of men.
He is the sovereign over all men.
He is the judge of all men.
He is the Sustainer of all things
He is infinitely superior to
anyone. He is beyond comparing.
He is infinitely transcendent.
He is the Creator of all men and
the Creator of all things

9. Using Isaiah 40, explain in your own words why God is awesome.

He is power

10. Give five reasons each of the following truths about God should cause you to fear Him. I'll give you one example—you fill in the rest.

    God is Creator.

    a. The fact that God is Creator means that He is different from me since I am the creation. As Creator He is greater than the creation; therefore I should fear Him.

    b.

c.

d.

e.

God is Judge.

a.

b.

c.

d.

e.

God is holy.

a.

b.

c.

d.

e.

God is Redeemer.

a.

b.

c.

d.

e.

11. In what ways is your view of God deficient? What are some practical steps you can take to develop a more biblical understanding of who God is?

10

THE FEAR THAT IS
GOOD FOR YOU

MANY REASONS can be given to support the statement that it is good for you to fear God.

For example, it is good to fear God because if you don't recognize how awesome and holy He is, you will never see your sinfulness as it really is. Instead you will live with a distorted, unhealthy view of yourself. You will never humbly see your need for mercy and grace. Without a correct sense of how big God is, you will never know how frail and small you really are. And if you live without an accurate sense of your own size, you will never know how much you need His presence, strength, wisdom, and support. If you don't celebrate His transcendence and true significance, you will deceive yourself into believing that your own endeavors, aspirations, and accomplishments are the truly significant things in your world. Simply put, any downsizing of God distorts your perspective on yourself, and on the life you live.

In the last chapter, we noted that one reason we should fear God is because of who and what God is—He is so great and awesome that He is worthy of being feared. In this chapter, we want to expand on another reason for fearing God, a reason that is often overlooked and even denied by some. Scripture tells us that we should fear God because the fear of God is good and beneficial for us. This is the clear teaching of Jeremiah 32:39 where God describes what He will do for His people. In this passage, God says, "I will give them one heart and one way, that they may fear Me always, for their own good and for the good of their children after them."

Some time ago I went through the Bible and looked up every verse on the fear of God. As I did this study, I was impressed, almost surprised, to find that many of the commands (and they are many) to fear God were followed by promises of incredible blessing to people who do so. I came away from this exercise thinking that nobody in his or her right mind would consider the fear of God something undesirable, that no one who believed that God is a faithful and true God, a God who cannot lie, would ever think that developing and sustaining the fear of God would ruin his or her life. Nothing could be further from the truth! Given the benefits that the Bible says come to the person who fears God, we would be absolute fools not to want to experience more of this fear.

The Bible is filled with incredible promises to the person who fears God. In this chapter, we don't have time or space to consider but a small portion of them. I do, however, want to point you to several of them and encourage you to personally do a more thorough study on your own. In a concordance, look up every reference to the fear of God. You'll be surprised at how many there are! I also encourage you to read John Bunyan's rather exhaustive study on the fear of God. In that study, Bunyan's reminders of the numerous blessings that come to people who fear God will amaze you and bless your Christian walk.

THE BENEFITS OF FEARING GOD

What are some of the benefits that come to the person who fears God? To expound on all the Bible references to these benefits would take a very large book! Because this chapter is part of a book with a larger focus, we will limit its scope to several of the truths that describe the good that God promises to those who fear Him. We hope this limited exposition will whet your appetite to do a more thorough study on your own.

The books of Psalms and Proverbs are filled with statements about the positive value of the fear of God. Psalm 25 describes several of the benefits that come to the person who fears God. Verse 12 begins by asking the question, "Who is the man who fears the LORD?" It concludes by telling us what will happen to the person who fears the Lord. Of this person, the psalmist says, "[God] will instruct him in the way he should choose." In his comments on this phrase, J. H. Jowett writes that this means that this man "shall be guided in his choices. He shall have the gift of enlightenment. His discernment shall be refined so as to perceive the right way when the ways are many. . . . The moral choice shall be firm and sure. . . . The practical judgment shall also be nurtured and refined in the Lord's school."[1]

Imagine what it would be like to have the most intelligent, most learned, wisest human being in all of history as an instructor as you went through life. Suppose that person would be available to you in every situation and every circumstance. Suppose you could run every decision you have to make by that person. What difference would that make as you live out your life? What would that mean in terms of your being a success in life? It would make a huge difference in your overall effectiveness.

But what is promised in Psalm 25:12 is even better than that! This verse assures us that if a person knows and fears God, if God is in His rightful place in that person's life, this all-wise, all-knowing, never-makes-a-mistake, and never-lacks-in-understanding God will help that person to make wise choices. And that will make a person a success in the way God defines success. How could it be otherwise?

Certainly you would agree that a successful person is a person who makes one wise decision after another. Conversely, it is true that a failure is a person who makes one unwise decision after another. Obviously if someone is able to make right choices, it will be good for that person, for his spouse, for his children, and for the church of Jesus Christ. Obviously if a person is consistently able to make right choices in life, his life will count for something, and he will make an impact on the world for Christ.

1. John Henry Jowett, *Brooks by the Traveller's Way*, Christian Classics Ethereal Library, accessed December 10, 2013, http://www.ccel.org/ccel/jowett/brooks.iv.xxii.html.

Do you want to be a person who makes wise decisions, a person who knows what you ought to do in every situation? Well, this passage says that the man who fears the Lord is the man whom God "will instruct . . . in the way he should choose." Write it down, and accept it as true—the fear of God is good for you.

It Is Good for Your Soul

But in this psalm there's more about the benefits of fearing God. Verse 13 tells us that the soul of the person who fears God "will abide in prosperity." Do you want to be prosperous in the most important ways? Do you want to experience that which is really good? Well then, pay attention to this psalm.

There are different kinds of prosperity and good that God brings to the person who fears Him. Sometimes the prosperity or good may come in the form of financial blessing. But sometimes financial prosperity is not really good for us, and so God, in love, withholds that from us. Financial prosperity is not the primary focus here. There is a kind of prosperity and experience of good that far exceeds financial prosperity.

What is the prosperity or good that far exceeds financial prosperity? Note that God says this person will have a wealthy, or good, soul. He may not have millions of dollars in the bank or in investments. In fact, he may be as poor as the proverbial church mouse, but he will have the kind of prosperity that is much more valuable than having all the money in the world. He will have soul prosperity.

What does it mean to have a wealthy, or good, soul? Who is it that has a prosperous or good soul? It's the person who is experiencing inner peace, the person who has the rare jewel of internal contentment. It's the person who has a life that is characterized by the fruit of the Spirit—"love, joy, peace, patience, kindness, goodness, faithfulness, gentleness, self-control" (Gal. 5:22–23). It's the person who is rich in faith and mercy, full of hope, and an heir of the kingdom (2 Cor. 8:9; Eph. 1:18; James 2:5).

Soul prosperity includes having direction and meaning in life, and knowing where you're going and how to get there. It means being filled with an inner joy and satisfaction that is not dependent on outward circumstances. It means being like Peter as he is described in Acts 12. He had been arrested and thrown in jail because he had preached the gospel. His life was in danger. A fellow Christian, James, had just been beheaded for the same offense. Yet Peter slept soundly. Why could Peter respond to his difficult circumstances in this way? The answer: he had a wealthy soul because he feared God.

To have a prosperous soul means to be like Paul as he is described in Acts 16. In this chapter we find that Paul had been beaten, threatened, bound hand and foot—and who knew what tomorrow would bring. Yet Paul was singing and giving praise to God. Why could Paul respond to his difficult circumstances in this way? He had a wealthy soul because he feared God.

To have a prosperous soul means to be like David as he described himself in Psalm 3. David's own son Absalom had rebelled against him and was seeking to wrest the leadership of the country away from him. Absalom was pursuing David with the intention of bringing harm to him. Yet in the midst of all this David could say,

> I laid me down and slept; I awaked; for the LORD sustained me.
> I will not be afraid of ten thousands of people, that have set themselves against me round about. (Ps. 3:5–6 KJV)

Why was David able to handle this difficult, unpleasant circumstance in this way? Why could he lie down and sleep? Why was he not afraid? The answer comes from David's own pen: "Stand in awe, and sin not: commune with your own heart upon your bed, and be still. . . . I will both lay me down in peace, and sleep: for thou, LORD, only makest me dwell in safety" (Ps. 4:4, 8 KJV).

Before we leave this phrase, it's important to consider one other important word—the word *abide*. The Hebrew word used here means "to lodge or to dwell, to be at home, to dwell at ease, to continue undisturbed."[2] In other words, the benefit promised here is not a temporary but a permanent one.

2. Joseph Alexander, *The Psalms* (Grand Rapids: Zondervan), 116.

The text does not say that prosperity will occasionally pay a visit to the soul of this person. It says that the person who continuously fears God can have a continuous experience of soul prosperity. His experience of soul prosperity will not be an up-and-down, every-now-and-then matter. As he rightly fears God, the kind of internal prosperity this verse is referring to will make its home, its dwelling place, in his inner being. What a blessing this is! Could a person want for anything more than this? Is there any good that can exceed this kind of good? We think not! And all this can be ours if we rightly fear God. Again, Scripture is clear in saying that the fear of God is good for you.

It Is Good for Your Descendants

Continuing in Psalm 25:13, we are specifically reminded of the blessings that come to the descendants of a God-fearing person. "His descendants shall inherit the earth" (author's paraphrase). Since this is in the Old Testament, the Hebrew word used here probably is referring to the land that God promised to Abraham (Gen. 12:1; 17:8). In other words, God is saying that He will fulfill His promises to the children of those who fear Him. He is saying that His blessing will not only come to the parents but also to their descendants; fearing God will be good for a person's progeny as well as for himself. A God-fearing person will have a positive impact on his children and on his grandchildren. In explaining the meaning of this phrase, J. H. Jowett writes, "Children become heirs when parents become pious. The God-possessed transmits a legacy of blessing. . . . It would be a profitable exercise to calculate what one may inherit because another man was good."[3] Moses was expressing the same truth when he wrote that God shows lovingkindness to the descendants of those who love Him and keep His commandments (Ex. 20:6).

Turning to Psalm 112 we find the same theme being repeated. The psalm begins with the words, "Praise the LORD!" Verse 1 then gives a general reason why people who fear God should praise the Lord: people who fear God are blessed, or fortunate. "How blessed [how fortunate] is the man who fears the LORD, who greatly delights in His command-

3. Jowett, *Brooks by the Traveller's Way*, http://www.ccel.org/ccel/jowett/brooks.iv.xxii.html.

ments." Then, becoming more specific about the blessings God-fearers enjoy, the writer reminds us again of the way a God-fearing person will affect his children and their children: "His descendants will be mighty on earth; the generation of the upright will be blessed" (v. 2).

Psalm 128:1–4 also emphasizes the benefits that come to the descendants of God-fearing people:

> How blessed is everyone who fears the LORD,
> . . . .
> Your wife shall be like a fruitful vine
> Within your house,
> Your children like olive plants
> Around your table.
> Behold, for thus shall the man be blessed
> Who fears the LORD.

In Proverbs 14:26–27 God says that the children of the person who fears God will have a place of refuge and will be recipients of a fountain of life that flows from that God-fearing parent. Proverbs 31:10–31 goes to great lengths to describe the way a God-fearing wife and mother will benefit her family in particular, and society in general.

In *Your Family, God's Way*, I wrote this about the Proverbs 31 woman:

> A careful reading of Proverbs 31 presses us to one conclusion. A God-fearing wife and mother is a family-oriented person. . . . This woman takes excellent care of her family. Though clearly not restricted to the home (vv. 13, 14, 16, 20), she is utterly devoted to her family as her number-one ministry. Her family is not neglected while she does other important things.
>
> "Her husband has full confidence in her" (v. 11, NIV), or as the New American Standard Bible puts it, "The heart of her husband trusts in her." He knows she is committed to him, and he trusts her without reservation. This means he depends upon her for support and help, knowing that he will not look in vain. The Hebrew verb found in this phrase literally means "to lean upon." It implies that this woman is dependable. . . .

Her husband's public praise attests to his approval of how she relates to him. He values her more than all the women in the world (vv. 28–29). . . .

The passage also says a lot about this woman's relationship with her children. We read that her children rise up and bless her. Along with her husband they say, "Many daughters have done nobly, but you excel them all" (v. 29). They are impressed by her godliness, manifested in noble character and conduct. . . .

What she did was a *consequence* of her commitment to and relationship with God. Her deep reverence for God had produced within her a nobility of character, which then expressed itself in the exemplary attitudes and actions described in the passage.[4]

Being a conduit of blessing to their descendants is one of the primary concerns of all godly parents. In fact, by God's common grace, it is even a major concern of many non-Christian parents. I have never yet met parents, Christian or non-Christian, whose stated goal in their relationship to their children was to bring a curse upon them. I believe most parents do not want to harm their children in any way. Some may unintentionally bring great harm to their children, but I've not encountered any parent who has openly stated that this was his or her goal.

Many parents rightly have a concern about being a blessing to their children. Generally speaking, it would seem people want to be good parents—they want to have a positive impact on their children. The validity of this statement is demonstrated in many ways. A visit to your local bookstore will convince you that learning how to be a good parent is a major concern for many people. Magazine article after magazine article illustrates the deep level of interest people have in this subject. The fact that some of the most popular seminars, both Christian and non-Christian, are seminars about how to be a good parent indicates that people are vitally interested in this subject; that people want to raise their children properly; that they want their children to be secure, well adjusted, productive, and stable.

4. Wayne Mack, *Your Family, God's Way* (Phillipsburg, NJ: Presbyterian & Reformed, 1991), 25–26, 28.

So how can parents make certain that they are conduits of real blessing, of good, to their children? Psalm 25:12–13 suggests the answer is to develop and sustain a healthy fear of God. In many places in Scripture, God, who is the expert on good child rearing and who knows everything about everything, says the most important key in being a good parent is for you to develop and sustain a healthy, robust fear of Him. Do you want to be a blessing to your family? Do you want your children to be mighty on the earth? Well then, develop and sustain a healthy, robust fear of God. It will be good for you and for your family (Jer. 32:39). That's God's promise. All the promises of God found in His Word are magnificent and great (2 Peter 1:4). But more than that, they are all certain to be fulfilled, for as the apostle Paul said: "As many as are the promises of God, in Him [Christ] they are yes; therefore also through Him is our Amen to the glory of God" (2 Cor. 1:20).

God Is the Friend of God-Fearing People

"The secret of the LORD is for those who fear Him" (Ps. 25:14). Joseph Alexander indicates that a literal translation of these Hebrew words would be "the friendship of Jehovah is to those fearing Him."[5] Alexander indicates that in the original language, the word translated *friendship* means "a company of persons sitting together," as in Psalm 111:1. Then by derivation, it means "confidential intercourse, intimacy, friendship," as in Proverbs 3:32. Still further, he explains that in most English versions the Hebrew word is translated *secrets*, because most friendships involve intimacy and sharing of confidences.[6]

Scripture informs us that Abraham, the great Old Testament patriarch, who is called the father of all who believe, and whose great faith is extolled in Hebrews 11 and Romans 4, was called a friend of God (2 Chron. 20:7; Isa. 41:8; James 2:23). To be known as a servant of God or as an acquaintance of God is a tremendous privilege. But to be called a friend of God goes far beyond this. In some ways it even goes beyond being called a son of God, because it's possible to be someone's son and

5. Joseph Alexander, *The Psalms Translated and Explained* (1864; repr. Grand Rapids: Zondervan, 1960), 116.
6. Ibid.

still not be a friend. Could anything have been more heartwarming and thrilling to Abraham than for him to be regarded in this way by God?

This text in Psalm 25 tells us that the privilege of being God's friend is not reserved for Abraham alone. It can be a privilege enjoyed by many others—by you and me. Imagine that: you and I, along with the great hero of the faith, Abraham, can enjoy the incredible honor and distinction of being known as friends of God, with all the privileges and benefits that come with that position. Being considered one of God's friends is a blessing that is almost too much to believe. If the Bible didn't teach it, it would almost seem blasphemous and irreverent to speak in these terms.

What are some of the benefits of being a friend of God? One benefit is intimacy, sharing confidences and secrets. When people become God's friends, God does what people who have developed a deep friendship do—He shares His secrets with them. In His friendship with them, God opens to them insights and perspectives that He doesn't share with just anyone and everyone. In keeping with New Testament teaching, God shares with His friends "a wisdom . . . not of this age, nor of the rulers of this age, . . . the hidden . . . wisdom which none of the rulers of this age has understood" (1 Cor. 2:6–8). With certain people He shares insights and understanding that most people never experience. He shares with His friends, through His Word and by His Spirit, the very mind of Christ (John 15:15–16; 1 Cor. 2:6–9, 14–16). Because of their relationship with Him as His friends, God is pleased to let them know His very thoughts, concerns, and desires.

What a tremendous blessing this is to us! Who would think that being a friend of God is not a great honor and privilege? But before we leave this phrase in Psalm 25:14, it is important to note that this blessing of being intimate with God is not for everyone. True, being a friend of God is not a privilege reserved only for Abraham, but it is not a privilege that God bestows indiscriminately. No, the text says, it is a privilege experienced only by those who fear God. Again, it is clear that fearing God is not only reasonable in the light of who and what He is, it is also something we should greatly seek.

God Has a Warehouse Filled with Goodness for God-Fearing People

Psalm 31:19–20 is another passage describing the blessings that come to the person who fears God.

> How great is Your goodness,
> Which You have stored up for those who fear You,
> Which You have wrought for those who take refuge in You,
> Before the sons of men!
> You hide them in the secret place of Your presence from the
>   conspiracies of man;
> You keep them secretly in a shelter from the strife of tongues.

This psalm tells us that God has stored up goodness for those who fear Him. It's as if He has an immense warehouse filled with blessings just for them.

Concerning the goodness God has stored up, Alexander Maclaren writes:

> There are, as it were, two great masses of what the Psalmist calls "goodness"; one of them which has been plainly manifested "before the sons of men," the other which is "laid up" in store. There are a great many notes in circulation, but there is far more bullion in the strong-room. Much "goodness" has been exhibited; far more lies concealed.
>
> . . . God's riches are not like the world's wealth. You very soon get to the bottom of its [the world's] purse. Its "goodness" is very soon run dry.[7]

Not so with God's purse of goodness. It never runs dry. It never becomes empty.

J. R. Miller's comments on the same passage are very helpful:

> For those who fear God and walk in His ways there is not a real need of any kind along the entire path to heaven's gate, without its goodness

7. Alexander MacClaren, *Expositions of Holy Scripture: Psalms, Christian Classics Ethereal Library*, accessed December 10, 2013, http://www.ccel.org/ccel/maclaren/psalms.ii.xxi.html.

laid up in reserve.... The Rabbins say that when Joseph had gathered much corn in Egypt, and the famine came on, he threw the chaff into the Nile, that when the people who lived in the cities below saw it on the water they would know there was corn laid up for them. So, what we have in this world of Divine goodness is little more than the husks of the heavenly fruits, which God sends down upon the river of Grace as intimations to us and assurances of glorious supplies laid up for us beyond the grave.... If we are God's children we shall find in heaven the blessed substance of every empty shadow we have chased in this world in vain, and the full fruition of every fair hope that on earth seemed to fade. The best is yet on before.[8]

W. Forsyth also explains the meaning of this text in a vivid way:

What is seen [of God's goodness], may, as it were, be measured; but what is unseen, is boundless. What is a river to the ocean! What is the landscape, that the eye can reach, to the vast unseen realms of the earth! What are the thousand stars that crowd the winter sky, to the millions upon millions that are hid in the depths of space! So with the goodness of God.[9]

The goodness of God is immense. In fact, it is immeasurable, inexhaustible, beyond comprehension. But note carefully what this verse states about the identity of the people for whom this goodness is stored. This goodness is not stored up for everyone. It is stored up for none but the people who fear God. These are the only people who have any reason to expect they will participate in the blessings of His goodness.

"O taste and see that the LORD is good" are the words of the psalmist in Psalm 34:8. And how is this goodness manifested? The psalmist explains that God's goodness comes to us in the form of His watchful care over us, in the form of God providing for all our needs, in the form of constant renewal and refreshment as we travel through life (34:8–10).

8. J. R. Miller, quoted by *The Bible Illustrator, StudyLight*, accessed December 10, 2013, http://www.studylight.org/com/tbi/view.cgi?bk=ps&ch=31.

9. W. Forsyth, quoted by *The Bible Illustrator, StudyLight*, accessed December 10, 2013, http://www.studylight.org/com/tbi/view.cgi?bk=ps&ch=31.

But again, it's important to notice that this goodness is only for those who fear God and have taken refuge in Him.

IT BRINGS A VARIETY OF CHOICE BLESSINGS

Psalm 112 contains a description of numerous other benefits that come to God-fearing people. Again, as we noted while looking at Psalm 25:13, the writer of Psalm 112 mentions the prosperity that comes to the person who fears God. "Wealth and riches are in his house" (v. 3). This repeated emphasis on prosperity for God-fearers is His way of helping us to remember what we so easily seem to forget. He wants us to be absolutely convinced that fearing Him will promote the well-being of man's whole nature: morally, spiritually, socially, relationally, practically, behaviorally, physically, and intellectually.

Continuing, verse 3 tells us about another benefit: "And his righteousness endures forever." People who fear God live righteous lives, not just temporarily, but continuously throughout their lives on earth and through eternity. Proverbs 8:13 tells us that the fear of the Lord causes a person to hate evil, pride, arrogance, and unwholesome, ungodly speech.

Psalm 112:4 mentions the benefit of receiving peace in the midst of distressing, chaotic, and difficult circumstances: for God-fearing people, "light arises in the darkness" (v. 4). Verses 4–5 also indicate that the fear of God produces the kind of character that is gracious, compassionate, generous, unselfish, and considerate with other people. It makes a person just and fair in his dealing with others. He is "gracious and compassionate and righteous." He "is generous and lend[s] freely" and "conducts his affairs with justice" (NIV).

The second part of verse 6 points out that the person who fears God will make a positive impact on other people. "The righteous will be remembered forever." Each of us have met and forgotten hundreds, probably thousands of people. But as we have journeyed through life, we meet some people whom we remember. Why do we remember a few and forget most? In general, I think it may be said that the people we remember for a long time are those who have made a significant impression on us. According to the psalmist, people who fear God stand out; they make an impression. Their deep relationship with God has so impacted them that they impact others.

One example of this was Abel, the son of Adam and Eve. Scripture indicates that he was a righteous, godly man while he was alive. He feared God, and his faith, obedience, and lifestyle showed it. Scripture tells us that even though he is now dead, Abel is yet speaking; he is still influencing and encouraging others in the way of righteousness. Even today, thousands of years after his death, he is still remembered as a righteous person. According to Psalm 112:6, so it will be with every person who truly fears God. He will influence others while he is alive, and he will continue to be an influence after his death. His body will be put in the ground, but his reputation and influence will continue to be a positive influence after he dies.

Several phrases in this psalm serve to calm our fears and bring peace to our hearts. They describe the positive effect the fear of God will have on a person's emotions: "He will never be shaken" (v. 6). "He will not fear evil tidings; his heart is steadfast, trusting the LORD. His heart is upheld, he will not fear" (vv. 7–8). In other words, this person won't come apart at the seams, he won't commit suicide, he won't fear other people, and he will never be shaken. He's not always focusing on the worst. This person will not live in constant fear of unpleasant circumstances. He will view the future with confidence rather than apprehension. He will not be intimidated by the responsibilities and challenges God sets before him. He doesn't overreact to unpleasant news.

In this psalm, God is telling us that the fear of evil tidings and the fear of God are incompatible. They can't exist in the same person at the same time. They are like oil and water; they can't be mixed. It's an either/or proposition. You will either be controlled by the wrong kind of fear, or you will be controlled by the fear of God. One or the other will be your master, but not both at the same time. Simply put, this psalm shows you that when you fear God, you won't be constantly wondering if something terrible is going to happen, you won't go through life fidgeting and worrying. You won't be constantly waiting for the next shoe to drop. Your theme song in life is not in a minor key. You're not constantly focusing on the negative. You're not constantly telling yourself and others, "You know, I might lose my job, or I might get sick, or I might get some kind of terminal illness, or my marriage might fall apart. I just know something horrible is going to happen to my children. I just know they are going to be molested, or they will get some kind of awful disease, or they are going to fail in school!"

No, if you fear God, you will not fear evil tidings! You will have peace in your soul. Your heart will be steadfast because you trust in the Lord. God will uphold your heart; you will not be ruled by destructive fear. If you have a healthy and robust fear of God, you are going to turn whatever happens to you—your difficulties, your adversities—over to God.

When you fear God you know that He is far more capable than you are to take care of your problems. You also know for certain that God will take care of you, because He has promised that He would (Ps. 23; 51:22; Isa. 41:10; 1 Cor. 10:13; 1 Peter 5:7). You are convinced that God will overrule your enemies. You know that nothing can happen to you that God cannot turn for His glory and your good.

Proverbs 14:26 tells us, "In the fear of the LORD there is strong confidence." What else can this verse mean except that if you fear God in the correct way, you will be a confident person? It means that you won't be afraid of people, circumstances, responsibilities, the future, death, or judgment. Certainly, what God is telling us in these verses is that when we are racked with anxiety or fear, when we seem to be coming apart at the seams, we are to trust in Him and fear Him alone.

Some might say people experience fear and a lack confidence because they were born with a nervous temperament, but God's Word says that it is because they lack the fear of God. Some might say the primary reason people are inordinately fearful is because of the way they were raised or because they have had a number of traumatic experiences. But God's Word says otherwise. Traumatic experiences don't make people fearful; they just bring to light a lack of the fear of the Lord. They don't cause a person to lack confidence; they just reveal the fact that he doesn't have it. And he doesn't have it because he doesn't fear God!

The Bible says, "The wicked flee when no one is pursuing, but the righteous are bold as a lion" (Prov. 28:1). If we are right with God, if God is in His rightful place in our lives, and if we truly fear Him, we will be bold as a lion. We are not going to fear men! Write it down and accept it as a fundamental truth: the answer to the fears that control you, rip you apart, and hinder you, is to develop and sustain a healthy, wholesome, awesome fear of the living God.

We hope that by this time you have been convinced by the overwhelming scriptural evidence that the fear of God is reasonable and beneficial. We also hope that you are eager to learn a more complete explanation of what the fear of God involves. Along the way in this book, we've given you bits and pieces of information about the essence of the fear of God. In the next chapter, we'll deal with the essence of the fear of God in a much more complete way.

Ask God to show you areas in your life in which you need to fear Him more, then turn the page and continue the journey with us.

QUESTIONS FOR DISCUSSION

1. What does Jeremiah 32:39 teach about the fear of God?

   It will be good for them to always fear me, for their own good and the good of their children after them.

2. Why is this study of the benefits of the fear of God woefully inadequate?

3. What promise is given in Psalm 25:12?

    a. In specific terms, what is being promised in this verse?

    He will instruct the man who fears the Lord in the way chosen for him.
    Instruction

    b. Why is the promise in this verse so beneficial?

    Having God's guidance in the way we should go is the most marvelous gift.

    c. What attitudinal, emotional, and behavioral differences should this promise make in your own life and family?

    I should learn to relax and let God guide me.
    It will bring peace and clarity.

    d. To whom and for whom is this promise intended?

    For all that fear God

4. What promise is given in Psalm 25:13a?

a. In specific terms, what is being promised in this verse?

He will spend his days in prosperity, and his descendants will inherit the earth.

b. Why is the promise in this verse so beneficial?

His descendants will inherit the land
It is an assurance that He will provide all that we need.

c. What attitudinal, emotional, and behavioral differences should this promise make in your own life and family?

Hopeful attitude.
A soul that prospers will give love and attention to those in need.

d. To whom and for whom was this promise given?

5. What promise is given in Psalm 25:13b?

   a. In specific terms, what is being promised in this verse?

   Protection in His shelter

   b. Why is the promise in this verse so beneficial?

   c. What attitudinal, emotional, and behavioral differences should this promise make in your own life and family?

   d. To whom and for whom was this promise given?

6. What promises are given in Psalm 25:14?

   a. In specific terms, what is being promised in this verse?

The Lord confides in those who fear Him; He makes His covenant known to them

   b. Why are the promises in this verse so beneficial?

It offers protection in His shelter

   c. What attitudinal, emotional, and behavioral differences should these promises make in your own life and family?

   d. To whom and for whom were these promises given?

7. What promises are given in Psalm 31:19–20?

   a. In specific terms, what is being promised in these verses?

   b. Why are the promises in these verses so beneficial?

   c. What attitudinal, emotional, and behavioral differences should these promises make in your own life and family?

   d. To whom and for whom were these promises given?

8. What promises are given in Psalm 112:3–5?

   a. In specific terms, what is being promised in these verses?

   b. Why are the promises in these verses so beneficial?

   c. What attitudinal, emotional, and behavioral differences should these promises make in your own life and family?

   d. To whom and for whom were these promises given?

9. What promises are given in Psalm 112:6–8?

a. In specific terms, what is being promised in these verses?

b. Why are the promises in these verses so beneficial?

God will come to the person who conducts his affairs with justice.

c. What attitudinal, emotional, and behavioral differences should these promises make in your own life and family?

d. To whom and for whom were these promises given?

10. How have you personally been affected by this study?

11

THE FEAR THAT OVERCOMES FEAR

IN THE LAST two chapters we have discussed why the fear of God is important, and we have given some reasons why you should fear God. In doing this, we have noted the wonderful blessings that come to the person who has the proper fear of God. This kind of godly constructive fear is the supreme antidote to all forms of ungodly, destructive fear with which we are so frequently plagued. It's the antidote to every form of the fear of man: the fear of judgment, the fear of the future, the fear of rejection, the fear of failure, the fear of persecution, the fear of death, the fear of suffering, and the fear of being mocked and ridiculed, among others.

It's easy to see that the fear of God has tremendous practical implications for us as we seek to live in a way that is pleasing to God. But just knowing the importance of something is not helpful unless we know what that something is. I may, for example, know that it is important to have good health, but if I don't know what good health is, my knowledge of the importance of good health will do me little good. I may know, and even *agree*, that I should love my wife, but if I don't know *how*, the knowledge that I *should* is of little practical value. So it is with the matter of godly fear. Knowing its importance is of little use unless we know what godly fear actually is. That answer is the purpose of this chapter.

We first want to examine several verses that will provide a biblical understanding of what the fear of God is. Having done that, we will pull together the truths found in these verses about the fear of God to summarize what it truly means to fear God. Finally, we want to make some application of this definition to our own lives.

BIBLICAL PASSAGES ON THE FEAR OF GOD

God-Fearing People Trust God

Exodus 14:31 tells us that "when Israel saw the great power which the LORD had used against the Egyptians, the people feared the LORD, and they believed in the LORD." Interestingly, this verse connects the fear of God with believing in Him. Proverbs 29:25 makes the same point when it uses the words *fear* and *trust* interchangeably. Frequently in the book of Proverbs, the first part of a verse makes a statement and the second part of the verse gives us a contrast. This is certainly true in Proverbs 29:25: "The fear of man brings a snare, but he who trusts in the LORD will be exalted."

What does it mean to fear man? It's the same as putting your trust in man. What does it mean to trust in the Lord? It's the same as fearing the Lord. So whatever else the fear of God includes, it does include faith in God. Faith, or trust, in God and the fear of God are inseparably joined. You simply can't have one without the other.

People who fear God trust God. They trust in God as He reveals Himself to be in the Bible. They trust in His omnipotence—that He is all-powerful. They trust in His omniscience—that He is all-wise and all-knowing. They trust in His omnipresence—that He is present everywhere and they can never be out of His presence. They trust in His goodness—that He is loving, gracious, merciful, patient, and willing to forgive. They trust in His veracity and truthfulness—that He will not and cannot lie, He will keep all His promises, and whatever He says in His Word is true. They trust in His immutability, His faithfulness, and His changelessness—that He is the same yesterday, today, and forever; that He isn't one thing one day and something else the next. They trust in His interpretation of reality—that He knows exactly what is happening, why it happens, and what to do about it to make it right; that what He has to say about man's basic problem and how to solve that problem is accurate. They trust what He has to say about their own sinfulness and their need of a Savior. They trust what He has to say about the way they should live, about what is right and wrong; they trust that His ways are the best ways. They make His Word the standard by which they evaluate all things and believe that any idea that does not line up with Scripture is wrong. People who fear God just flat-out trust God. They don't put their ultimate trust in man—themselves or others. They put their trust in God.

If you are a God-fearing person, you are a person who trusts in God's justice; you believe that God will judge the world in righteousness and with equity (Pss. 96:13; 98:9, author's paraphrase). You are a person who will not pay back evil for evil, who does not take your own revenge, because you leave room for the wrath of God. You are a person who believes and acts on the belief that vengeance belongs to God and that God will repay evildoers (Rom. 12:17–20). You believe, as Deuteronomy 32:4 states, that "all His ways are justice; a God of faithfulness and without iniquity, just and right is He" (author's paraphrase). You believe that it is appointed unto man once to die and that after death men and women will appear for judgment before God who is perfectly righteous, who knows every detail of their inner and outer lives (2 Cor. 5:10; Heb. 9:27; Rev. 20:11–15). You believe that God "has fixed a day in which He will judge the world in righteousness" through Jesus Christ (Acts 17:31).

If you are a God-fearing person, you are a person who believes that God's Word is perfect, sure, right, pure, clean, true, and righteous altogether (Ps. 19:7–11). You fear God, you trust God, and you know that what God says is trustworthy. You simply can't fear God and not trust His Word. The two cannot be separated.

If you are a God-fearing person, you are a person who "does not trust in mankind, does not make mankind his strength nor allows his heart to turn away from the Lord. Rather, he puts his trust wholly in the Lord and makes God his trust. Even during those times when he walks in darkness and has no light, when he can't understand or make sense out of what is happening around him or to him, he trusts in the name of the Lord and relies upon Him" (Jer. 17:5–8; Isa. 50:10, author's paraphrase).

God-Fearing People Love God

Several verses make it clear that the fear of God and the love of God are closely related. Deuteronomy 10:12 tells us that God requires that we fear Him and love Him. Deuteronomy 6:2 declares that God wants us to fear Him, and verse 5 says that He wants us to love Him with all our heart, soul, and might. Fearing God involves loving God; loving God involves fearing God.

Many people in our world would say that you can't love someone you fear. Some books about parenting put fear of parents and love of parents in juxtaposition. The authors of these books (usually psychologists) warn parents not to use any form of punishment that encourages fear. They indicate that this will be harmful to the child's psyche and could encourage violence on the part of the child. They suggest that developing any kind of parental fear in the child will most certainly harm the child emotionally and psychologically, and will damage the parent's relationship with the child.

Recently I had an extensive discussion with a man who had been powerfully influenced by this kind of teaching. Encouraged by purveyors of these ideas, this proud and self-righteous man was excusing, even justifying, his bitterness and hatred toward his parents by saying that they had disciplined him when he was growing up. When asked how he knew this was the reason for his problems, he indicated that this was what psychologists—who incidentally had never met his parents, nor talked to them—had told him. Their premise: you can't really love someone whom you fear.

This kind of thinking is problematic for at least several reasons.

First, many people who learned to fear their parents also love them very deeply. The man I just mentioned had several siblings who loved their parents deeply and considered their parents to be their best friends. These siblings had the same parents and were raised in the same way, yet they disagreed entirely with this person's assessment of their parents and their upbringing.

Second, many people who were taught to fear their parents are very well adjusted emotionally and psychologically. They are not violent or cruel to others. They are not adult or child abusers. To the contrary, they are kind, gentle, and loving to others. In addition, many of them are incredibly productive people who make significant contributions to the church and society.

Third, the people who create this great divide between fear and love assume that all discipline that may produce fear must be administered in an angry, violent, abusive manner. They can't conceive that any discipline administered in a respectful, considerate, and loving manner could possibly induce fear, because to them fear is only the result of a threatening or dangerous situation. They can't conceive that fear and love can coexist in the same person.

Fourth, this kind of thinking flies in the face of the clear teaching of Scripture. Scripture indicates that the proper kind of discipline is an expression of love; conversely, the Bible teaches that parents who fail to discipline are expressing hatred to their children (Prov. 13:24). In keeping with this truth, Hebrews 12:5–11 reminds us that God's discipline of us is a proof of His love for us. God's discipline and parental discipline (when administered in an appropriate manner) are intended to produce a constructive, wholesome kind of fear, a fear that is entirely compatible with real love. Children who rightly fear their parents love their parents, and children who rightly love their parents also fear their parents. Similarly, it may be said that people who rightly fear God also love God. These two qualities cannot be separated. You can't really have one without the other. After studying the subject of the fear of God, Jerry Bridges describes the relationship between the fear of God and the love of God this way: "The fear of God also denotes the love and humble gratitude of the person who, conscious of his own sinfulness and exposure to divine wrath, has experienced the grace and mercy of God in the forgiveness of his sins."[1]

---

1. Jerry Bridges, *The Joy of Fearing God* (Colorado Springs: WaterBrook Press, 1997), 98.

God-Fearing People Obey and Serve God

No truth about the fear of God is made more evident in Scripture than the fact that the fear of God involves glad-hearted, diligent obedience and service. Often in Scripture, the mention of the fear of God is followed by a statement indicating that God-fearing people keep His commandments. Here are a few examples:

> What does the LORD your God require from you, but to fear the LORD your God, to walk in all His ways . . . and to serve the LORD your God with all your heart and with all your soul. (Deut. 10:12)

> How blessed is the man who fears the LORD,
> Who greatly delights in His commandments. (Ps. 112:1)

> How blessed is everyone who fears the LORD,
> Who walks in His ways. (Ps. 128:1)

> The conclusion, when all has been heard, is: fear God and keep His commandments, because this applies to every person. (Eccl. 12:13)

All these Scriptures emphasize the fact that the people who fear God obey Him; they keep his commandments, they structure their lives according to His Word, and they greatly delight in His commands. They obey with delight, with all their hearts, with all their souls. In other words, their obedience is not a grudging or forced obedience. They don't serve Him or walk in His ways because they have to, but because they want to. God-fearing people obey God because they consider it a privilege to please Him. God-fearing people don't have to be coerced, manipulated, or threatened into obedience. They don't have to be sent on a guilt trip or dragged kicking and screaming away from sin and into a life of righteousness.

God-fearing husbands delight in loving their wives as they love themselves. They delight in living with their wives in an understanding way, in honoring their wives, and in being heirs together of the grace of life. God-fearing wives consider it a privilege to be their husbands' helpers, to be their cheerleaders, their confidantes, their co-laborers, their encouragers, their supporters, and their teammates. They delight in building their homes rather than tearing them down. They delight in submitting themselves to their husbands as to the Lord.

God-fearing parents are joyfully careful not to provoke their children to wrath. They eagerly accept and fulfill the responsibility of bringing their children up in the discipline and instruction of the Lord. They willingly accept the responsibility of teaching their children, by word and example, the commandments of God, and make their family a priority in their lives. The fear of God and the love of God inevitably incline them in this direction. God-fearing children want to honor and obey their parents. They listen to them and are willing to help them. They care for them; they seek their counsel, protect them, and encourage them. This is what the fear of God is and does.

In Job 1:1, God's description of Job illustrates this truth about the fear of God. This verse tells us that Job was blameless and upright, and that he turned away from evil. The verses that follow indicate how devoted he was to his family. What was it that motivated Job to be this kind of person, the kind who walked in God's ways? He feared God. This was the great explanation for the kind of man Job was, the kind of life he lived.

If you were to ask the God-inspired writer of Proverbs what the fear of God was, he would have responded with these words: "The fear of the LORD is to hate evil; pride and arrogance and the evil way, and the perverted mouth, I hate" (Prov. 8:13). People who fear God hate evil; they hate pride, arrogance, and unwholesome speech, especially in themselves. Why? Because, as the text says, they fear God, and God hates these things. Conversely, they love godliness, righteousness, holiness, humility, and God-honoring, edifying communication. God is their reference point. So what pleases God pleases them, and what displeases God displeases them.

God-Fearing People Hope in God

Behold, the eye of the LORD is on those who fear Him,
On those who hope for His lovingkindness,
. . . .

Our soul waits for the LORD;
He is our help and our shield.
For our heart rejoices in Him,

. . . .

Let Your lovingkindness . . . be upon us,
According as we have hoped in You. (Ps. 33:18, 20–22)

These verses tell us that those who fear God do three things: (1) they hope for the Lord, (2) they wait for the Lord, and (3) they rejoice in the Lord.

When you find a person who has a robust, wholesome, healthy fear of God, you find a person whose life is characterized by hope, expectation, and joy.

Hope, as defined biblically, is not a "hope-so" kind of thing. It is a biblically based, rock-solid certainty that what God has promised in His Word will most assuredly come to pass. God-fearing people know His promises are based on His immutability and faithfulness. For the believer, hope is an anchor that keeps the soul from drifting into discouragement and despair. For the believer, hope is an unmovable and unshakable pillar that holds him up and provides stability. Still further, as defined biblically, hope is not based on fortuitous circumstances, or on your own personality, or on your own worthiness. It is based on the character and nature of God. The psalmist mentions God's lovingkindness twice in the passage we quoted from Psalm 33. The English Standard Version translates this Hebrew word as "steadfast love." Whether translated "lovingkindness" or "steadfast love," the idea is that the believer's hope is based on a very important attribute of God. God is full of lovingkindness, and He is steadfast in His love. He is a good God, full of grace, kindness, mercy, compassion, and love. It is His very nature to be this way. It is an aspect of His divine character to steadfastly be this way. He cannot waver in exercising this attribute, because it is part of His immutable nature. Consequently, the psalmist fears Him and confidently expects and anticipates His help and protection.

Then too, as defined biblically, hope is a rock-solid, take-it-to-the-bank certainty that the best is yet to come. This believer's fear of God means that he does not fear evil tidings, that his heart is steadfast

(Ps. 112:7). It means that he is realistically optimistic about the future. His knowledge of who God is and what God has promised encourages him to believe that God's thoughts toward him are thoughts of peace and not of harm or disaster. He is convinced that God will bring him to a desired end (Jer. 29:11).

People around him who don't fear God may be giving up, thinking pessimistically about the present and the future. They may be falling into the clutches of despair, but not this person. The focus of others may be on the enormity of their own personal problems or on the magnitude and insolvability of the problems they see around them. They may not be able to see any way out or through. They may think that things for them, for the world, or for the church are going to get worse and worse. They may think that they are trapped and things are hopeless. For them, life may be like a downhill slide into futility and despair. They may have the attitude that nothing will ever get better.

Their attitude may be similar to the attitude of the man described in the first chapters of Ecclesiastes. This man tried to find meaning and purpose in life apart from God, but he didn't and couldn't. He tried to make some sense out of what he saw happening "under the sun," but initially he couldn't. He tried to find meaning, satisfaction, and solutions to the dilemmas confronting him in his own life and in the world. He turned to education for help but didn't find it there. He tried to find meaning in pleasure, then in collecting wealth, and then in productive activity—constructing magnificent edifices and planting beautiful gardens—but he couldn't. Finally, after giving it his best shot, he concluded that

> there is no lasting remembrance of the wise man as with the fool, inasmuch as in the coming days all will be forgotten. . . . So I hated life, for the work which had been done under the sun was grievous to me; because everything is futility and striving after wind. . . . I completely despaired of all the fruit of my labor for which I had labored under the sun. When there is a man who has labored with wisdom, knowledge and skill, then he gives his legacy to one who has not labored with them. This too is vanity and a great evil. For what

does a man get in all his labor and in his striving with which he labors under the sun?" (Eccl. 2:16–17, 20–22)

At this point in his life this man became very pessimistic. And in this he became a representative of many throughout past and present history.

"Not so for me," said the psalmist. "I don't see things that way. That's not my perspective on life. Yes, I face humongous problems in my own life. Yes, I see horrific difficulties in the world around me, but I fear God, and because I fear God I have hope. My fear of God includes a well-grounded confidence and a realistic optimism as I live life 'under the sun.' I fear God, therefore I have hope, and my soul rejoices, I have confidence. I know that the eye of the Lord is upon me. God knows, God cares, God understands, God is loving, God is good, God is sovereign, He is in control, and He will deliver my soul from destruction and keep me in my times of difficulty. There is a way out. God will work all things together for good. He will not abandon me." This man's fear of God changed his whole attitude toward everything (Ps. 33:18–22).

An eighty-six-year-old man gave his testimony. This man had lived a very active and productive life. He had been involved in many Christian ministries. He had written many books and contributed in various ways to the cause of Christ. He was now legally blind, losing his hearing, unable to walk without assistance, and spent much of his time in a wheelchair. Yet his testimony was a buoyant one. He was still rejoicing in Christ; serving Christ in whatever way he could; active in counseling others; traveling, with his wife's assistance, to board meetings and speaking engagements; declaring wherever he went that God is good, upright, and trustworthy. This man had hope, joy, and confidence as he faced the present and future. He had this hope not because of his own strength, nor because of fortuitous circumstances, nor because he had no problems, nor because everything was going well in the world. No, he had hope because he feared God—and that made all the difference. So it will be with us: the more we fear God, the more hopeful, joyful, and confident we will be (Prov. 14:26–27).

God-Fearing People Are Awestruck by God

No biblical definition of the fear of God would be complete without mention of the attitude of reverence and awe. Psalm 33:8 uses the words *fear* and *awe* as synonyms. "Let all the earth fear the LORD; let all the inhabitants of the world stand in awe of Him." To fear God is to stand in awe of Him; to stand in awe of God is to fear Him.

In Revelation 15 the apostle John told us that God gave him a vision of what the Christians who had died and are now in heaven were doing and experiencing. He wrote that he had seen them standing before God singing:

> Great and marvelous are Your works,
> O Lord God, the Almighty;
> Righteous and true are Your ways,
> King of the nations!
> Who will not fear, O Lord, and glorify Your name?
> For You alone are holy;
> For all the nations will come and worship before You;
> For Your righteous acts have been revealed. (Rev. 15:3–4)

As these believers stood before God, they sang of His glory and majesty, His might and power, His righteousness and holiness, and His infinite uniqueness. Their response to this revelation of God was a holy fear and a desire to glorify Him. Their fear consisted of a holy awe and reverence that turned their focus away from thinking about themselves or other people or even the glories of heaven, to being consumed with God. These people in heaven were a God-conscious, God-centered people. They had lost their concern about proclaiming or displaying their own glory. The primary topic of their conversation was not about themselves. Their primary focus was not on themselves. Rather they were taken up with a desire to glorify and magnify God.

God-fearing people are consumed with and enthralled by God. They stand in awe of God. With Jeremiah, they say of God and to God:

> There is none like You, O LORD;
> You are great, and great is Your name in might.

Who would not fear You, O King of the nations?
Indeed it is Your due!
For among all the wise men of the nations
And in all their kingdoms,
There is none like You. (Jer. 10:6–7)

With Jeremiah, God-fearing people recognize the uniqueness of God, the greatness of God, the power of God, the sovereignty of God, and the worthiness of God. They think about Him all the time, and therefore stand in awe of Him. They are awestruck and reverent before Him.

Psalm 10:4 indicates that one of the characteristics of an ungodly person is that God is not in all his thoughts. His mind is not filled with thoughts of the God of the Bible. He lives in the futility of his own mind. The God of the Bible doesn't factor into the way he lives life, understands life, makes his decisions, relates to people, makes and spends his money, uses his time, and faces and solves problems. He thinks and lives autonomously—as though the God of the Bible doesn't even exist. For him, the God of the Bible, who has revealed Himself in Jesus Christ, is not a factor and certainly is not the primary factor in his life.

Conversely, Scripture indicates that God-fearing people can't get God out of their minds. To fear God means that you think about God all the time. God is in all your thoughts. It means that God will not be an appendage to your life—He will be your life. It means that God will not simply be Someone you think about on Sunday or occasionally throughout the week. God will be a factor, the primary factor, in the way you live life, understand life, make decisions, relate to people, make and spend your money, use your time, and face and solve problems.

With Paul, when the fear of God is at its maximum in the life of a person, he says and means, "My earnest expectation and my hope [is] that . . . Christ will even now, as always, be exalted in my body, whether by life or by death. For to me, to live is Christ and to die is gain" (Phil. 1:20–21). "We . . . have as our ambition [our goal in life, that which we live for, that which we want to accomplish more than anything else] . . . to be pleasing to Him" (2 Cor. 5:9).

Paul, as a person whose fear of God was at its maximum, was entirely consumed with Christ—living for Christ, thinking about Christ, pleasing Christ, proclaiming Christ, and magnifying Christ was his passion in life. He stood in awe of Christ, God manifest in the flesh. He reverenced Him. If we compare Paul's life to a compass, we could say that the direction needle on the compass of his life was always pointing to Christ. If we compare Paul's life to a wagon wheel, the hub at the center of the wagon wheel of his life was Christ, and the band around the circumference of that wheel was Christ. In his life every word spoken proceeded from Christ and led to Christ. That is the ultimate meaning of what it means to be a God-fearing person.

John Bunyan wrote,

> I take this grace of fear to be that which softens and mollifies the heart and makes it stand in awe of both the mercies of God and the judgments of God. This is that which retains in the heart that due dread and reverence of the heavenly Majesty that is fitting to be in and kept in the heart of sinners. . . . This is that . . . which makes the sinner stand in awe of God.[2]

According to Bunyan, and in keeping with Scripture, when a person fears God, his heart is mollified, softened, and caused to stand in awe of God. He experiences in his heart a proper dread of and reverence for God. This is fitting and should be a characteristic manner of life for the believer. This was true of the psalmist, of the Christians in heaven, of Jeremiah, and it ought to be true of every person in this world (Ps. 33:8).

PULLING IT ALL TOGETHER

The fear of God is a reflex, an attitudinal and emotional reaction to an accurate understanding and awareness of the glory and majesty of the God of the Bible that causes a person to trust God, love God, obey God,

2. John Bunyan, *Complete Works of Bunyan*, vol. 2 (Marshallton, DE: National Foundation for Christian Education, 1968), 422.

hope in God, and be consumed with God—wanting to honor, magnify, glorify, please, and serve Him in every area of life. This fear of God will involve your intellect, your emotions, and your attitudes and actions.

The Fear of God Involves Your Intellect, Your Thought Processes

People who fear God have big thoughts of God, His majesty, and His glory. They think of Him as He is described in Scripture. Their view of God is not based on their own opinion or the opinions of others, but rather on God's self-revelation of Himself in the living Word (Jesus Christ) and in His written Word (the Bible).

The Fear of God Involves Your Emotions

People who fear God stand in awe of Him. Awe is dread, wonder, and reverential fear. Scripture says of the early Christians that they "kept feeling a sense of awe" (Acts 2:43) and that "great fear came over the whole church" (Acts 5:11, also see v. 5). People who fear God don't act in a flippant manner toward Him; they are not careless, irresponsible, or casual before Him. They know the experience described in numerous passages of Scripture:

> Worship the LORD with reverence
> And rejoice with trembling. (Ps. 2:11)

> Tremble, and do not sin. (Ps. 4:4)

> I will bow in reverence for You. (Ps. 5:7)

> Worship the LORD in holy attire;
> Tremble before Him, all the earth. (Ps. 96:9)

> Tremble, O earth, before the LORD. (Ps. 114:7)

> My flesh trembles for fear of You. (Ps. 119:120)

According to these texts, people who fear God are affected emotionally in at least four ways:

1. They tremble before Him.
2. They rejoice.
3. They experience a sense of reverence or awe.
4. They bow down, an outward evidence of something that is happening on the inside, particularly in their emotions.

They are not forced to do this. They just instinctively do so because their emotions of dread and awe have been ignited. In other words, an accurate biblical understanding of who and what God is will affect your emotions.

In an excellent book titled *The Knowledge of the Holy*, A. W. Tozer writes,

> The church has surrendered her once lofty concept of God and has substituted for it one so low, so ignoble, as to be unworthy of thinking, worshiping men. . . .
>
> The low view of God entertained almost universally among Christians is the cause of a hundred lesser evils everywhere among us. A whole new philosophy of the Christian life has resulted from this one basic error in our religious thinking.
>
> With our loss of the sense of majesty has come the further loss of religious awe and consciousness of the divine Presence. We have lost our spirit of worship and our ability to withdraw inwardly to meet God in adoring silence. Modern Christianity is simply not producing the kind of Christian who can appreciate or experience the life of the Spirit. . . .
>
> The decline of the knowledge of the holy has brought on our troubles. It is impossible to keep our moral practices sound and our inward attitudes (and emotions) right while our idea of God is erroneous or inadequate. If we would . . . bring back spiritual power in our lives, we must begin to think of God more nearly as He is.[3]

In these statements, Tozer accurately describes how our present-day evangelical culture has downsized God and lost the concept that God

3. A. W. Tozer, *The Knowledge of the Holy* (New York: Harper & Brothers, 1961), 6–7.

is to be feared. But a person who comes to an accurate understanding of who and what God is will inevitably have an emotional response of reverence, holy fear, joy, caution, and perhaps some shame.

The Fear of God Will Affect Your Attitudes and Actions

An accurate fear of God will motivate you to trust and hope in Him, obey and serve Him, love and admire Him, worship and praise Him, depend and rely on Him, submit and yield to Him, and magnify and glorify Him.

Scriptural support that combines the concept of the fear of God with these attitudes and activities we've just mentioned is found in many passages:

> You shall fear only the LORD your God: and you shall worship Him. (Deut. 6:13)

> You shall keep the commandments of the LORD your God, to walk in His ways and to fear Him. (Deut. 8:6)

> You shall fear the LORD your God; you shall serve Him and cling to Him. . . . He is your praise and He is your God, who has done these great and awesome things. (Deut. 10:20–21)

> Only fear the LORD and serve Him. (1 Sam. 12:24)

> Worship the LORD with reverence. (Ps. 2:11)

> You who fear the LORD praise Him;
> . . . glorify Him,
> And stand in awe of Him. (Ps. 22:23)

> You who fear the LORD, trust in the LORD. (Ps. 115:11)

> Those who fear You . . . [will] be glad. (Ps. 119:74)

> You who revere the LORD, bless the LORD. (Ps. 135:20)

You shall worship the Lord your God, and serve Him only. (Matt. 4:10)

Fear God, and give Him glory. (Rev. 14:7)

What do these sample verses teach about God-fearing people? They teach that God-fearing people will worship God, serve the Lord, walk in His ways, cling to Him, praise Him, glorify Him, trust in Him, rejoice in Him, and bless the Lord.

All these characteristics describe what it means to fear God in such a way that all other forms of destructive fear will be diminished and eliminated. We encourage you to apply all these to yourself to determine your "Fear of God Quotient." To put this chapter to work in your life, rate yourself on the following issues using this evaluation scale: (4) Always, (3) Often, (2) Sometimes, (1) Seldom, or (0) Never. Put a circle around the number that best describes your usual fear of God. This exercise will replace the Questions for Discussion.

As you live your life on a daily basis and face challenges and difficulties:

1. Do you find yourself struggling with the fear of man as defined in earlier chapters of this book?

   (4) Always   (3) Often   (2) Sometimes   (1) Seldom   (0) Never

2. Does the truth of God's omnipotence keep you from worry, frustration, and discouragement?

   (4) Always   (3) Often   (2) Sometimes   (1) Seldom   (0) Never

3. Does the truth of God's omniscience keep you from worry, frustration, and discouragement?

   (4) Always   (3) Often   (2) Sometimes   (1) Seldom   (0) Never

4. Does the truth of God's omnipresence keep you from worry, frustration, and discouragement?

   (4) Always   (3) Often   (2) Sometimes   (1) Seldom   (0) Never

5. Does the truth of God's justice keep you from worry, frustration, anger, resentment, retaliation, and discouragement?

   (4) Always   (3) Often   (2) Sometimes   (1) Seldom   (0) Never

6. Does the truth of God's goodness, grace, and mercy keep you from worry, frustration, anger, resentment, and discouragement?

   (4) Always   (3) Often   (2) Sometimes   (1) Seldom   (0) Never

7. Does your love for God remain strong and manifest itself in practical ways as described in John 14:21, 23 and 1 John 4:20–21; 5:3?

   (4) Always   (3) Often   (2) Sometimes   (1) Seldom   (0) Never

8. Do you render to God glad-hearted, diligent obedience and service?

   (4) Always   (3) Often   (2) Sometimes   (1) Seldom   (0) Never

9. Do you find yourself hating and turning from your own sin, pride, arrogance, and unwholesome speech?

   (4) Always   (3) Often   (2) Sometimes   (1) Seldom   (0) Never

10. Do you possess a realistic optimism about what is happening in your life and in the world?

    (4) Always   (3) Often   (2) Sometimes   (1) Seldom   (0) Never

11. Do you reflect on and believe in God's lovingkindness and find it to be of practical, experiential comfort to you?

    (4) Always   (3) Often   (2) Sometimes   (1) Seldom   (0) Never

12. Are you enthralled with and consumed by God?

    (4) Always   (3) Often   (2) Sometimes   (1) Seldom   (0) Never

13. Are you a God-conscious, God-centered person?

    (4) Always   (3) Often   (2) Sometimes   (1) Seldom   (0) Never

14. Do you consciously think about how you can please God?

    (4) Always   (3) Often   (2) Sometimes   (1) Seldom   (0) Never

15. Do you find yourself being awestruck by God's majesty and glory?

(4) Always (3) Often (2) Sometimes (1) Seldom (0) Never

Now add up your score and identify the areas of strength and weakness you have in your fear of God. If you rated yourself "always" on each item or even on many items, you're probably being unrealistic. In our opinion, only Jesus Christ and the saints that are already in heaven could say they always do all or even most of these things. Be honest and let this exercise bring areas of weakness to your attention. Identifying areas in which you need to grow is a vital part of fostering that growth. Then, having identified the areas in which you need to improve, move on to the next chapter, where we will discover how to develop, increase, and sustain a healthy, robust, wholesome fear of God.

12

YES, BUT HOW?

"YES, but how?"

I have asked this question many times after Bible studies or church services. The speaker may have faithfully interpreted and explained the meaning of a Bible passage, opened the text so that I understood what the passage meant, even admonished me to put it into practice. Perhaps he exhorted me to repent, pray, love my neighbor as I love myself, worship, or witness. He may have clearly told me what to do. But then he stopped. After hearing him, I knew what I should do and I may have even been motivated to do it, but he never told me how to actually do what he was exhorting me to do. So I left asking the question, "Yes, but how?"

By this time you may be saying, "All right already! I understand why we should fear God and what it means to fear God. I really do want to develop a more healthy fear of God and be a truly God-fearing person. Now will you please tell me how I can become that kind of person? Please give me some help in knowing how to do it."

That's the very thing we want to do in this chapter. If the fear of God is as important for Christians as we have indicated, we would expect that God would not only give us information about the why and what of this issue, but also the how. And indeed He has! We're going to see that God has a great deal to say about this aspect of developing, increasing, and sustaining the fear of God in our lives.

FACTOR NUMBER ONE: A CHANGE OF HEART

To understand how to develop and sustain a healthy fear of God, it's important for us to note that we don't just naturally fear God. With all that we've noted so far about this quality—its importance, its reasonableness, its meaning—we might be tempted to think that men would automatically fear God.

Understanding who God is, what He has done and still does, and the benefits that come to people who fear Him, we might be inclined to ask the same questions that Jeremiah and the people in Revelation asked: "Who would not fear You, O King of the nations?" (Jer. 10:7); and "Who will not fear, O Lord, and glorify Your name?" (Rev. 15:4). It seems irrational, absurd, and almost unbelievable that people would not automatically fear and give reverence to Someone as great and majestic as God is, Someone who has the power and ability that God has, Someone who has done and still does what God has done and continues to do.

Yet the Scripture declares, and our experience illustrates the fact, that men don't naturally fear God. In God's description of the human race since the time of Adam, He says, "There is no fear of God before their eyes" (Rom. 3:18). In this verse Paul is probably quoting an Old Testament text that says essentially the same thing: "There is no fear of God before his eyes" (Ps. 36:1).

"There is no fear of God in this place" was the way that Abraham described the culture in which he lived (Gen. 20:11). The situation has not changed. The twenty-first-century society in which we live is still devoid of the fear of God. Instead of fearing God, unregenerate, unredeemed men automatically fear man (Prov. 29:25; Rom. 1:23, 25). By nature, men are more concerned with the approval of other men than the approval of God (John 12:43).

The question that naturally arises is: what must happen in order for men who don't naturally fear God to begin to do so? Thankfully the Scriptures give a very clear answer. In Jeremiah 32, God spoke about His people: "I will give them one heart and one way, that they may fear Me always. . . . I will put the fear of Me in their hearts so that they will not turn away from Me" (vv. 39–40). For people to fear God, He has to supernaturally put that fear in their hearts.

Earlier in Jeremiah, God described the original hearts of men as being deceitful above all things and desperately wicked (Jer. 17:9). Before God gives men new hearts, they oppose the God of the Bible; they resist and rebel against this God (Gen. 6:5; Eccl. 9:3; Isa. 1:5; Mark 7:21–23; Rom. 1:18–25; 8:5–8). Sometimes this resistance and rebellion is covert and sometimes it is overt, sometimes it is violent and easily recognizable, and sometimes it is subtler and even disguised. Nonetheless the hearts of all men resist God and don't fear Him in the way that they should. For a person to truly fear God, some important internal changes must take place, changes that only God can make. These changes are variously described in Scripture. Jeremiah indicates that for this change to occur, God must perform heart surgery: He must give that person a new heart. He must change that person on the inside, at the very core of his being.

In the book of Ezekiel, God described this same indispensable operation in two passages: First in Ezekiel 11:19–20: "I will take the heart of stone out of their flesh and give them a heart of flesh, that they may walk in My statutes and keep My ordinances and do them." Then again in Ezekiel 36:25–27:

> I will sprinkle clean water on you, and you will be clean; I will cleanse you from all your filthiness and from all your idols. Moreover, I will give you a new heart and put a new spirit within you; and I will remove the heart of stone from your flesh and give you a heart of flesh. I will put My Spirit within you, and cause you to walk in My statutes.

In both of these passages in Ezekiel, God made it clear that the problem with mankind's attitude toward and relationship with Him is a heart problem. They have hearts of stone, hearts that are impervious to God and His Word, hearts that are insensitive and inflexible, hearts that lack the fear of God. These hearts must be replaced with hearts of flesh—hearts that are soft, impressionable, and responsive; hearts that are sensitive, tender, and compliant to God and His Word.

Ezekiel 36 refers to filthiness and idolatry. Where was the primary location of that filthiness and idolatry? The references to needing a new heart and a new spirit indicate that the cleansing that was needed was internal. Ezekiel 14 states that the problem with human nature is idolatry of the heart (vv. 1–9). Ezekiel 11:21 mentions that it is the heart that moves toward detestable things, those things that are an abomination to the Lord. The problem of mankind, then and now, is a heart problem. So the cleansing that Ezekiel 36 says people need is an internal one.

For us to become God-centered, God-fearing, we need to be cleaned up on the inside; we need to receive a new heart, a new disposition, a new spirit. No one fears God appropriately until this change has occurred. In his comments on this passage, Matthew Henry has rightly said, "We cannot sanctify God's name unless He sanctify our hearts, nor live to His glory, but by grace alone."[1]

We find the same truth in the New Testament about our need for an inner change. First Corinthians 6:9–10 describes what the Corinthians were like before they became Christians. They lived lives of debauchery and immorality with no fear of God before their eyes. They lived for themselves, only to please themselves. They did what they wanted to do, with no regard for the God of the Bible. They had the hearts of stone about which Ezekiel had written. But Paul indicated that something had happened to them that changed them; his comment, "such were some of you" (1 Cor. 6:11) implied that they were no longer living that way.

What had happened to change their orientation to life? Verse 11 explains what made the difference: they had been washed (cleaned up on the inside), and they had been justified (declared righteous) through the person and work of the Lord Jesus Christ on their behalf. And even beyond that, the change had occurred because they had been set apart by the Holy Spirit. They had heard the Word of God, and as they had, the Spirit of God had convicted them of their sin, brought them to repentance, and prompted them to faith in Christ. Through the work of the Holy Spirit, God's Word, and the atoning work of Jesus Christ,

1. Matthew Henry, *Matthew Henry's Commentary*, vol. 4 (New York: Revell), 962.

they had been cleansed on the inside and their attitude had changed toward themselves and God.

In the words of Jeremiah and Ezekiel, God gave them a new disposition that enabled them to do what they could not have done previously. He replaced their old hearts, which had been under the control of sin, with new hearts under the control of God. Or in the words of Paul, Christ had made them new creatures (2 Cor. 5:17–21). As a result, they could bring glory to God and live a God-fearing life (1 Cor. 6:19–20; 10:31).

How can we develop the fear of God? The first requirement for developing and sustaining a God-fearing life is to be cleaned up on the inside, receiving forgiveness through the sacrificial death of Christ (2 Cor. 5:21; 1 John 1:7), and being declared righteous by God's grace through the redemption that is in Christ (Rom. 3:24–25) by faith in Christ alone. When that happens, a person becomes a new creature in Christ, receives a new heart and spirit, and becomes indwelt by the Holy Spirit. He or she is enabled to live a God-centered and God-honoring life (Rom. 8:9–13; 1 Cor. 12:13; Eph. 3:17–19).

As Peter wrote, when a person is redeemed by Christ, he or she should, and can, live his or her entire life on this earth as a God-fearing person. Experiencing redemption from the penalty and power of sin sets us free to live our lives in the fear of the Lord (1 Peter 1:17–19). This kind of life is only possible for those who have been redeemed, but it is possible for all who are redeemed.

John Bunyan explained:

> This fear flows from a new heart. This fear is not in man by nature; the fear of devils they may have, as also an ungodly fear of God, but this fear is not in any, but where there dwelleth a new heart, another fruit and effect of this everlasting covenant, and of this distinguishing love of God.... So then, until a man receive a heart from God, a heart from heaven, a new heart, he has not this fear of God in him.... This fear of God must not be, cannot be found in old hearts; old hearts are not bottles out of which this fear proceeds, but it is from an honest and good heart, from a new one, from such an one that is also the effect of the everlasting covenant, and the love of God to

men. He therefore that has not received at the hands of God a new heart, cannot fear the Lord.[2]

This, then, is the first factor in answering the question, "Yes, but how?"

FACTOR NUMBER TWO: DEVOTION TO PRAYER

But that's only the beginning. A second key factor in developing and sustaining a healthy fear of God involves your prayer life. In Psalm 86:11 the writer is an example for all of us who want to be more God-fearing in our lives. Here we find him praying, "Unite my heart to fear Your name."

David, who wrote this psalm, teaches us several things about becoming a more God-fearing person.

First, he made it clear that you must begin with the heart. The fear of God is developed in the heart before it is ever experienced anywhere else. If you have a powerful fear of God, it will emerge from the heart. But if you do not have the fear of God, something is wrong in your heart.

Second, David realized that in order to have a robust fear of God, his heart must be united—he couldn't allow himself to be drawn several different directions at once. David knew that his heart was the control center of his life; he realized that if his heart was not united, nothing else would come out right in his life; he was aware that a person whose heart is divided is unstable in all his ways (James 1:8). David knew that his heart was the reservoir from which all the issues of his life flowed (Prov. 4:23). He realized that frequently our hearts are divided in terms of their focus. He knew that sometimes our hearts begin to drift or become distracted from what is really important.

Sometimes, like Martha, we lose our focus. We divide our attention among many things rather than the one thing that is needful (see Luke 10:38–42). When our hearts get out of control and move in many different directions, we forget that the fear of God should be a priority.

2. John Bunyan, *Complete Works of Bunyan*, vol. 2 (Marshallton, DE: National Foundation for Christian Education, 1968), 423.

Third, David knew that he couldn't control his heart on his own. He knew that this was too big a task for him. He knew that if his heart was to be united, God had to give him the strength to do it. This petition was both an expression of his desire and an expression of his weakness. He realized that he desperately needed the help of God if he were to have a united heart controlled by the fear of God.

In essence David had learned the lesson that Jesus was teaching when He gave us the model prayer in Matthew 6:9–13. In this prayer Jesus used different words from the ones David used, but the meaning is the same. He said that when we pray we should begin by praying that God's name (which represents who and what He is) would be hallowed. And what is it to hallow God's name? It is to set it apart as holy, unique, and worthy of reverence and holy respect. By indicating that this is the first petition we should pray, Jesus was teaching us that reverence for God should be the primary focus of our lives and prayers. And the fact that He taught us to pray that God's name would be hallowed indicates that we can't do this without the help of God.

Developing and sustaining a healthy, robust fear of God should be a primary emphasis in your prayer life. Apart from His help, you will never be able to give God the respect and reverence that is due Him. Show me a person who isn't praying the way David prayed in Psalm 86:11 and the way Jesus taught us to pray in Matthew 6:9, and I'll show you a person in whose life the fear of God is very small or nonexistent.

FACTOR NUMBER THREE: STUDY OF THE WORD

A third key factor in developing and sustaining a healthy fear of God is suggested by numerous verses in which the fear of God is mentioned. A few of these verses are quoted below. Certain words that will help us get an answer to the "yes, but how?" question are stressed with bold type.

> Remember the day you stood before the LORD your God at Horeb, when the Lord said to me, "Assemble the people to Me, that I may

let them **hear My Words** so **they may learn** to fear Me all the days
they live on the earth." (Deut. 4:10)

This is the commandment, the statutes and the judgments which the
LORD your God has commanded me to **teach you** . . . so that you and your
son and your grandson might fear the LORD your God. (Deut. 6:1–2)

Therefore, you shall keep the commandments of the LORD your God,
to walk in His ways and to fear Him. (Deut. 8:6)

You shall . . . fear Him; and . . . **listen to His voice.** (Deut. 13:4)

So that **you may learn** to fear the LORD your God always. (Deut.14:23)

He shall read it [God's Word] all the days of his life, that he may
learn to fear the LORD his God. (Deut. 17:19)

All Israel **will hear** of it and fear. (Deut. 21:21)

Assemble the people . . . so that they may **hear and learn** and fear the
LORD your God. (Deut. 31:12)

Come, you children, **listen to me;**
I will teach you the fear of the LORD. (Ps. 34:11)

By noting the emphasized words in these verses, we may draw several
conclusions about how to develop and sustain the fear of God in our lives.

First, several times we see that hearing and listening are associated
with developing the fear of God. Romans 10:17 informs us that "faith
comes by hearing, and hearing by the word of God" (NKJV). In other
words, if you want to have strong faith, you must put yourself in a place
where you will hear God's Word being faithfully preached. Faith doesn't
just float around in the air and mysteriously grab you. God uses His
preached Word to strengthen your faith.

Similarly, we might say that the fear of God comes by hearing
God's Word. Faithfully, diligently, and attentively hearing God's Word

being preached is one of the primary instruments God uses in building this quality into our lives. People who want to develop a stronger fear of God must make this a priority in their lives, and they must do it regularly. And they must make sure that the preaching they are listening to is really an expository ministry—that is, that it gives a detailed description of the Scriptures and focuses on explaining the meanings and implications of the text.

It is not some man's ideas, nor is it the theories of psychologists or philosophers or sociologists that promote the fear of God. It is the faithful proclamation of God's Word. There can be no neglect of nor substitute for this.

Second, another set of words indicates that the fear of God is produced by teaching and learning. These two words indicate that developing and sustaining the fear of God will involve the use of the mind. To become a God-fearing person, you must be a student; you must put forth an effort to learn. Being a student obviously involves studying. If you don't study, you have no right to think of yourself as a student. Sitting around watching television or even sitting in a church auditorium or classroom doesn't necessarily mean you are a student or that you are learning anything. You may just be sitting there occupying space. You may not be learning, retaining, or processing anything that is being said. No one can be considered a learner unless he or she retains, processes, and benefits from what is being said. Again, please note that growing in the fear of God is associated with being taught, studying, and learning the Word of God.

Earlier we gave a definition of the fear of God, which stated that the fear of God is a reflexive, attitudinal, and emotional reaction to an accurate understanding of who and what God is. We explained the attitudinal and emotional part of that statement, but we didn't explain what is meant by the words *reflexive* and *reaction*.

The word *reflex* means that your attitudes and emotions automatically respond to something. When your hand touches an extremely hot surface, you don't have to tell your hand to move away from that surface. Because of the nerve endings in your hand, your hand just automatically jerks away from the hot surface. When we use the word *reflexive* in association with the development of the fear of God, we mean that when a certain thing happens, we will naturally and automatically respond with the fear of God.

The word *reaction* conveys a similar idea. It should be clear that the fear of God is more of a *reaction* than it is an action. It is something that happens rather than something you directly make happen. Only in an indirect way do you make the fear of God happen. The fear of God happens because something else has happened. And unless that something else happens, you will never develop and sustain the fear of God.

Third, what is it that causes the fear of God to develop? What must take place for the fear of God to happen? The rest of our definition answers these questions.

The fear of God comes about as you gain and maintain an accurate understanding of who the God of the Bible is. In other words, as you hear and listen to God and His Word, as you study and learn about Him, as you continue to accurately think about and meditate on God and His Word, the fear of God will develop. This is the method God uses to make your fear of Him stronger.

Fourth, in his treatise on the fear of God, John Bunyan writes,

> The fear of God flows from . . . a sound impression that the Word of God makes on our souls; for without an impress of the Word, there is no fear of God. Hence it is said that God gave Israel good laws, statutes and judgments that they might learn them, and in learning them, learn to fear the Lord their God. . . . For as to the extent that a man drinks good doctrine into his soul, so to that extent he fears God; if he drinks in much, he fears Him greatly; if he drinks in but little, he fears Him but little; if he drinks not at all, he fears Him not at all.[3]

John Bunyan was absolutely convinced that a diligent study of God's Word played a crucial role in the development and maintenance of the fear of God in our souls. He could hardly have made that point clearer. Drink much of the Word of God, and you will have much of the fear of God; drink little, and you will have little; drink not at all, and

3. Ibid., 424.

you will have none, is his conviction. And according to the Scripture, he was right!

FACTOR NUMBER FOUR: MEDITATION ON THE TRUTH

Ask God the question, "How can I develop and sustain a robust fear of God in my life?" and one of the answers He will give you is, "Be still, and know that I am God" (Ps. 46:10 NKJV). "Do you want to know Me, who I really am, what I am like? Do you want to have an experiential knowledge of My greatness, My glory, My majesty? Well then, you must be still; you must be willing to think; you must take charge of your mind and control your thoughts and actions. You must stop frenetically running around, keeping yourself so busy mentally or physically that you miss My presence. You must periodically, regularly, often make time to focus on Me, to think about Me. You must not let your mind think about whatever it wants. You must deliberately focus on who I am. If you are not willing to do this, you cannot know Me in an in-depth way, and you will not fear Me in a constructive, powerful way. To know me as I really am and to fear Me as you ought, you must 'be still, and know that I am God.'"

Don't misunderstand what God means by being still. He's not telling you to just sit around and relax and be passive. He's telling you to be still for the purpose of knowing Him. What then should you think about while you're being still that would help you know and fear Him more? In the remainder of this chapter, we will explain in detail several important things you should do while you are being still that will help you grow in your understanding and appreciation of God.

First, be still, and reflect on your own sinfulness, your own unworthiness, your own inadequacy. People tell you that you should think about how great you are, about your own value, about how important you are. But Scripture tells you the opposite.

Again and again throughout Scripture God reminds us of how desperately wicked and undeserving we are apart from Him and His grace. Read through Romans 1–3; Ephesians 2; Colossians 1–3;

1 Timothy 1; and 2 Timothy 3; and note what these passages say about your nature. Reflect on the verses we studied from Jeremiah 17 and 32, and Ezekiel 11 and 36, about the condition of your heart. Memorize and meditate on verses that remind you of who and what you are and what you deserve apart from Christ. Review verses such as Isaiah 64:6; Romans 7:14–23; 1 Corinthians 15:8; Ephesians 3:8; and 1 Timothy 1:15.

Most of the Bible was written to people who were already the professing people of God. Why then does it include so many references to our sinfulness and depravity? Professing believers already know that they are sinners and can only be saved by grace. So why does it repeat this fact again and again? Because God knows we are prone to forget this fact. He knows it is good for us to remember what we were and, to some extent, still are, so that we will appreciate Him and the great cost of our salvation even more.

If you want to increase your fear of God, make a point of frequently reflecting on your sins: sins of attitude, thought, word, actions, and reactions; what you do that you shouldn't do; what you don't do that you should do; and your internal and external sins. Do a thorough Bible study on the biblical doctrine of sin. Write down your reflections and review your notes frequently—this will be of great help to you in developing and sustaining a healthy fear of God.

Read a Puritan book about sin such as Edward Reynolds's *Sinfulness of Sin* or Thomas Goodwin's *Man's Guiltiness before God*. Study a good systematic theology book such as those written by Louis Berkhof or Robert Raymond and study the section on the doctrine of sin.

Second, be still, and ponder God's so great salvation (Heb. 2:3). The apostle Peter believed that an understanding of and a reflection upon our so great redemption should motivate us to live all our lives in the fear of God (1 Peter 1:17–19). Paul's life is also a testimony to the motivating power that thoughts about redemption can have in developing and sustaining a God-centered lifestyle. In Galatians 6:14, Paul wrote that he had only one thing to brag about, and that was the cross of Jesus Christ. At that point in his life, he could have listed a number of accomplishments to brag about, but he didn't. Why? Because he knew what he had been and still was—a sinner in need of God's grace. Paul understood and appreciated the cross of Christ because he knew how desperately he needed grace, how freely God offered that grace, and the price Christ had paid on the cross. This continual lifestyle of reflection became a motivating factor in keeping God as his primary focus.

When we turn to 1 Timothy 1:13–17, we see the same scenario played out again in Paul's life. In verse 13 he described what he was like before God saved him—extremely sinful; he then went on in verse 15 to describe what he had become: the chief of sinners. The impact that these reflections had on Paul is twofold:

1. In verses 14–15 he wrote that he was motivated to magnify the grace of God for the salvation that he had experienced through Christ Jesus. He'd been a Christian for many years by that time. He had been mightily used of God. He had founded many churches and had been used of God in bringing many to faith in Christ. He had written many powerful letters, which are now included in our Bible and which contain many important doctrines of the Christian faith. Yet he had the same zeal about God, God's grace, Christ Jesus, salvation, and ministry as he had had when he had first become a Christian. Why? Because he frequently took the time to be still and remember God's so great salvation.

2. The reflection on God's so great salvation motivated Paul to give God the praise and glory. "For this reason I found mercy, so that in me as the foremost [sinner], Jesus Christ might demonstrate His perfect patience as an example for those who would believe in Him for eternal life. Now to the King eternal, immortal, invisible, the only God, be honor and glory forever and ever" (1 Tim. 1:16–17). Do you see what effect Paul's reflection had on him? It motivated him to trust, love, obey, serve, hope in, stand in awe of, glorify, and magnify God.

Many years ago John Bunyan wrote this about the development of godly fear: "Godly fear flows from a sense of the love and kindness and mercy of God by Jesus Christ. There can be none of this fear, but rather wrath and despair, which produces a fear that is . . . devilish . . . but godly fear flows from a sense of hope and mercy from God by Jesus Christ."[4]

In a similar fashion, John Brown wrote, "Nothing is so well suited to put the fear of God . . . into the heart, as an enlightened view of the cross of Christ. There shine spotless holiness, inflexible justice, incomprehensible wisdom, omnipotent power, holy love. None of the excellencies darken or eclipse the other. But every one of them rather gives luster to the rest."[5]

To help you in your thoughts about salvation, grace, and godly fear, conduct your own thorough study on the subjects of the grace of God, the cross of Christ, justification, forgiveness, and redemption. Select verses on these subjects from your studies to memorize and meditate on. Do a verse-by-verse study of Romans 3:24–6:23. Writing down your reflections and reviewing your notes frequently will be of great help to you in developing and sustaining a godly fear. Read and meditate on books such as Jerry Bridges's *Transforming Grace* and *The Disciplines of Grace*, Charles Spurgeon's *All of Grace*, John Bunyan's *Grace Abounding to the Chief of Sinners*, Thomas Goodwin's *Object and Acts of Justifying Faith*, James White's *God Who Justifies*, John MacArthur's *Murder of Jesus*, and Michael Horton's *Putting Amazing Back into Grace*. Study the section on the doctrine of salvation in a good systematic theology book such as those by Louis Berkhof or Robert Raymond.

If you want to develop and sustain a robust fear of God, be still, and reflect often on your so great salvation. Think much about the greatness of your salvation and you will have much fear, think little about the greatness of your salvation and you will have little fear, think not at all about the greatness of your salvation and you will have no fear of God at all.

4. Ibid.

5. John Brown, *Expository Discourses on 1 Peter*, vol. 1 (Edinburgh: Banner of Truth Trust, 1975), 472–73.

Third, be still, and think about God's attributes. We've probably all heard the saying, "Out of sight, out of mind." Like it or not, that statement is usually true. We tend to be influenced by the things that we keep in our sight, whether literally or mentally. What we actually see tends to influence us the most. What we focus on mentally is what will influence our feelings, our desires, our choices, and our actions. If you stop thinking about God or if you think of Him wrongly (i.e., unbiblically), His influence in your life will be minimized, if not eliminated altogether.

When Isaiah "saw the Lord sitting on a throne, lofty and exalted, with the train of His robe filling the temple" (Isa. 6:1), he was powerfully affected. He saw his own sinfulness, and he cried out, "Woe is me, for I am ruined! . . . For my eyes have seen the King, the LORD of hosts" (v. 5). He gladly volunteered for ministry and said, "Here am I. Send me!" (v. 8). He never even asked where God was going to send him or what it would involve, when he would have to go, what sacrifices he would have to make, or how easy or difficult his ministry would be. He had seen the Lord and that provided all the motivation he needed.

When the apostle John saw the greatness and majesty of Christ, he fell down before Him as a dead man, and then arose and gladly accepted the ministry Christ gave him to do (Rev. 1:12–19). He saw the Lord, and his inevitable, reflexive reaction to that sight was godly fear, which included all the aspects of that fear we have already studied.

When Moses saw the Lord as He really is, Moses "made haste to bow low toward the earth and worship" (Ex. 34:8), and throughout the rest of his life he was motivated to maintain a godly fear.

When Job was reminded of the greatness, power, sovereignty, wisdom, majesty, and uniqueness of God (Job 38–41), his response illustrated what it means to fear God. He said,

> I know that You can do all things,
> And that no purpose of Yours can be thwarted.
> "Who is this [referring to himself] that hides counsel without
>   knowledge?"
> Therefore I have declared that which I did not understand,

Things too wonderful for me, which I did not know.
"Hear, now, and I will speak;
I will ask You, and You instruct me."
I have heard of You by the hearing of the ear;
But now my eye sees You;
Therefore I retract,
And I repent in dust and ashes. (Job 42:1–6)

At that point in his life, Job became still and focused on the greatness and majesty of God.

The result? Trust, humility, confession, repentance, love, hope, awe, reverence, praise, adoration, and submission—the fear of God.

In his comments on the importance of a proper understanding of who God is, John Bunyan writes,

> God may well be called the fear of His people ... because of the dread and terrible majesty that is in Him. "He is a mighty God, and terrible, and with God is terrible majesty" (Daniel 7:28; 10:17; Nehemiah 1:5; 4:14; 9:32; Job 37:22).
>
> His people know Him, and have this dread upon them, by virtue whereof there is begot and maintained in them that godly awe and reverence which is agreeable to their profession of Him. "Let Him be your fear; let Him be your dread." Set Him before the eyes of your souls, and let His excellence make you afraid with godly fear (Isaiah 8:12–13).[6]

To help you focus your thoughts about God's attributes, do a thorough study on such subjects as the holiness, goodness, sovereignty, power, eternality, immutability, omnipresence, wisdom, knowledge, patience, love, and wrath of God. Select meaningful verses on these subjects from your studies to memorize and meditate on. Reflect on passages such as Psalms 104–108; 135–136; and Isaiah 40. Review these passages regularly. Writing down your reflections and reviewing your notes frequently will be of great help to you in developing and sustaining a healthy fear

6. Bunyan, *Complete Works of Bunyan*, 424.

of God. Read and meditate on books such as Jerry Bridges's *Trusting God* and *The Joy of Fearing God*, J. I. Packer's *Knowing God*, Stephen Chamock's masterful book *The Existence and Attributes of God*, A. W. Pink's *Attributes of God*, John MacArthur's *God: Coming Face to Face with His Majesty*, or John Bunyan's *Treatise on the Fear of God*. Study the section on the doctrine of God in a good systematic theology book such as those by Louis Berkhof or Robert Raymond.

If you want to develop and sustain a healthy fear of God, be still, and reflect often on the attributes of God. Think much about the greatness of your God and you will have much godly fear, think little about the greatness of your God and you will have little godly fear, think not at all about the greatness of God and you will have no fear of God at all.

Fourth, be still, and reflect on the mighty works of God. The connection between doing this and developing godly fear is clearly illustrated in Exodus 14:31. God's people were between a rock and a hard place. They had just been released from cruel slavery to the Egyptians and were making their way toward the land of Canaan. They had arrived at the Red Sea only to discover that the Egyptians had changed their minds about letting them go and were now pursuing them with the intention of either making them return or murdering them.

On the one side they faced the Red Sea, and on the other they faced the powerful armies of Egypt with their chariots and horsemen. In marvelous ways God protected and delivered them.

> The angel of God, who had been going before the camp of Israel, moved and went behind them; and the pillar of cloud moved from before them and stood behind them. So it came between the camp of Egypt and the camp of Israel; and there was the cloud along with the darkness, yet it gave light at night. Thus the one did not come near the other all night.
>
> Then Moses stretched out his hand over the sea; and the LORD swept the sea back by a strong east wind all night and turned the sea into dry land, so the waters were divided. The sons of Israel went through the midst of the sea on the dry land, and the waters were like a wall to them on their right hand and on their left. Then the

Egyptians took up the pursuit, and . . . went in after them into the midst of the sea. At the morning watch, the LORD . . . brought the army of the Egyptians into confusion. He caused their chariot wheels to swerve, and He made them drive with difficulty; so the Egyptians said, "Let us flee from Israel, for the LORD is fighting for them.". . .

Moses stretched out his hand over the sea, and the sea returned to its normal state . . . then the LORD overthrew the Egyptians in the midst of the sea. . . . Not even one of them remained. . . .

Thus the LORD saved Israel that day from the hand of the Egyptians. (Ex. 14:19–30)

God did a mighty thing for His people that day, something that no man or group of men could ever have done. What a manifestation of God's power, protection, and concern for His people! What impact did this mighty act have on the Israelites? Scripture tells us that "when Israel saw the great power which the LORD had used against the Egyptians, the people feared the LORD, and they believed in the LORD" (Ex. 14:31). Miriam put their God-fearing response into words, composing a song which is found in Exodus 15. In it Miriam sang, "Who is like You, majestic in holiness, awesome in praises, working wonders?" (Ex. 15:11). As Miriam and the other Israelites reflected on God's mighty acts, their fear of God was increased.

Psalm 46:10, which speaks about being still and knowing who God is, is surrounded by reminders of God's great and mighty acts. In the context, the psalmist wrote about God's provision of a river whose streams make glad the city of God. He declared God to be our refuge and strength, a very present help. He referred to His ability to melt the earth with His voice. He encouraged us to "come, behold the works of the LORD" (v. 8). He declared God's ability to bring desolation and make wars cease to the end of the earth. He reminded us that God can overcome and destroy the mightiest of military weapons—that such weapons are no match for God. It is easier for God to snap our mightiest weapons in two than it would be for us to snap a toothpick in two. Through all these examples, the psalmist was encouraging us to be still, but while being still to meditate on the mighty acts of God.

Scripture tells us that God "made known His ways to Moses, His acts to the sons of Israel" (Ps. 103:7). From beginning to end, the Bible is filled with reminders of the great things God has done. This ought to cause us to ask, "Why does God do this? Why is He constantly reminding us of His mighty acts? Why are they recorded for us? Were they recorded just for informational, historical purposes?" Obviously not! They were recorded to motivate us to a deeper and fuller sense of awe and respect of God.

To help you focus your thoughts about God's mighty acts, look up the different references to the power of God and references to what His people praise Him for. Read through some of the books of the Bible, noting some of the mighty acts of God. Start with the book of Psalms. In the Psalms, you'll find the psalmist has already made lists of God's mighty acts. Psalms 103–107 and Psalm 136, for example, are classic examples of lists that extol the mighty acts of God. Make a list of these mighty acts and frequently pull it out to meditate on what those mighty acts reveal about God. Writing down your reflections and reviewing your notes frequently will be of great help to you in developing and sustaining a godly fear.

If you want to develop and sustain a healthy fear of God, be still, and reflect often on the mighty acts of God. Think much about the mighty acts of your God and you will have much fear, think little about the mighty acts of your God and you will have little fear, think not at all about His mighty acts and you will have no fear of God at all (Deut. 4:9; Josh. 4:20–24; 1 Sam. 12:24).

Fifth, be still, and reflect on the judgments that God has sometimes pronounced on men for their lack of godly fear.[7] Study, for example, the story of Nadab and Abihu found in Leviticus 10:1–3. These men were burned to death with fire from heaven because they trifled with God and His worship. Study the example of judgment that came on Achan (Josh. 7), Eli's sons (1 Sam. 2), Uzza (1 Chron. 13:9–10), or Ananias and Sapphira (Acts 5). Reflect on the warnings of Psalm 52:5. God said that He will break down certain people forever, snatching and uprooting

7. Ibid.

them from their homes. Who are these people? They are people who do not fear God—people who boast in evil, those whose tongues devise destruction, who love evil more than good, who speak falsehood more than truth, who will not make God their refuge, who trust their riches rather than God, and who are strong in their own evil desires (Ps. 52:1–4, 7). Verse 6 indicates that righteous people ought to take notice of the judgment that comes on ungodly people and be motivated to fear God.

Psalm 64:7–10 teaches the same truth. It tells us that God will shoot at and wound the ungodly, He will cause them to stumble and will use the words of their mouths against them, He will bring them to shame. What will be the result of reflecting on those judgments of the ungodly? Men will be motivated to "fear, and they will declare the work of God, and will consider what He has done. The righteous man will be glad in the LORD and will take refuge in Him; and all the upright in heart will glory" (v. 9–10).

To help you in your thoughts about the judgments that God has sometimes pronounced on men for their lack of godly fear, study the different references to God's judgment, wrath, anger, discipline, or chastening. Find scriptural examples of God's judgment on people for their ungodliness. Sometimes God's judgment came on totally ungodly people, and sometimes some form of chastening came on professing believers. (We've given you a few examples, but there are many more such as Adam and Eve, Cain, Lot's wife, Jacob, etc.) Think of God's specific warnings about ungodliness—such as the one found in Hebrews 12:5–11. Compile a list of these warnings and frequently pull out and meditate on that list.

If you want to develop and sustain a healthy fear of God, reflecting on the judgment of God on ungodliness can be a great aid to you. Think much about the judgments of your God and you will become a person with a strong fear of God, think little about the judgments of your God and you will be neglecting something the Bible says will aid you in developing godly fear, think not at all about the judgments of God and you will be greatly hindered in this area of your spiritual life.

Sixth, be still, and reflect on the blessings God has brought into your life and into the lives of others. Psalm 67 indicates that when people observe the blessings of God in the lives of others they are motivated to fear God. It declares, "God blesses us, that all the ends of the earth may fear Him" (Ps. 67:7).

In Psalm 34:2, David made a statement about a commitment he had made. He said, "My soul will make its boast in the LORD." In the second part of the verse, David described what would happen when he bragged about God: "The humble will hear it and rejoice." In other words, his recounting of God's greatness and blessings would affect the way other people thought about God.

This same concept is repeated in Psalm 40:1–3. David began this psalm by describing a serious problem he had encountered. He was in grave danger. It was as though he were in a pit where he was being, or could have been, destroyed. He seemed to be in miry clay, in danger of slipping into destruction, lacking stability, having no firm footing, and not making any progress at all. We don't know what the specifics of the situation were, but whatever they were, David was desperate. But then God came to David's rescue, brought him up out of the pit, gave him stability, set his feet on a rock, made his footsteps firm, and put a new song into his mouth, a song of praise to the Lord. God had marvelously blessed David, and David wanted everyone to know about it. Why did David do this? We don't have to guess; he told us the effect he expected his testimony of God's goodness and blessing to have on others: as a result of God's blessings to him, "many will see and fear and will trust in the Lord" (v. 3).

The lesson as related to developing godly fear is unmistakable. Focusing on God's blessings and the honorable, lovely, pure, just, right, excellent, and praiseworthy things God brings into our lives (Phil. 4:8) will help us become a God-fearing, God-centered people.

To help you focus your thoughts on God's blessings, review different scriptural references to the blessings of God. Note how God has blessed His people throughout the ages. In particular, make a list of all the blessings you have received from God—spiritual, physical, social, economic, relational, educational, occupational, and others. Make a list of the promises God has made to you about your past, your present, and your future. Memorize some of these promises and meditate on them regularly. Determine with the psalmist that you will bless the Lord at all times (Ps. 34:1; 57:7) and that you will never forget all His benefits (Ps. 103:1–3).

At the beginning of this chapter, we suggested that some of you might be saying, "All right already! I understand why we should fear God and what that means. I truly do want to develop or increase and sustain a more healthy, wholesome, robust fear of God. I want to become a God-fearing person. Now will you please tell me how I can become that kind of person? Please give me some practical help."

As we conclude this chapter, we hope the "Yes, but how?" question has been answered for you. We've done our part. Now it's up to you. Remember, the fear of God is not something that you get in one big inoculation. It's something you must work on day after day, week after week, year after year. As long as you're in this world, you'll never be able just to "coast" in your ability to fear God.

We hope you have understood the importance of seeking after godly fear. Ecclesiastes 12:13 tells us that godly fear is the whole duty of man. It's what God requires of us. To take this lightly is to disobey God. And more than that, the Bible mentions on numerous occasions that godly fear is good for us. In particular, the fear of God is what will overcome and even cast out all ungodly, debilitating, destructive fear. Remember, much godly fear will bring the benefits described earlier in this book, little godly fear will bring little of those blessings, and no godly fear will bring none of those blessings. Which will it be for you? How seriously will you take the challenges of these chapters? It's up to you now. You have been told what to do, and you now know why and how you should do it. The only question remaining is: will you do it?

QUESTIONS FOR DISCUSSION

1. Why is it important to understand that the fear of God doesn't come naturally?

2. What lesson do we learn from Deuteronomy 4:10 about the fear of God?

3. What must happen before men who don't naturally fear God can begin to do so?

4. Explain the significance of this statement: "For a person to truly fear God, some important internal changes must take place."

5. Have you experienced this heart change?

6. What do we learn from Psalm 86:11 about developing the fear of God?

7. What do we learn about prayer from Matthew 6:9–13? How does this relate to the fear of God?

8. What do we learn about developing the fear of God from Deuteronomy 14:23; 31:12; and Psalm 34:11?

9. How often do you listen to God's Word? What are the attributes of a good listener? How can you improve your listening skills?

10. Are you a learner? What changes need to take place for you to become a more effective student?

11. What do we mean when we use the word *reflexive* in association with the development of the fear of God?

12. Why do you think the Bible is called "the fear of the Lord"? What connection might there be between the Bible and the experience of "the fear of the Lord"?

13. What does it mean to "be still, and know that I am God"?

14. Why should we be still?

15. Look back over the past month of your life. Can you identify several times when you were still, in the way the psalmist describes? If you cannot, what can you do to incorporate that into your next month?

16. Why does Scripture refer so much to man's depravity?

17. What steps will you take to become more aware of your own sinfulness?

18. What enabled Paul to stay so continually passionate about his salvation?

19. In complete honesty, how does your attitude toward your salvation compare to Paul's?

20. What specific steps do you plan to take to develop a greater aware-
    ness of God's love?

21. What steps do you plan to take to get to know God better?

22. What five attributes of God amaze you the most? Why?

23. What specific acts of God are you thankful for today?

24. What blessings in your life are you praising God for today?

25. Summarize the five most important lessons you have learned from this chapter. Explain how you are going to implement these principles into your life over the course of the next month.

13

LEARNING FROM
THE MASTER

WHEN I STUDIED COUNSELING, one of my requirements was to sit in on a seasoned counselor's sessions so I could learn from him as I watched. In this chapter I want you to imagine yourself doing that. In this case, Jesus is the counselor, the disciples are the counselees, and the problem is fear.

We've seen the importance of courage, we've gained insight into the nature of fear, and we've studied many of the general biblical principles on overcoming fear. Now I want you to learn from Jesus as He brings those principles together to deal with a very specific and very common land of fear—the fear of sharing the gospel.

God has given every believer a responsibility. You may not like it, and you may not be comfortable with it, but if you are going to obey Him, you can't avoid it. God wants His people to spread the good news. We learned at the beginning of this book that fear can be spiritually crippling. And we considered one particular type of sinful fear, the fear of man. One of the primary ways the fear of man has crippled the church is that it is behind our failure to proclaim the good news.

Peter wrote, "Sanctify Christ as Lord in your hearts, always being ready to make a defense to everyone who asks you to give an account for the hope that is in you, yet with gentleness and reverence" (1 Peter 3:15). Paul echoes this same command in Colossians 4:5–6:

Conduct yourselves with wisdom toward outsiders, making the most of the opportunity. Let your speech always be with grace, as though seasoned with salt, so that you will know how you should respond to each person.

Peter explained that this is one of the primary reasons God has chosen us as believers:

You are a chosen race, a royal priesthood, a holy nation, a people for God's own possession, so that you may proclaim the excellencies of Him who has called you out of darkness into His marvelous light. (1 Peter 2:9–10)

Jesus' commission applies to all His disciples:

Go therefore and make disciples of all the nations, baptizing them in the name of the Father and the Son and the Holy Spirit, teaching them to observe all that I commanded you; and lo, I am with you always, even to the end of the age. (Matt. 28:19–20)

Each one of us has different personal tendencies. Some of us like to talk, others don't. Some of us are bold, others aren't. Some of us love to meet strangers, others don't. But regardless of our personal tendencies, every one of us is commanded to stand up for Christ and do what we can to make the gospel known.

And really, we must admit, those aren't surprising commands. If God became man in order to die for us, it makes sense to tell others about that. If there is a heaven and a hell, and God has provided a way for man to go to heaven and stay out of hell, obviously we ought to share that way with others. If God has blessed us with every spiritual blessing in the heavenly places, if He has lavished His love upon us, if He cares about us, of course we must stand up for Him and talk about Him with others. These commands are clear and reasonable.

But the problem is, if we all agree that these instructions to proclaim the gospel are both clear and reasonable, why are so many of us so slow to do it? If we know enough to nod our heads and say, "Amen," when the pastor says we need to be telling others about Christ, why is it that so few of us actually do?

The answer is pretty simple. We're afraid. We are afraid of what people might think about us, we are afraid of what people might do to us, we are afraid of what people might say about us. So we keep quiet. Fear sits us down and shuts us up.

It might comfort you to know that this is not a new problem. Jesus had to deal with this exact issue the very first time He sent His disciples out to proclaim the gospel (Matt. 10). He commanded them, "As you go, preach, saying, 'The kingdom of heaven is at hand.' . . . What I tell you in the darkness, speak in the light; and what you hear whispered in your ear, proclaim upon the housetops" (vv. 7, 27). Boldly, clearly, proclaim the truth.

But Jesus knew it wouldn't be easy. "I send you out as sheep in the midst of wolves" (v. 16). "You will be hated by all because of My name" (v. 22). And as a result, you will be tempted to become afraid, to sit down and shut up. The fear of man could destroy your ministry.

We live thousands of years after the disciples, but our mission is the same: proclaim the gospel. So is our temptation: the fear of man. It's every believer's responsibility to do everything within his or her power to take the truth of God's Word and make it known! It's because we disobey Christ by fearing man that we are often so ineffective in fulfilling the mission He has laid out for us.

That's why Jesus reminded them three times, "Therefore do not fear them" (v. 26), "Do not fear those who kill the body but are unable to kill the soul" (v. 28), "So do not fear" (v. 31). It's wrong for a follower of Christ to fear man. Failure to share the gospel because of fear is not excusable—it's rebellion.

Good news! Jesus didn't merely say to us, "Do not fear," and leave it at that. He didn't just slap us in the face and tell us to get with the program. No, He reasoned with us. He explained why it is that we should not fear. He wasn't calling on us to be irrational or to close our eyes to reality, put on a happy face, and be fearless. No, He gave four rock-solid reasons in verses 24–31 why we as believers should courageously stand up for Christ.

PERSECUTION ISN'T SURPRISING

"A disciple is not above his teacher, nor a slave above his master. It is enough for the disciple that he become like his teacher, and the slave like his master. If they have called the head of the house Beelzebul, how much more . . . the members of his household!" (Matt. 10:24–25).

If you are someone's disciple, you are there to learn from that person. That person knows more than you, otherwise you wouldn't be the disciple. And if you are someone's slave, you are there to serve that person. It's the slave's job to serve the master, not the other way around. Both the teacher and the master hold a position of greater importance and authority than the student and the slave.

Believers are disciples and slaves of Christ. He is the teacher, we are the students. He is the master, we are the slaves. He is above us, He is more important than we are, and He is more valuable than we are.

Every true believer's basic life goal is to be like Jesus. As Jesus explained in verse 25: "It is enough for the disciple that he become like his teacher, and the slave like his master." We realize that we aren't even worthy to untie Jesus' shoelace, so the great goal of our life is not to surpass Him but to imitate Him.

The name *Christian* is meaningless if it doesn't mean this. The apostle John explained that "the one who says he abides in Him ought himself to walk in the same manner as He walked" (1 John 2:6). If you are a Christian, you are saying, "I abide in Christ." And if you say that you abide in Christ, you ought to live your life like Christ lived His. There's more to being a disciple and a slave than merely saying you are a disciple and you are a slave. You need to act.

If you claim to love Christ, love Him. If you talk about being a Christian, live like one. Christians aren't simply people who buy fire insurance, who "sign up just to avoid an unpleasant afterlife. A Christian is . . . one whose faith expresses itself in submission and obedience. A Christian is one who follows Christ, one who is committed unquestionably to Christ. . . . His basic aim is to be in every way a disciple of Jesus Christ."[1] The disciple's goal is to be like his teacher.

Those aren't revolutionary statements. They are very basic truths. But have you ever stopped and thought about what that means for your life? Every Christian should take a good hard look at the way the world treated Jesus. Before you say you want to be like Christ, stop and think about what it will mean if you really do live like Him.

Jesus faced constant opposition. He was insulted—called a blasphemer, a Sabbath breaker, and a companion of sinners. In Matthew 10 we read that they called Him Beelzebul, which means "the ruler of demons." God came into the world, and man had the audacity to call Him Satan. Jesus was unjustly accused. They couldn't catch Him doing anything wrong, so they made up lies about Him. He was persecuted—there were times when people became so angry they wanted to throw Him off a cliff! Isaiah 53 tells us: "He was despised and forsaken of men, a man of sorrows and acquainted with grief; and like one from whom men hide their face, He was despised, and we did not esteem Him" (v. 3). And He was executed for crimes He did not commit.

If that's how they treated the head of the household, Jesus says, it is just as certain that they will do the same to you if you are one of His followers. If they don't love Jesus—who is the King—they won't love you who are His disciples.

Christians shouldn't go around looking for persecution. They just shouldn't be surprised when it comes. Jesus was perfect. He was full of grace and truth. He went about preaching the kingdom and healing people, and the world responded to His love with hatred. That means if you identify with Christ and do His will, you can expect to be treated the same way He was treated by the world. The world hated him, so the world will hate you (John 15:20).

Remember why Jesus is telling us all this: He wants to help us overcome our fear of man. Knowing they persecuted Jesus should help you not to fear when they persecute you.

---

1. John MacArthur, *The Gospel according to Jesus* (Grand Rapids: Zondervan, 1988), 197.

Fear often contains an element of surprise. Something takes you by surprise, you are not prepared to handle it, and as a result you become afraid. Well, persecution shouldn't shock you. That's Jesus' point. Don't live in a fantasy world. He promises that it is going to happen. Be ready for it.

We only need to read some biographies of great Christian men and women to see that it is not always easy to do the right thing. John Calvin once said, "I have had no other purpose than to benefit the church by maintaining the pure doctrine of godliness. Yet I think that there is no one who is assailed, bitten and wounded by more false accusations than I."[2] The missionary William Carey and his coworkers were mocked as "fools, madmen, tinkers, Calvinists, and schismatics."[3] Toward the end of his life, Charles Spurgeon summarized the attacks that had been made on him by saying, "Men cannot say anything worse of me than they have said. I have been belied from head to foot, and misrepresented to the last degree."[4] By observing these faithful servants, we are reminded that if we aren't opposed, it might actually be because we are doing something wrong!

When you are opposed, you need to remember—this is not the first time this has happened! You don't have to be associated with some outstanding Christian leader or Bible expositor to figure that out; you need to read how the world treated Christ, the perfect Son of God. Thinking about Christ should give you strength and courage.

If you are a disciple of Christ, you will face persecution. Christ did. Christ was victorious, and by God's grace, you will be too. It may feel as though you are failing, it may feel as though everyone is against you, it may feel as though you are defeated. But if what you are doing is right, if you are faithful to Christ, you are not failing. You are not

2. John Calvin, *Calvin: Institutes of the Christian Religion*, Volume 1 and 2, ed. John T. McNeill, trans. Ford Lewis Battles, The Library of Christian Classics (Philadelphia: The Westminster Press, 1975), 4.

3. George Smith, *The Life of William Carey, Shoemaker and Missionary* (Fairford, UK: Echo Library, 2006), 355.

4. Quoted by John Piper, "Charles Spurgeon: Preaching through Adversity," *Desiring God*, January 31, 1995, accessed November 20, 2013, http://www.desiringgod.org/resource-library/biographies/charles-spurgeon-preaching-through-adversity.

defeated, and not everyone is against you—because God Himself is on your side. And if God is for you, even if the entire world is against you, you win, because God never loses.

ALL WRONGS WILL BE MADE RIGHT

"Therefore do not fear them, for there is nothing concealed that will not be revealed, or hidden that will not be known" (Matt. 10:26).

Looking to the past should give you courage, and so should looking to the future. Jesus told us, "View your present situation with an eternal perspective."

Specifically, He was talking about judgment day. Understand that the way things look right now is very different from the way they will look on that great day. What man has tried to cover, God will reveal; and what man has tried to hide, God will make known.

There's a day coming when each and every person who has ever lived will be summoned to stand before God and be judged. Read Hebrews 9:27: "It is appointed for men to die once and after this comes judgment." "For we will all stand before the judgment seat of God" (Rom. 14:10).

You won't be presenting your life to God. He'll reveal it to you, and He will do so in great detail. He will judge men for their speech: "I tell you that every careless word that people speak, they shall give an accounting for it in the day of judgment" (Matt. 12:36). He will judge men for their deeds:

> But because of your stubbornness and unrepentant heart you are storing up wrath for yourself in the day of wrath and revelation of the righteous judgment of God, who will render to each person according to his deeds. (Rom. 2:5–6)

He will judge men for their thoughts: "Wait until the Lord comes who will both bring to light the things hidden in the darkness and disclose the motives of men's hearts" (1 Cor. 4:5).

Man is proud of himself because he thinks no one sees his sin, but he's wrong—God sees. And on that judgment day He will take off the cover and disguises, and everyone's sin will be seen for what it really is. All wrongs will be made right.

Men won't be able to run from the judgment, because God is everywhere:

> Where can I go from Your Spirit?
> Or where can I flee from Your presence?
> If I ascend to heaven, You are there;
> If I make my bed in Sheol, behold, You are there. (Ps. 139:7–8)

Men won't be able to overpower Him at the judgment, because He is all-powerful:

> For great is the LORD and greatly to be praised;
> He is to be feared above all gods.
> For all the gods of the peoples are idols,
> But the LORD made the heavens. (Ps. 96:4–5)

Men won't be able to fool Him, because He knows all things:

> For His eyes are upon the ways of a man,
> And He sees all His steps.
> There is no darkness or deep shadow
> Where the workers of iniquity may hide themselves. (Job 34:21–22)

> God will bring every act to judgment, everything which is hidden, whether it is good or evil. (Eccl. 12:14)

> There is no creature hidden from His sight, but all things are open and laid bare to the eyes of Him with whom we have to do. (Heb. 4:13)

If all we looked at was this life, we'd be tempted to give up in despair. The psalmist felt that way in Psalm 73. He looked around and saw the wicked prospering. He wrote, "Surely in vain I have kept my heart pure and washed my hands in innocence" (v. 13). In other words, he was saying, "I'm living a holy life, and my life is a disaster—yet these unbelievers are hating God and doing great—so what's the point of being holy?"

But then the psalmist went into the sanctuary of God, and God reminded him of the way things will eventually end: "Surely You set them in slippery places; You cast them down to destruction. How they are destroyed in a moment!" (v. 18–19). God will have the last word. They may oppose Him now, they may look like they are winning now, but it won't be that way forever. When you are tempted to become fearful, when you are tempted to become discouraged, when you look around and think the wicked are winning—you need to stop and remember— now is not all there is. There will be a judgment day. There is more to life than just the here and now.

A day is coming when that which is hidden will be revealed, and that which is covered will be made known, when God will pour out eternal blessings on His people for their faithfulness in the midst of suffering, and when He will punish the enemies of Christ forever.

So don't be so concerned about what the world says now. If you are doing what is right, you will be vindicated! The applause of men is not nearly as valuable as the approval of God. Live with an eternal perspective.

ETERNITY IS FOREVER

"Do not fear those who kill the body but are unable to kill the soul; but rather fear Him who is able to destroy both soul and body in hell" (Matt. 10:28).

Jesus looked His disciples straight in the eyes and continued, "Don't fear man, because he can only kill you." That doesn't sound like much comfort, does it? Imagine the disciples looking at each other thinking, "Oh great, that makes me feel better."

But if you are going to overcome the fear of man, you need to step back and get some perspective. Sometimes in tense situations, things happen so fast that you can't think straight. As a result you make foolish decisions that only make your problem worse. Imagine a teenager learning to drive. He's alert. He sees a squirrel running in front of his car, reacts, swerves, and hits a truck. He tried to avoid a minor problem, and he ended up in major trouble.

Jesus doesn't want us to make that mistake. He said, "Do not fear those who kill the body but are unable to kill the soul; but rather fear Him who is able to destroy both soul and body in hell" (v. 28).

The only way you can find comfort in a statement like that is if you have your values in order. You shouldn't fear men when they threaten to kill your body, because your body isn't your most precious possession. The life of your soul is much more valuable than the life of your body.

If someone said to you, "You'd better not do that, because if you do, I'm going to take away one of your socks," that wouldn't be much of a threat, would it? If you lose a sock, so what? But if someone said, "You'd better not do that, because if you do, I am going to take away your house," that's more of a threat, because your house is much more valuable than a sock. If you had to make a choice—do this and lose a sock, or do this and lose a house—which would you choose? You would choose to lose the sock, of course. No doubt. And if someone made a choice and said, "Take my $300,000 house. I want to keep this sock," you'd say, "Something is wrong with you! You should value your house more than your sock!"

There is something worse than physical death, and that is spiritual death. There is something better than life here on earth, and that is life in heaven! Your soul and your eternal future are much more valuable than your earthly body and your time here on earth. Eternity is longer than our time here on earth, and hell is worse than any amount of physical suffering you might have to endure here on earth. So don't be a fool and value a few years here on earth over eternity.

When you are in a tight spot, you've got to think straight. You are going to be placed in situations where people are against you. You are going to be tempted to fear them and, as a result, compromise and dishonor God. When you do that, you are not thinking properly. You are afraid of the wrong person. Don't fear man. Fear God.

GOD WON'T FORGET ABOUT YOU

Are not two sparrows sold for a cent? And yet not one of them will fall to the ground apart from your Father. But the very hairs of your head are all numbered. So do not fear; you are more valuable than many sparrows. (Matt. 10:29–31)

One of the reasons we become scared is because we feel alone and powerless. We're in a desperate financial situation, and there seems to be no way out. We know that we don't have the resources, so we become frightened. Or people are opposing us, and we are the only ones who are standing up for truth; it is lonely, and we are fearful. Jesus wants us to remember that we are not alone. God is always with us. He knows exactly what is going on in our lives. And what is more, He cares about us.

Can you tell the difference between one sparrow and another? Do you even notice the sparrows from day to day? Have you ever noticed when a sparrow or a bird was missing? We never wake up in the morning and think, "Oh no, one less sparrow in the world today!" No, life goes on; we don't even notice when a sparrow dies.

But God does. "Are not two sparrows sold for a cent?" (v. 29). God is so involved in the events of the world that "not one of them will fall to the ground apart from your Father" (v. 29). Millions and millions of sparrows have lived and died since God created the world. But not one sparrow has lived and died apart from God's knowledge.

God did not create the world and then just go away and leave it. Moment by moment He is sustaining and governing this universe in which we live. He is the Ruler of the universe, the Sovereign Lord. This means that He is actively at work directing everything and causing all events to ultimately fulfill His great purpose. Augustine explained, "Nothing, therefore, happens unless the Omnipotent wills it to happen. He either permits it to happen, or He brings it about Himself."[5] God is involved in even the most "minute events—even the life and death of an almost worthless sparrow."[6]

5. Quoted by Roger Ellsworth, "The Sovereignty of God and Pastoral Ministry," *Founders Ministries*, November 22, 2013, accessed November 22, 2013, http://www.founders.org/journal/fj51/article2.html.

6. Jerry Bridges, "Is God in Control?" Life Action Ministries, March 1, 2002, accessed November 22, 2013, https://www.lifeaction.org/revival-resources/revive/view-god/god-control/.

You should find great comfort in that thought. God's in control. That should make you happy. Jerry Bridges explains,

> While it is certainly true that God's love for us does not protect us from pain and sorrow, it is also true that all occasions of pain and sorrow are under the absolute control of God. If God controls the circumstances of the sparrow, how much more does He control the circumstances that affect us. God does not walk away and leave us to the mercy of uncontrolled random or chance events.[7]

Rest in God's sovereignty. God does not do evil. He is not responsible for evil, but He is so awesome that He can use evil for your good and for His glory. You may not always be able to figure God out. You may not be able to see how He is working in your particular situation, but that's because you are not God and you don't see the whole picture.

God isn't unaware of what is going on in your life. He knows you better than you know yourself. Jesus told us, "[Even] the very hairs of your head are all numbered" (Matt. 10:30). You don't have any idea how many hairs there are on your head. You might find yourself thinking, "Oh no, I'm losing a lot of hair!" But God is so interested and involved in your life that He knows exactly how many hairs are on your head.

You may wonder why this example is relevant. The point is this: if God cares enough about you to know how many hairs are on your head—if He cares about something that, in the grand design of eternity, seems as insignificant as that—you can be sure that He cares about everything else going on in your life; He is concerned about every single thing that happens to you!

"So do not fear," Jesus said. "You are more valuable than many sparrows." He's not just in control; He's not just aware. He cares. If He exercises such control over nature that not even a sparrow falls to the ground apart from His knowledge, and if He knows so much about you that he knows how many hairs are on your head, you don't have to fear, because you mean much more to Him than many sparrows.

7. Jerry Bridges, *Trusting God* (Colorado Springs: NavPress, 1988), 30.

That gives us great hope. God's sovereignty wouldn't be much comfort to us if we didn't know that He cared about us. As Margaret Clarkson explains, "That God is, indeed, both good and powerful is one of the basic tenets of Christian belief."[8] Scripture commands us, "Cast all your anxieties on him, for he cares about you" (1 Peter 5:7 RSV). God is sovereign, and God is good. You don't have to choose between the two.

You don't have to be afraid, because nothing is going to happen to you that God doesn't allow, nothing is going to happen to you that God doesn't know about, and nothing is going to happen to you that ultimately isn't for your best interest! Jesus strips us of every excuse we could possibly come up with for not boldly proclaiming the gospel. He does so by reminding us of some very simple truths that every Christian acknowledges and confesses—the truths we've looked at so far throughout this book.

You're going to be tempted to fear. Don't be surprised by it. But as a Christian your response to those temptations should be radically different from the first response of the world. You look at life from an eternal perspective. You know and fear God, so you shouldn't fear man.

You must admit, that was quite a counseling session, wasn't it? Jesus really is the Master. He takes deep biblical truths and applies them to specific life situations. That's exactly what you must learn to do if you are going to overcome fear. You must learn to apply biblical truth to life.

The fact is, you may not be surprised by any of the principles you've studied so far. But the real question is, do they make any difference at all in the way you live? Truth is meant to transform. It's nice for you to know these truths, but it's better if you act on them.

Specifically, don't let fear cripple your witness. What Christ has told you in the darkness, speak in the light; and what you have heard whispered in your ear, proclaim on the housetops. Proclaim the Word! Do not fear!

QUESTIONS FOR DISCUSSION

1. What responsibility has God given to every believer?

8. Quoted in ibid., 32.

2. What are some excuses people give for not obeying those commands? What is often at the root of those excuses?

3. Can you give an example of a time when fear sat you down and shut you up?

4. Why is this responsibility to witness not surprising?

5. In Matthew 10, what problem did the disciples face?

6. It is a fact that you as a Christian are to be like Christ. What implications does this have for your life?

7. Why shouldn't you be surprised when you face opposition?

8. How does knowing you'll face opposition help you in your struggle with fear?

9. What hope do you have if you are obeying Christ?

10. How does the promise of an upcoming judgment day give you courage?

11. What are some practical steps you can take to begin living your life with an eternal perspective?

12. Why is Jesus' statement "Don't fear men; they can only kill you" not discouraging but encouraging? Give a thorough explanation.

13. What does the statement "When you are in a tight spot, you've got to think straight" mean?

14. How can you learn to rest in God's sovereignty?

15. If someone came to you and said he or she was afraid, how would you counsel that person using Matthew 10?

16. As a result of the truths you've studied in this chapter, what do you see in your life that needs to change?

14

A CALL FOR COURAGE

PERHAPS YOU'VE HEARD someone say, "Try Christianity. If Christianity is true and you're an unbeliever when you die, then you go to hell. But if Christianity is not true and you're a believer when you die, then at least you had a pleasant life on earth." The person speaking may have had good intentions, but Paul would have shuddered at such a statement.

Either Christianity is true or it isn't. If Christianity isn't true, then Christians are the biggest fools on the planet. Unbelievers shouldn't admire us. They should pity us. Paul wrote, "If we have hoped in Christ in this life only, we are of all men most to be pitied" (1 Cor. 15:19). Unbelievers should pity us because following Christ isn't easy. It's full of delight and gladness; but it is not now, has never been, and will never be easy.

J. C. Ryle explains:

True Christianity is a fight. . . . The true Christian is called to be a soldier and must behave as such from the day of his conversion to the day of his death. He is not meant to live a life of religious ease, indolence, and security. He must never imagine for a moment that he can sleep and doze along the way to heaven. . . . If he takes his standard of Christianity from the children of this world, he may be content with such notions, but he will find no countenance for them in the

Word of God. If the Bible is his rule of faith and practice, he will find his course laid down very plainly in this matter. He must fight.[1]

When God calls a man to come to Christ, He calls him to come and die: die to self, die to selfish desires, die to living for this world, and die to all the idols of his heart. Jesus made this very clear: "If anyone wishes to come after Me, he must deny himself, and take up his cross daily and follow Me. For whoever wishes to save his life will lose it, but whoever loses his life for My sake, he is the one who will save it" (Luke 9:23–24). Following Christ isn't for cowards.

Every Christian virtue requires courage. You can have all the good intentions in the world, but if you don't have courage, those intentions don't mean much. Anyone can talk about obeying God, but it takes courage to actually do so.

COURAGE REQUIRED

You Need Courage to Follow Christ

Jesus never promised that we would have it easy here on earth. Instead He said, "If you are going to be My disciple, you've got to deny yourself, and you need to love Me more than anyone or anything else. Pick up your cross and follow Me!" The gospel does not tell you to believe and then go and live for yourself. It tells you to repent, believe, and follow. True, it doesn't take much courage to pretend you are following after Christ. It doesn't take much strength to come to church and sing a few hymns and then go out and live for yourself. But it does take courage to deny yourself, pick up your cross, and truly follow after Christ.

You Need Courage to Stay Faithful to Christ

Life can be confusing. You will suffer, you will have difficulties, and you will sometimes feel like God is far off and doesn't care. There will be times when it will be easier to compromise your biblical convictions than to continue to obey, and times when the world's solutions

---

1. J. C. Ryle, *Holiness* (Moscow, ID: Charles Nolan, n.d.), 63.

seem far easier and far more attractive than following God's Word. If you are going to endure and not give up, you need strength to hold on and courage to stand strong when everything within you wants to give up, run, and hide.

You Need Courage to Stand Up for Christ

The Bible is full of promises. Paul told Timothy, "All who desire to live godly in Christ Jesus will be persecuted" (2 Tim. 3:12). That's one promise most people don't like. It's not easy to take a stand for Christ, because the world hates Him. You need courage if you are going to honor Christ when all the world is against you.

It takes courage to be a Christian. It always has. That's why we've written this book. We realize that fear can have a devastating impact on your life and ministry, and we want to help you overcome it. So far we've primarily looked at this problem by giving you biblical principles regarding overcoming fear. But now we want to close this book by looking at what Scripture teaches about developing courage.

You could look to many people in order to learn about courage. Church history is full of men and women who took bold stands for Christ. But if we had to pick just one person, apart from Christ, without hesitation we would choose to learn about courage from the apostle Paul.

Do you want to learn about computers? Ask Bill Gates. Investing? Warren Buffet. Basketball? Michael Jordan. Courage? Ask Paul.

To make it even better, God inspired Paul to speak on this very subject. In 2 Timothy 1:12, Paul spoke loud and clear about what it takes to be a person of courage. Paul didn't set out to define courage; he was simply encouraging Timothy to be bold. Paul knew that Timothy was struggling with fear, and he wanted Timothy to step up for Christ. To encourage him, Paul reminded Timothy of his personal testimony and of the difficult choices that he had made to follow after Christ. In doing so, Paul personified what it means to be courageous. "For this reason I also suffer these things, but I am not ashamed" (v. 12).

COURAGE DEFINED

Few virtues are more widely admired than courage, but few are more greatly misunderstood. Since the world has no objective or authoritative standard of truth, it has no objective, authoritative definition of courage. In our culture, people understand courage to be a good thing, but they don't really know what it is. That's why courage is desired by so many, but demonstrated by so few. It's hard to be courageous if you don't know exactly what courage is.

For every godly virtue, there is a negative, counterfeit quality that looks like the real thing and sounds like the real thing but is far from actually being the real thing. Our world is full of counterfeits of love, joy, peace, kindness, and all the other virtues. Courage is no different. Most of our world has been deceived by cheap imitations of courage.

I saw a perfect example of this misrepresentation of courage as my daughter and I watched *The Little Bear Movie* together. (It was her idea, I promise!) While Little Bear's father is away on a trip, Little Bear asks his mother if his daddy ever gets scared. Little Bear's mother basically tells him, "No, he doesn't get scared. Daddy's brave."

But Little Bear's mother doesn't have it quite right. Courage is not the absence of fear. That's a counterfeit definition. If Daddy Bear never gets scared, he's not brave—he's out of touch. Courage is controlling fear; courage is the ability to face whatever happens without being overcome by fear.

Courage is not about being reckless. Recklessness is not a virtue. If a man ran into a burning house and stayed there for a while just because he thought it would be exciting, you wouldn't think he was courageous. You'd think he was stupid. But if a man ran into a burning house to save a child, he would be given a badge of courage because he had a good reason for risking his life. Courage is not simply suffering or taking risks; courage is suffering and taking risks for a good reason.

Biblical courage is pressing forward to do what's right, even when there are painful consequences for doing so. Biblical courage is standing firm and refusing to compromise even when difficult circumstances arise.

Paul personified this definition. In 2 Timothy 1:12 he boldly pressed on in the midst of difficulties: "For this reason I also suffer these things"—and he didn't shrink back when things got tough—"but I am not ashamed."

Before Paul became a Christian, he had it all. He was on the fast track to success. He had a great background and an incredible education. He was an up-and-coming religious leader, admired and respected by his peers. He had basically everything that makes up what the world calls the "good life." But after God saved him, all that changed. Paul went from being the persecutor to being the persecuted.

When God called Paul (Acts 9), He told Ananias, "Go ... for I will show [Paul] how much he must suffer for My name's sake" (vv. 15–16).

How would you like that start to your Christian life? Become a Christian and, bang, immediately God reveals how much you are going to suffer for Him. That's not exactly an encouraging way to begin!

Paul began suffering immediately. He became a Christian, stayed in Damascus to fellowship with other believers, and began preaching the gospel. A group of men who didn't like what he had to say, got upset and plotted "to do away with him" (Acts 9:23). Paul was just a baby Christian, and he had to flee the city at night by hiding in a basket that was lowered down the city wall. He had gone to Damascus to persecute Christians, and he left Damascus being persecuted as a Christian.

But that was just the beginning. Paul's life didn't get any easier. Later Paul described what he had endured for Christ:

> Five times I received from the Jews thirty-nine lashes. Three times I was beaten with rods, once I was stoned, three times I was shipwrecked, a night and a day I have spent in the deep. I have been on frequent journeys, in dangers from rivers, dangers from robbers, dangers from my countrymen, dangers from the Gentiles, dangers in the city, dangers in the wilderness, dangers on the sea, dangers among false brethren; I have been in labor and hardship, through many sleepless nights, in hunger and thirst, often without food, in cold and exposure. (2 Cor. 11:24–27)

For following after Christ, Paul had almost every bad thing happen to him that you could possibly imagine. He was whipped five times—

that's 195 lashes—all for the gospel—but he kept on preaching. He was stoned and left for dead—but kept on serving Christ. Beaten, imprisoned, impoverished, tortured, hated, mocked—all for Christ, yet he refused to give up.

Imagine Paul coming to speak at your church. Can you picture him? His body is bruised and beaten from all the torture. He lifts up his shirt, and you see his back, lined with scars from all the whippings and beatings. He tells you stories of how he's been kicked out of cities, hunted, and tortured without mercy, and still he presses on. He keeps on following Christ despite the consequences.

That's courage.

As Paul wrote Timothy, he wasn't writing from some cozy little hideaway in Rome. Paul was suffering. "Timothy, as I write, I am currently experiencing suffering, but I am not shrinking back as a result, nor should you." Paul was writing in the present tense. He was in prison for the gospel. Paul could have been anything he wanted to be. He was a genius, yet because he chose to follow Christ, he ended his life in a jail cell, treated like a criminal, literally in chains for the gospel. And he knew he was about to make the ultimate sacrifice. He was about to die. He told Timothy, "I am already being poured out as a drink offering, and the time of my departure has come" (2 Tim. 4:6). In today's language he was saying, "I am about to be martyred for the gospel."

But what made everything worse was the loneliness he felt as he wrote. He had endured all these difficulties for the glory of God and the good of God's people, yet there he was, sitting in a prison cell all alone. "You are aware," he wrote in 2 Timothy 1:15, "of the fact that all who are in Asia turned away from me." From Paul's standpoint, it would have been easy to feel like a failure. He had done all this for Christ, and what was the result? He was in a jail cell, and everybody he loved was running away. What was the use?

Paul knew what it is to suffer. True, it doesn't necessarily take courage to suffer. Anybody can suffer. But the difference here is that Paul knew why he was suffering. In fact, he chose to suffer to do what was right.

He wrote in verse 12, "For this reason I also suffer these things." For this reason. Paul understood why he was suffering. It was not something that was happening randomly or by chance. Paul was suffering for a very specific reason: "the gospel . . . for which I was appointed a preacher and an apostle and a teacher" (vv. 8, 11). Paul was suffering because he loved Christ. Paul was suffering so that the good news could be spread. Paul was suffering because God had called Him to preach the gospel.

He was faced with the same dilemma time and time again: if he didn't preach the gospel, he wouldn't suffer; but if he did preach the gospel, he would suffer greatly. Yet he made the same choice time and time again: preach the gospel and suffer painful consequences. That's the choice he was making as he wrote Timothy, but this time the choice had become even more dramatic: Deny Christ and live. Preach the gospel and die.

Paul chose death over compromise. He refused to shrink back, saying, "I am not ashamed." When you are ashamed of something, what do you do? You hide it. Paul said, "I'm not hiding the gospel. I'm suffering, and I'm not pulling back. I'm not giving up; I'm still holding up."

That's Christian courage. That's the essence of spiritual strength. The storms of life may beat on you, you might experience great hardship for your stand for Christ, but don't run away. Stand strong, and press on doing what God has called you to do, no matter how high the cost.

COURAGE EXPLAINED

A coward lives by his feelings. They dominate him. He's emotionally up and down, depending on how he feels that day. The coward is not as concerned about what is true as he is about what is easy. He will gladly exchange truth for comfort. He's always taking the safe path, the easy way out. He backs away from challenges. He is always hedging his bets. He's a fence rider. He tries to live for both Christ and himself at the same time, but when there is a choice to be made, he chooses himself over Christ every time. When opposed, he compromises the truth.

The courageous person lives by principle. His feelings may go up and down, but he doesn't allow them to control his choices. In fact, he often has to act despite his feelings. That's what we see in Paul. Paul was not a masochist. He did not find some strange pleasure in pain. He was a person just like us. When he was whipped, it hurt; when he was beaten, it was painful; when he was shipwrecked, it was difficult. He didn't enjoy these experiences, but he endured them, and he did so with joy.

Why? The answer is found in the second half of 2 Timothy 1:12. "For I know whom I have believed and I am convinced that He is able to guard what I have entrusted to Him until that day." I know, I believe, and I am convinced. There was something more important to Paul than comfort or temporary pleasure, and that was the honor and glory of God. Paul acted on truth, even when it was difficult to do so.

The lesson? Courageous people are people of conviction. Their conviction flows out of their faith. And their faith is grounded on knowledge.

Frankly, the reason we have so few courageous people in our day is because our culture attacks convictions, mocks faith, ignores knowledge (Scripture), and promotes ignorance.

Instead of promoting truth, our culture promotes self.

G. K. Chesterton puts it like this:

> What we suffer from today is humility in the wrong place. Modesty has moved from the organ of ambition. Modesty has settled upon the organ of conviction; where it was never meant to be. A man was meant to be doubtful about himself, but undoubting about the truth; this has exactly been reversed. Nowadays the part of man that a man does assert is exactly the part he ought not to assert—himself. The part he doubts is exactly the part he ought not to doubt—the Divine Reason.[2]

The world has rejected basic absolutes. And when you reject absolutes, all that is left is yourself. You no longer have any conviction about right and wrong. Your only conviction is the protection and promotion of yourself. And if your only conviction is the protection and promotion of yourself, you won't have courage, because self-centeredness produces cowardice, not courage. You are not going to be courageous if the first,

2. G. K. Chesterton, *Orthodoxy* (Colorado Springs: Shaw, 2001), 38.

overarching commitment in your life is a selfish pursuit of happiness. True courage requires making sacrifices and doing things that are painful.

The world has it all wrong. We constantly hear, "You have a problem with fear? Your problem is that you don't love yourself enough." The idea is that you've got to think more about yourself, you've got to turn inward, if you are going to be courageous. But the truth is, if you look to yourself and really believe in yourself, you may become selfishly ambitious, you may become more willing to take risks to advance your own personal agenda, but you certainly won't become more courageous.

If you are going to be courageous, you've got to stop looking inward and start looking outward. You've got to stop being motivated by selfishness and empty conceit, and instead, with humility of mind, consider others as more important than yourself, looking out not only for your own personal interests, but also for the interests of others.

You won't naturally look out for the good of others. The only way that happens is if you become a person of conviction.

Do you need to be convinced of the truth of Scripture? Do you know how to become a person of conviction? You must build your faith. And how do you build your faith? You must grow in your knowledge of God.

That's what it all comes down to. Why do you fall when tough times come? Why are you so weak? Why do you start running away from God when things get a little bit difficult? Why don't you stand strong? You fail because your view of man is too big and your view of God is too small. That's the point of this book. You shrink back because you don't know God the way you should.

Why was Paul spiritually strong? Because he knew God. Why are people spiritually weak? Because they don't know God. Paul said there was no way he was going to pull back. He was going to continue to stand strong, even to death, because he knew in whom he believed.

In order to be courageous, you must get to know God.

When I was a boy, I struggled with fear. My vivid imagination plagued me. Many times when I was really scared, my mom would come to me and say, "Josh, do you really think God is that small? Do you really think that God can't take care of you in this situation? Do you really think that God could part the Red Sea but He can't help you when your room gets dark?" She was right! Why was I frightened? Now when I am in situations where I am tempted to shrink back and become fearful, I remind myself of who the Bible says God is, and I apply it to my situation.

When you are frightened, you need to go back to truth. You need to remember the attributes of God.

If God is all-powerful, and the Bible says He is, He certainly can give you the strength to do what He wants you to do. That means that you know without a doubt that nothing is too difficult for God. If God is good, He's not going to put you in a situation just to be cruel. That means you know that He's not playing games with you. If God is wise and knows all things, He understands why these things are happening to you. That means that He has a purpose for the things that are happening to you, and that purpose is for the best, even if you can't figure it out just yet. If God never changes and always keeps His promises, He will work out your situation for your good and for His glory since He has promised, "I will work all things together for good for those who love me" (see Rom. 8:28). That means you know that whatever situation you face will ultimately be for your good and for His glory!

If you are going to be spiritually strong, you must make knowing God the top priority in your life. You have to take out your Bible and ask the Lord to show you through His Word just who God is. You have to study His character. You have to think deeply about Him. You have to meditate, pray, and study! Spiritual weakness is the result of inadequate, unbiblical thoughts about God, for as Daniel wrote, "The people who know their God will display strength and take action" (Dan. 11:32).

Do you know the story of Shadrach, Meshach, and Abed-nego? They are a perfect example of this fundamental principle. King Nebuchadnezzar set up a golden image for everyone in his kingdom to worship. But these three Hebrew youths refused. King Nebuchadnezzar went into a rage, gave orders to bring the boys to him, and furiously demanded, "Is true . . . that you do not serve my gods or worship the golden image that I have set up?" (Dan. 3:14). Filled with anger, he issued an ultimatum: worship my statue or die.

Shadrach, Meshach, and Abed-nego could have given a number of different excuses for compromising and avoiding the punishment of death.

1. We're young. Everybody knows that young people aren't responsible for their actions, right?

2. We're refugees in a foreign nation. We're far away from home; we're in a difficult spot. Surely God will understand!

3. We'll bow down with our bodies but not with our hearts. Doesn't God care more about our heart attitudes anyway?

4. We don't want to die. We can do more good for God alive than we could if we were dead.

5. That furnace is hot. We just don't like pain.

But these three righteous young men refused to make excuses. They stood strong and would not compromise their belief in God. That's courage.

Here's the key. Consider the reason they gave for their courage: "O Nebuchadnezzar, we do not need to give you an answer concerning this matter" (Dan. 3:16). They were courageous because they had a proper view of man. They understood that Nebuchadnezzar was just an earthly king. He wasn't their God, and so he wasn't their standard of right and wrong. "If it be so, our God whom we serve is able to deliver us from the furnace of blazing fire; and He will deliver us out of your hand, O king" (Dan. 3:17). They were also courageous because they had a proper view of God. They understood that God was powerful enough to save them, even when it looked humanly impossible. "But even if He does not, let it be known to you, O king, that we are not going to serve your gods or worship the golden image that you have set up" (Dan. 3:18). They did not have some sort of fantasy view of God. They knew that God might not choose to deliver them. But that was fine, because God's glory was more important to them than their own lives. They knew God, and because they knew God, they were courageous and took action.

If you want to be spiritually strong, if you want to be able to rejoice in the midst of the storms of life, if you want to be courageous, you must make the pursuit of God a top priority in your life. It's that simple. That's what we see in 2 Timothy 1:12: "I am not ashamed; for I know whom I have believed." And that's what we've seen throughout this book.

Put your faith in God, not in men. Fear Him, not other people.

Paul gave another helpful insight at the end of verse 12. He told us specifically what it is about God that gave him strength in the midst of his trials. He wrote, "I am convinced that He is able to guard what I have entrusted to Him until that day" (v. 12). The Greek term translated here as *entrusted* literally means "a deposit," a legal term describing something one person places in trust to another's keeping. The word translated *guard* is a military term used of "a soldier on watch, who was accountable with his own life to protect that which was entrusted to his care."[3] Paul was saying that he had entrusted his life, his ministry, his welfare, and his very salvation to God. He had made a deposit, and he was courageous because he was persuaded that God was trustworthy and was able to guard that deposit until the day he stood before God. Paul went about doing God's business with great courage, because he had entrusted everything—his life, his safety, his salvation—to God. He knew that God was guarding his deposit.

Paul looked at his life with an eternal perspective: "I'm sitting here in a prison cell, and they are about to kill me, but I know that God is for me, and that He is guarding what I've entrusted to him. So they can take all this away from me, because all that is just temporary. One day soon I am going to stand before God, and I know that when I do, He will be pleased, and everything will be right. Therefore I have no reason to back down or be discouraged." In his own words he said,

> I have fought the good fight, I have finished the course, I have kept the faith; in the future there is laid up for me the crown of righteous-ness, which the Lord, the righteous Judge, will award to me on that

3. John MacArthur, *2 Timothy* (Chicago: Moody, 1995), 27.

day; and not only to me, but also to all who have loved His appearing. (2 Tim. 4:7–8)

God does not promise to protect us from painful circumstances, but He does promise something even better. He promises that those painful circumstances can't separate us from Him. Paul knew that "neither death, nor life, nor angels, nor principalities, nor things present, nor things to come, nor powers, nor height, nor depth, nor any other created thing" could separate him from the love of God, which is in Christ Jesus the Lord (see Rom. 8:38–39).

There is something much more important than physical safety, and that is the safety of your soul. If you are a believer, you can be certain that God Himself is protecting your soul. The world looked at Paul and said, "No way! That man sitting there in the prison cell is crazy! To give up life on this earth, to endure all this pain and not back down?" Paul looked at the world and responded, "You don't know who I know. You don't know that this apparent defeat is only a doorway to a great victory."

Paul was looking forward to eternity. He was viewing his life with an eternal perspective, saying, "I am in jail now, but soon I will be in heaven." As a result, he was courageous. He was strong. He took action.

We need more people like Paul today. Men and women who refuse to compromise the truth, who stand firm, and who press forward in obedience to God despite the painful and perhaps even fatal consequences that may come, because they know God, and they have entrusted their lives and their salvation completely to Him.

Courage comes from having the right perspective. As the apostle Paul explained, "The sufferings of this present time are not worthy to be compared with the glory that is to be revealed to us" (Rom. 8:18).

Frankly, if you don't believe in absolute truth, if you don't believe in God, if you don't believe in heaven and hell, then it makes sense to be cowardly. If you believe that when you die that is it, if you believe that there is no such thing as right or wrong, then your first concern should be self-protection. Your ultimate goal should be to keep yourself safe and remain alive. Therefore if you are an unbeliever, when you act courageously, when you put your life on the line for someone else, that is a great thing, but it doesn't make sense according to your philosophy of life. Your ultimate purpose in life must be all wrapped up in yourself, so why sacrifice yourself for someone else? As a result, it's surprising when any unbeliever is courageous.

Unfortunately the church today is filled with weak, cowardly people. That too is surprising, because if an unbeliever is acting out of character when he is courageous, a believer is also acting out of character when he is cowardly.

Christians believe in absolute truth. We believe in heaven and hell. We believe in right and wrong. Therefore our ultimate goal is not self-protection but the glory of God.

We're not saying that only Christians are courageous. That's not true. There are many courageous unbelievers. What we are saying is that only believers have a rock-solid reason for being courageous.

If the Lord is your helper, why are you afraid? What can man do to you?

Our prayer is that God will help you fulfill His purpose for your life, free you from being paralyzed by sinful fear, and mold you into a person who courageously obeys and glorifies Him. This book is only a beginning. If you are going to live all out for Christ, unhindered by fear, don't stop here. Get to know your God!

QUESTIONS FOR DISCUSSION

1. Why does Paul say, "If we hoped in Christ in this life only, we are of all men most to be pitied"?

2. Why is courage an essential requirement for Christian living?

3. What is the difference between courage and recklessness?

4. Can you think of any other counterfeits of courage? For example, what's the difference between courage and selfish ambition?

5. Define biblical courage in your own words.

6. How does 2 Timothy 1:12 illustrate biblical courage?

7. How does Paul personify courage?

8. How was Paul suffering when he wrote 2 Timothy 1:12? What does that teach us about courage?

9. Are there any specific examples of times when you demonstrated biblical courage? Have you done what was right even though it was difficult? Have you refused to compromise even though there were consequences? What caused you to act in a courageous manner? What about times when you displayed cowardice? What was it that caused you to respond in a cowardly manner?

10. Explain this statement: "A coward lives by his feelings. . . . The courageous person lives by principle."

11. What is the difference between courage and cowardice?

12. What reason does Paul give for his courage?

13. What reason does this chapter give for the lack of courageous people in our day? Explain.

14. What did G. K. Chesterton mean when he wrote, "Modesty has settled upon the organ of conviction; where it was never meant to be. A man was meant to be doubtful about himself, but undoubting about the truth; this has exactly been reversed"?

15. What happens when you reject absolutes? Why will you be unable to be courageous if your only conviction is the protection and promotion of self?

16. Explain this statement: "If you are going to be courageous, you've got to stop looking inward and start looking outward."

17. Why are people spiritually weak?

18. What must happen if you are going to become spiritually strong?

19. What can you learn about courage from the story of Shadrach, Meshach, and Abed-nego?

20. What is it about God that gave Paul courage in the midst of his trials?

21. What does an eternal perspective have to do with courage?

22. What steps can you take to develop an eternal perspective?

23. Why is it surprising for unbelievers to be courageous?

24. Why is it surprising for Christians to be cowardly?

25. What specific steps will you take to become courageous as a result of reading this book?

ALSO BY WAYNE A. MACK

Counselors needing specific assignments to give counselees or individuals seeking practical helps for their struggles will welcome Wayne Mack's homework manuals, which present a wealth of scriptural information for solving problems in each area covered.

The first volume deals with personal and interpersonal problems in over thirty categories, including anger, blameshifting, communication, dating, finances, obesity, pride, sexual problems, sleep, suffering, thought patterns, and work. The second offers assignments for husbands and wives and for parents and children on topics such as communication, marriage evaluation, child rearing, and family religion.

Where can we possibly find unfailing answers to our problems? Not in ourselves. Not in the world. Only God can diagnose our condition and equip us for real, lasting change. Wayne and Joshua Mack show how we can flee temptation, break free of sin, and live our lives as *overcomers*.

With discussion questions and writing space for personal responses, this book can be used for individual growth, for group study, or for homework assignments for those in counseling.

"Wayne and Joshua Mack teach us about an intentional and carefully lived life, about lifelong immersion in Scripture, about utter reliance on the grace and power of the Holy Spirit, about vigilant self-examination and willing self-denial, about devotion to Jesus Christ whole and simple."
— **David Powlison,** Executive Director, Christian Counseling and Educational Foundation

ALSO BY WAYNE A. MACK

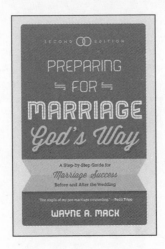

Preparing for Marriage God's Way is a marriage counseling resource that uses thoughtful self-examination to reveal the personalities, background, and expectations that you and your partner are bringing to your union. Through rigorous Bible study, you will learn about God's expectations for marriage and be equipped with His solutions for dealing with typical marriage conflicts. Three follow-up lessons after your wedding help you to reflect on all that's happened after you said, "I do."

"Oh, the problems that could be prevented if couples anticipating marriage worked their way through this book with a caring Christian prior to the wedding ceremony! Wayne Mack's knowledge both of the Scriptures and of marital problem solving is evident in the order of topics; the clear, practical teaching; and the application assignments."

　　—**Randy Patten,** Director of Training and Advancement, Association of Certified Biblical Counselors